Reference MWAPI

Reference MWAPI

James Hay

Digital Press

Boston • Oxford • Johannesburg • Melbourne • New Delhi • Singapore

Recognizing the importance of preserving what has been written, Butterworth–Heinemann prints its books on acid-free paper whenever possible.

Butterworth–Heinemann supports the efforts of American Forests and the Global ReLeaf program in its campaign for the betterment of trees, forests, and our environment.

Library of Congress Cataloging-in-Publication Data
Hay, James (James Darren)
    Reference MWAPI / James Hay.
        p.   cm.
    Includes index.
    ISBN 1-55558-208-7 (alk. paper)
    1. Application software—Development.   2. Microsoft Windows
(Computer file)   I. Title.
QA76.76.D47H399   1998
005.13'3—dc21   98-28424
                                                            CIP

British Library Cataloguing-in-Publication Data
A catalogue record for this book is available from the British Library.

The publisher offers special discounts on bulk orders of this book.
For information, please contact:
Manager of Special Sales
Butterworth–Heinemann
225 Wildwood Avenue
Woburn, MA 01801-2041
Tel: 781-904-2500
Fax: 781-904-2620

For information on all Butterworth–Heinemann publications available, contact our World Wide Web home page at: http://www.bh.com

Printed and bound by CPI Group (UK) Ltd, Croydon, CR0 4YY

Transferred to Digital Print 2011

For Laura

Forever in our hearts

Contents

Preface

Imagine developing independent Graphical User Interface (GUI) applications with a simple, straightforward, robust Application Programmers Interface (API) tool! *Reference MWAPI* will demonstrate the reality of such an API. This book introduces an innovative, time-efficient approach to programming that you will find indispensable regardless of the computer language you use for GUI development. In addition, our hands-on experience, research, and careful study of the M Windowing API (MWAPI) specifications combine to make this book a concise reference for the MWAPI extension to the M (MUMPS) language.

As developers of state-of-the-art software, we owe it to our customers and to ourselves to take an innovative approach to our work. If you are experienced with M, you will likely find some differences in your usual usage of the language. Micronetics Design Corporation's conformance to the MWAPI specification provided the development environment used to create the sample code and illustrations that demonstrate object creation and use.

If you are not an M user or are unfamiliar with use of the M language, we have furnished an introductory explanation of the M syntax required to use the MWAPI so you will get an idea of its use. You may find *M Programming*, also published by Digital Press, to be a good reference.

It is my hope that this book will stir your imagination and offer a fresh look at existing issues.

I am grateful for the patience my wife and daughter have shown to me over the course of writing this book.

Foreword

I think it was in 1992 when I first learned about the M Windowing API (or MWAPI). At the time I was working on Micronetics's GUI implementation (MSM-GUI) and was also chairman of the MUMPS Development Coordinating Committee—Europe (MDCC-E). MSM-GUI grew from some work by one of our partners to provide graphical capabilities within the M language on an IBM X/Windows workstation. After all, these were the days before the domination of Microsoft on the desktop—and when X-Windows was considered by many to be the future of graphical user interfaces.

The MDC, a user-community/body that continues to develop the M standard, had been trying for some time to balance the views of the vested interests represented by implementers such as us. Already we implementers had separately developed mechanisms by which our M products could control and manipulate GUI interface elements, including a function-based approach that applied special mnemonics to a pseudo-device type and a binding to the underlying X-Windows system.

After prolonged and often heated discussion during the course of various meetings of the MDC, it became obvious that no compromise could be reached. The time was ripe for lateral thinking! A totally different approach was put forward by MDC. This approach was very "M-like," elegant, and high-level, and it had the potential to provide the M programmer with flexible, easy access to GUI interface elements. The writing was on the wall: as many MDC members burned gallons of midnight oil to massage the nascent MWAPI into shape, plans were developed by MDC to produce a MWAPI interface layer to Micronetics's existing MSM-GUI implementation and to migrate to a pure MWAPI implementation as soon as possible.

The MWAPI was built to be culture neutral and to run on any underlying windowing platform, which is why its terms do not correspond with those we are now used to (courtesy of Microsoft Windows). This was a conscious decision; a great deal of effort was put into ensuring that nothing prevented implementers from porting the MWAPI to any windowing platform. For example, Microsoft Windows has "Controls and Properties," OSF/Motif has "Widgets and Resources," and the MWAPI has "Gadgets and Attributes." But as Shakespeare wrote: "What's in a name? That which we call a rose by any other name would smell as sweet."

Over the next few years I often found myself giving talks or tutorials on the MWAPI during seminar tours or at various M-related conferences. One of the examples that I often used to illustrate the power and simplicity of the MWAPI was the "Hello World" example. This involves the production of a simple window on which the words "Hello World" appear. In order to write this example in real C/C++ code (that is without benefit of generated code or MFC) requires hundreds of lines of C code. And what of the MWAPI? All that is needed is to create the following two node structure:

```
WIN("TITLE")="Hello World"
WIN("TYPE")="LABEL"
```

and issue the following M command:

```
MERGE ^$WINDOW("Window","G","Gadget")=WIN
```

Everything else about the window and the "Hello World" label is defaulted for you. What could be more simple or elegant?

Flash forward six years, to today. What has happened?

- Microsoft now dominates the desktop and has the de facto standard GUI interface (so the efforts to make the MWAPI portable were to no avail).
- The MWAPI is now an ISO and ANSI standard—ANSI/MDC X11.6-1994, approved in October 1995—and continues to be enhanced as part of the MDC standardization process.
- The MWAPI is used as the foundation for a sophisticated development environment used in the 32-bit Microsoft Windows environment.

Many people around the world are using the technology with little or no extension to develop and deploy sophisticated stand-alone and client-server applications that harness the power of the M environment. These are often produced with little or no knowledge of the MWAPI itself, the code being generated by the development environment. It is my hope that this book will give the reader the potential to take a look under the hood and discover what the MWAPI is all about.

To the readers of this book, I sincerely hope that you find the time while learning this technology to appreciate both its simplicity and elegance.

> Keith Snell
> Support and Development Director
> Micronetics Europe Ltd.
> Chairman of MDC MWAPI task group

Introduction

1

This book will teach you how to use the M Windowing Application Programmer Interface (MWAPI) to develop standard windows applications. The MWAPI is an American National Standards Institute (ANSI) extension of the M language designed for the development of Graphical User Interface (GUI) applications. The specification defines syntax and methods for creating applications that take advantage of windowing environments and provides support for legacy code through terminal emulation. The MWAPI eliminates the need for an in-depth knowledge of any particular target platform by providing a platform-independent development environment where applications may be freely ported among windowing systems without source code modification. Regardless of the host platform, the look-and-feel characteristics are maintained by abstracting these attributes into a standard set of syntax and methods. If the reader wants a book that provides the in-depth coverage necessary to develop powerful applications using a standard approach, this is it.

The MWAPI's high-level approach shields the developer from the lower-level operations of any particular windowing platform while retaining the functionality permitted of any other application running in the environment. The MWAPI uses a natural hierarchical syntax of Structured System Variable Names (SSVN) to maintain the definitions of windowing objects. Creating objects is as simple as assigning values to these SSVNs. It is much easier to use a familiar syntax and a few commands than to work with the numerous function calls of typical windowing APIs to accomplish the same task.

The MWAPI's approach to detecting and processing user interactions with graphical objects differs from traditional methods. The typical approach to processing events is to poll the underlying windowing system's event queue for the appropriate action. This lower-level approach requires knowledge of a particular windowing platform and is not as portable. A high-level approach referred to as *callback processing* is used to process the events for MWAPI applications. Chapter 2 discusses event processing in depth, and most of the other chapters discuss it with respect to their focus.

The structure of this book is designed to serve as a learning tool and reference during applications development. Numerous examples, tables, illustrations, sample programs, images, and discussions provide a "how-to" look at this powerful system. We demonstrate the simplicity of the MWAPI by writing the code to develop applications without the aid of a GUI builder tool. The reader will discover why it is important to learn the methods and syntax of this system even if a GUI builder tool is used.

The integration of the MWAPI is covered in seven chapters that focus on particular components of the system. Chapter 2 presents an overview of event processing and builds a foundation of required knowledge, and Chapter 9 ties all the components together with a complete and detailed application. Exercises test the knowledge of the reader on selected highlights of each chapter.

History

The MWAPI was developed in response to a growing need to enable the development of window applications using the M language. Several years ago, the M Development Committee (MDC) charged its Task Group Four, Subcommittee 11, to come up with a proposal to extend the M language standard (X11.1) to windows development. The result is a new standard specifically for windows development. In June 1993 version 1.0 of the MWAPI specification (X11.6) was granted type A status. In October 1995, version 1.0 was granted standard approval by the American National Standards Institute (ANSI), and shortly afterwards the MDC made version 1.1 of the MWAPI a type A specification. Version 1.1 adds functionality to the version 1.0 specification and modifies others. Some of the syntax specified in version 1.0 has been removed in the version 1.1 specification, causing the former to be not completely upward compatible to version 1.1. The changes to version 1.0 by 1.1 are noted throughout this book, and include:

- Clarifications to previous text.
- The ability for an MWAPI application to control pointer appearance.
- The addition of a Table gadget.
- The addition and deletion of attributes available for different objects.
- The specification for keyboard, character, and pointer button codes.
- Modification to the error codes to conform with the standard M error coding scheme.

The compatibility issue between versions 1.0 and 1.1 presents few programming difficulties. Most vendors tend to implement the features of the latest type A specification.

At the time of publication, the MWAPI is so new that version compatibility is unlikely to be an issue.

Structure

The structure of the MWAPI is hierarchical and is descended from a windowing platform. The specification does not require an underlying windowing platform and permits an MWAPI implementation to serve as the platform. In descending order from the windowing platform are *logical displays, windows,* and *elements.* Physical display devices may contain multiple logical displays, and each logical display may contain numerous windows. A single window can consist of many elements and have many other (child) windows associated with it. Figure 1.1 shows the structure of the MWAPI.

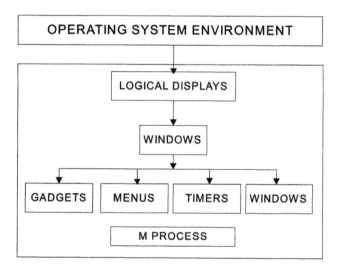

FIGURE 1.1: *MWAPI Hierarchy*

Each M process may consist of one or more logical displays descended from the root. These conceptual objects describe the environments where their descendants may exist and function. The children of all logical displays are windows, and they serve as the basis for communication between the users and applications. There are two distinct types of windows: *application* windows and *MTERM* windows. All the benefits of a graphical windowing environment can be realized via application windows; legacy code is supported in the windowing environment through the MTERM window. MTERM windows, which resemble "DOS boxes" in an MS Windows environment, are for terminal emulation, and may not have descendants. The children of application windows can be other windows, or they may be *elements.* Elements

3

provide the parent window with abilities to perform specialized tasks including I/O, event timing, and choice selection, and include gadgets, menus, and timers. A conceptual event loop detects and processes specified interactions with windows and elements. Processing events is the "handshaking" between the interface and application code.

The MWAPI can be compared to a family lineage with the windowing platform as the common ancestor. Children of the windowing platform pass down to their children certain defining characteristics, and these characteristics are in turn passed down from parent to child. Once modified, these characteristic values are inherited by subsequently created children. The inheritance of visual characteristics from parent to child is one mechanism used for obtaining the goal of maintaining the host's look-and-feel characteristics. The MWAPI differs from the natural process of inheritance by allowing an application to modify inherited characteristics. If the MWAPI implementation is acting as the windowing platform, the look and feel is determined by the implementation.

This method of programming differs from the linear model of traditional programming. To account for the nonlinear ways a user can interact with objects, windowing applications require a shift in programming technique. Windows programming employs an event model where user interactions with objects may cause events to occur.

SSVNs

Structured System Variable Names (SSVNs), which are specified by the M standard language, are an array-like structure. Unlike most of the SSVNs specified by the M standard language, MWAPI-specified SSVNs can be modified by application code. Such modifications are an essential for the creation and use of objects.

The MWAPI introduces three new SSVNs for the maintenance of the characteristics of window objects: ^$DISPLAY, ^$WINDOW, and ^$EVENT. They correlate with the hierarchy shown in Figure 1.1. The characteristics that make up logical displays are maintained in ^$DI[SPLAY]. The Window SSVN (^$W[INDOW]) houses the characteristics of windows, gadgets, menus, and timers (entities). The Event SSVN (^$E[VENT]) describes the characteristics of events as they occur to and from the structure.

Attributes

Attributes are special keywords used to specify the characteristics that make up logical displays, entities, and events, and are maintained as subscripts to ^$DI, ^$W, and ^$E respectively. These keywords maintain an intuitive correspondence to the characteristic they describe. An object's COLOR attribute describes a color characteristic of the object, and the POS attribute describes its position. Characteristics are qualified or quantified by the values assigned to their attribute nodes. The value that may be assigned to an attribute's node must lie within a specified domain determined by its function, and the keywords assigned to an object must be specified for its use. Attributes are discussed throughout this book.

Attributes assigned to ^$DI and ^$W descend from the name of the object they describe. Certain attributes are implicitly defined using default values derived from the operating system environment, implementation, or parent (inheritance). Default values may be modified from their original assignments. If a modified attribute has a default value, the use of the M KILL command on the attribute's SSVN node reference will cause the value to be restored to its default assignment; if the attribute does *not* have a default value, the operation will leave the SSVN node reference undefined.

How It Works

MWAPI entities are created by the assignment of attributes descended from the entity's name in the Window SSVN. The minimum number of attributes specified and syntax required to create an entity depends on the type of entity. The assignment operators used to create and modify attributes are SET and MERGE, and the effects of both commands are realized at the conclusion of the command. Attributes assigned by the SET command will take effect immediately. The MERGE command syntax allows for the assignment of multiple attributes at one time, and depending on the number of required attributes, may be the assignment operator needed to create the object. If multiple attributes are assigned via the MERGE command, the effect of each attribute will occur only after all of the characteristics have been assigned.

The following modifications have been made to the M language to support the MWAPI extension:

- The maximum stringlength of a variable has been extended for the CLIPBOARD Display Attribute to include the size of the clipboard.

- The maximum stringlength for the value of a Document Gadget has been modified to allow up to 32,767 characters.

- The M KILL command has been extended in scope to allow for the reestablishment of an attribute's default value.

Support is provided for exchange of data among all applications that may access the clipboard by using a clipboard feature. These applications may consist of non-M applications as well. If the underlying windowing platform provides this feature, any application that can access the windowing platform's clipboard is able to share data with MWAPI application(s) running on the same platform. If the underlying windowing platform does not provide a clipboard capability, or the MWAPI is acting as the underlying windowing system, the MWAPI implementation will provide the functionality.

5

About This Book

Chapters 2 through 8 present in-depth coverage of the syntax and use of the MWAPI from processing events to object manipulation to new functions and variables. This "one-stop shopping" approach allows the reader to find all about an object in one chapter. At the end of each chapter there are Exercises; the answers can be found in Appendix B. The information discussed is brought together into a complete application in Chapter 9. Appendix A discusses actual codes and Appendix C summarizes the book's content.

Attributes are extremely important for the creation of MWAPI objects. The use of attributes is the main focus of each chapter that deal with objects. Each attribute is thoroughly described, including notes of how they relate to other attributes and objects and other information on their usage. Since version 1.0 was approved by ANSI about the time version 1.1 became a type A specification and the MWAPI is so new, it is very likely all implementations will conform to the later specification. In the event your implementation conforms solely to version 1.0, differences in the two specifications are well documented. Commands, attribute keywords, and SSVN names are shown in uppercase, and italicized text are subscripts, command arguments, and parameters.

The reader is shown the practical aspects of MWAPI programming through the use of sample programs complete with illustrations, source code, and comments. The sample programs incorporate material covered up to the current point in the book, and lead to a complete MWAPI application in Chapter 9.

The concepts discussed in each chapter are reinforced by highlights and exercises.

Highlights

The MWAPI extends the M language to the development and operation of standard graphical user interface (GUI) applications. MWAPI applications may operate in conjunction with an underlying windowing platform, but the specification does not require this.

An application using standard MWAPI syntax will run virtually unmodified on any target windowing system and hardware platform running a conforming implementation of the MWAPI, and adhere to its host's look-and-feel characteristics.

The hierarchical structure of the interface to an MWAPI application is similar to the structure of a family tree complete with ancestor-descendant relationships and inheritance. This hierarchy is descended from the underlying windowing platform, or the MWAPI implementation to include one or more logical displays, windows and elements per M process. A conceptual event loop exists for each M process running an implementation of the MWAPI to notify objects of event occurrences.

The characteristics that make up MWAPI objects are defined by values assigned to attribute nodes descended from their names. Three SSVNs are introduced to maintain object definitions: Display (^$DI), Window (^$W), and Event (^$E).

The next chapter covers event processing. A good understanding of how to capture and process events is central to MWAPI applications.

Exercises

1. Does a developer need to have an in-depth knowledge of the low-level API of a particular windowing platform to program a complete windows application using the MWAPI?
2. Does the MWAPI attempt to maintain the look and feel provided by its host windowing platform?
3. Can an MWAPI application run without an underlying windowing platform?
4. Name the relationships in the structure of an MWAPI application.
5. What does the MWAPI specification use SSVNs for?
6. What is an attribute used for?
7. Can any value be assigned to an attribute?
8. Can any attribute be assigned to any object?
9. How are MWAPI entities created?
10. Can existing applications benefit from the MWAPI?

Event Processing

2

The focus of this chapter is on the processing of events. Most events are caused by a user interacting with the interface, and the rest are caused by the driving application. Events, and their processing, are the methods of communication between an MWAPI interface and application code; they can occur for windows, menu choices, timers, and most gadgets. This chapter presents a solid foundation upon which to build an MWAPI application through a detailed discussion of the event object.

The MWAPI uses a high-level callback method for notifying entities of events in the windowing environment's event queue, while more mainstream windowing APIs use a low-level polling approach. Callback processing simplifies event handling and does not require the developer to possess an in-depth knowledge of any particular windowing system or event queue. The callback processing technique standardizes the process of event handling across windowing platforms to give portability to a conforming application.

An understanding of the fundamentals for "hand shaking" between an interface and the applications code is crucial to the functioning of a windowing application. An MWAPI entity can process several types of events, which are discussed below in the Event Types section. The Event Processing section takes an in-depth look into the mechanics of event processing. The Event Information Attributes section focuses on the characteristics that make up event objects and the Implementation section discusses various schemes for processing events that are demonstrated in the remaining chapters. This chapter ends with Highlights and Exercises.

Event Types

Event type keywords allow an MWAPI developer to identify the events that can be processed. The MWAPI standard defines 28 event types and permits implementation-defined event types. Each keyword describes the type of an event that can be processed by an entity (see Table 2.1). Event types beginning with "Z" are reserved for implementation values and may not be portable across implementations.

The developer uses the syntax shown in Example 2.1 to specify the event type that may receive callback processing. The use of this syntax and the event types specified for each object are covered in more detail in later chapters.

TABLE **2.1**: *MWAPI Defined—Event Types*

CHANGE	GODOWNBIG	PDRAG
CHAR[1]	GOTOP	PMOVE
CLICK	GOUP	PUP
CLOSE	GOUPBIG	RESIZE
DBLCLICK	HELP	RESTORE
DESELECT	KEYDOWN	SELECT
FKEYDOWN[2]	KEYUP	TIMER
FKEYUP[2]	MAX	UNFOCUS
FOCUS	MIN	
GOBOTTOM	MOVE	
GODOWN	PDOWN	

[1] This keyword was added by the version 1.1 specification for the MWAPI.
[2] These keywords were deleted by version 1.1. The KEYDOWN and KEYUP keywords describe the events these event types did.

```
S ^$W(entity reference,"EVENT",event type)=value
```

EXAMPLE **2.1**: *Event Type Assignment Syntax*

An *entity reference* is a reference to a window, gadget, timer, or menu that is specified to receive the event. The *event type* subscript is one of the keywords listed in Table 2.1. The object referred to by *entity reference* determines the event types that can be used. The argument (*value*) specifies the routine and offset where the event can be processed.

Event types can be grouped into eight categories, shown in Table 2.2. Only MWAPI-specified event types are listed. Categories of event types include:

1. The entity type that can receive callbacks from the category. Not all event types can occur for all entity or element types.
2. A description of the event category.
3. The event types that make up the category.

The descriptions for the categories, except the Timer category, pertain to the event occurring due to user interaction. The Timer event category is particular to the timer element and the expiration of a time interval (see Chapter 7). All event types can be triggered by application code (see the ETRIGGER command in the Application Trigger section).

TABLE 2.2: *MWAPI Event Classifications*

Event Category	Entity	Description	Event Types
Focus	Window and Gadget	Focus events occur when an entity receives or loses input focus.	CHANGE FOCUS UNFOCUS
Help	Window and Gadget	Help events occur when a request for help occurs by pressing a designated key.	HELP
Keyboard	Window and Gadget	Keyboard events occur when the user presses and releases a key on the keyboard.	CHAR KEYDOWN KEYUP
Long List Box	Gadget	Long List Box events occur when a user selects a movement control in a Long List Box gadget.	GOBOTTOM GODOWN GODOWNBIG GOTOP GOUP GOUPBIG
Pointer	Window and Gadget	Pointer events occur for certain pointer actions that occur within a window or gadget.	CLICK DBLCLICK PDOWN PDRAG PMOVE PUP
Select	Window, Gadget, and Menu choice	Select events occur when a user selects or deselects a choice.	DESELECT SELECT
Timer	Timer	Timer events occur when an interval timer expires.	TIMER
Window State	Window	A window state event occurs when certain characteristics of a window change.	CLOSE MAX MIN MOVE RESIZE RESTORE

Event Processing

Event processing involves the detection and processing of interactions with entities. The MWAPI uses a method of event notification referred to as callback processing. If event processing is active, and an event occurs as a result of user interaction for an active entity with focus (reference ^$DI($PD,"FOCUS"), see Chapter 3), the MWAPI implementation checks the immediate subscripts of the entity's EVENT attribute node for an event type keyword that matches the event that occurred (see Example 2.1 for the syntax). If a matching keyword is found, the program flow can be directed to the node's value for processing.

The value of an EVENT attribute node must be a valid argument to an M DO command listing one or more processing routines. During callback processing, the Event SSVN (^$E) automatically returns information related to the triggered event. The type of event, and the object for which it occurred, are examples of the information that can be found by referencing the Event SSVN. Before and after callback processing, ^$E is undefined. Event information is returned as arguments to ^$E attribute nodes. When the callback routine terminates, control returns to the event loop to await another callback. Callback processing can also be triggered by an application executing an ETRIGGER command and the expiration of a timer's interval (see Chapter 7). Imagine callback processing as similar to a baseball game where events are thrown to the batter and hit to the object with focus. In the case of ETRIGGER execution, the SSVN node referenced in the syntax temporarily takes the place of the focus.

Events triggered by user action can cause a sequence of events to occur. For example, the sequence of events for CLICK events is PDOWN, CLICK, and PUP; for DBLCLICK events, the sequence of events is PDOWN, CLICK, PUP, PDOWN, DBLCLICK, and PUP. The MDC's version 1.1 specification for the MWAPI changed the sequence for CLICK events from PDOWN, PUP, and CLICK, while for DBLCLICK events the specification was PDOWN, PUP, CLICK, PDOWN, DBLCLICK, and PUP.

A sequence of events will also occur when the user causes focus to change from an entity with an enabled UNFOCUS or CHANGE event type node to an entity with an enabled FOCUS event type node. Both entities will receive callbacks in this situation. In order for a PDRAG event to be generated, PDOWN and PUP events will also be generated. If the callback was triggered by ETRIGGER execution, the stated event type is the only one that will occur.

Events do not occur as the result of an application modification of an SSVN. When programming an MWAPI application, the programmer should keep in mind the events that can occur due to another event. The next section discusses how EVENT nodes are used for processing events.

Callback processing can be restricted using ENABLE and FILTERIN Event Specification Attributes. Example 2.2 shows the syntax for the assignment of Event Specification Attributes. The ENABLE attribute is used to toggle whether a matching EVENT node may receive a callback. Event processing is enabled for all EVENT attribute nodes by default. The processing of an event may be disabled by assigning a value of zero to the subscript. Event processing is further restricted with the FILTERIN attribute. The programmer can use the FILTERIN attribute to restrict pointer or keyboard events to certain character, pointer, or keyboard codes before callback processing can occur. Appendix A lists keyboard and pointer button codes.

```
S ^$W(entity reference,"EVENT",event type,event specification attribute)=value
```

EXAMPLE 2.2: *Event Specification Attribute Syntax*

The MWAPI specification gives the programmer three commands to control event processing: ESTART, ESTOP, and ETRIGGER. The specifics of each command is discussed in the next few subsections, and their use are demonstrated in later chapters with applications.

Activating

The ESTART command turns on, or activates, event processing for an M process running the MWAPI. The syntax for this command is shown in Example 2.3.

```
ESTA[RT][:post conditional] [time-out]
```

EXAMPLE 2.3: *ESTART Command Syntax*

The activation of event processing permits enabled EVENT attribute nodes to process events. The user can interact with and trigger events for entities, and events triggered through application code can also occur. Event processing is temporarily deactivated at the initiation of callback processing, and reactivated when complete. However, if an enabled event occurs while event processing is temporarily deactivated during callback processing, it can be deferred until event processing is once again active. The MWAPI standard specifies no limit to the number of allowed deferred events, and events can be lost if not processed quickly. The allowed number of deferred events is determined by the size of the windowing platform's event queue.

Deferring

Event processing can be stacked by the execution of an additional ESTART command during callback processing. Information contained in ^$E is saved on the stack and the SSVN becomes undefined. The stack is popped and ^$E restored as event processing for each stack level is terminated. When a nested ESTART command is executed, the value of ^$DI($PD,"FOCUS") must indicate the name of a window whose MODAL window attribute is defined as APPLICATION during callback processing, and before execution of the nested ESTART command. The Long List Box demonstration in the Implementation section of Chapter 5 shows use of nesting ESTART commands.

A window with its MODAL attribute set to "APPLICATION" disables all other windows defined in the current copy of ^$W. If the window does not have this value for its MODAL attribute when the nesting ESTART is executed, an error is generated with a code of "M55."[1] If the window's MODAL attribute is correctly assigned, the nested ESTART saves the current variable context, increments the stack level, and activates event processing for the window, identified by ^$DI($PD,"FOCUS"), and all its elements, as well as any enabled timer events for all other windows.

13

Deactivating

When event processing is active, it will remain active for the stack level until either the ESTOP command is executed, the activating ESTART command times out, or the initiation of callback processing for an event occurs. Upon termination of an event processing stack, program execution continues with the code following the most recently executed ESTART command.

If a time-out is associated with an ESTART command, the value of $TEST is modified to indicate how the ESTART was terminated: if the value of $TEST equals one, event processing was terminated by execution of an ESTOP command; if its value equals zero, the ESTART timed out. The value of $TEST is not modified for event termination when there is no associated time-out specified.

The ESTOP command explicitly terminates event processing for the current stack level. The syntax of this command is shown in Example 2.4.

```
ESTO[P][:post conditional]
```

EXAMPLE 2.4: *ESTOP Command Syntax*

The ESTOP command implicitly executes the number of M QUIT commands necessary to return execution to the previous stack level and terminate the most recently executed ESTART command. When an ESTART is terminated, program execution continues with the line of code following the terminated command. No effect is realized if an ESTOP is executed when event processing is not active.

Application Trigger

The ETRIGGER command is used to trigger events and send a callback to a desired entity for a selected action. The syntax for this command is shown in Example 2.5.

```
ETR[IGGER][:post conditional] SSVN node reference [:data structure name]
```

EXAMPLE 2.5: *ETRIGGER Command Syntax*

The *SSVN node reference* parameter is a reference to the EVENT attribute node, indicating the event type to trigger for a window, gadget, menu choice, or timer. If the entity specified by the reference does not exist, an error will occur with a code equal to "M48."[2] If the event type specified does not exist in ^$W for the entity, an error will occur with a code equal to "M47."[3] The *data structure name* component is the name of an array containing Event Information Attribute nodes to be defined in ^$E. Event Information Attributes are keywords that identify characteristics of an event, and are covered in the next section. Additional examples of the ETRIGGER command are shown in the Implementation section of Chapter 4 and the sample program in Chapter 9.

An event caused by an ETRIGGER directs callback processing to the value of the referenced EVENT node. The only event that can occur when an ETRIGGER is executed is the one specified in its argument. An event that occurs due to the execution of an ETRIGGER command will not cause subsequent events to occur. Events that occur due to user interaction with MWAPI entities are directed to the entity with focus. The value of ^$DI($PD,"FOCUS") specifies where user-triggered events are directed (see Chapter 3 for more information on ^$DI). Events triggered by an ETRIGGER command can be directed to any active window regardless of where the focus is directed in ^$DI($PD,"FOCUS"). An ETRIGGER event will not alter focus.

The characteristics of an event triggered by ETRIGGER execution may not be sufficient to process the same event when triggered by a user. The processing routine may be designed to react to a certain event characteristics such as pointer button or keycodes, or the FILTERIN node can restrict the callback to certain codes. The user has the pointer device and keyboard to indicate these characteristics, but the same event triggered by an application does not have this advantage. The codes will need to be defined by the application by assigning the appropriate Event Information Attributes to the array named in the *data structure name* component of the ETRIGGER syntax. An event that occurs for a valid ETRIGGER execution returns some information about the event, although not all of the information normally returned when the same event is triggered by user action. If additional Event Information Attributes are needed, the application must supply them. Information specified for inclusion in ^$E must meet the following two conditions:

1. The event attribute must be allowed for the event type triggered.

2. The event attribute must not be automatically provided for the triggered event.

Table 2.4 identifies the Event Information Attributes automatically defined in ^$E for user-triggered events, and those permitted for each event type.

Example 2.6 demonstrates use of the ETRIGGER command to trigger a click event to occur for window "W" with additional characteristic keywords to be defined in the Event SSVN.

```
S DATA("NEXTFOCUS")="ANOTHER_WINDOW"
S DATA("SEQUENCE")=3
S DATA("PBUTTON")="PB1"
ETR ^$W("W","EVENT","CLICK"):DATA
```

EXAMPLE 2.6: *ETRIGGER Command*

The characteristics of the click event triggered by the syntax in Example 2.6 includes the "PBUTTON" subscript and its value because it is specified for a click event and is not automatically defined. DATA("NEXTFOCUS") is not included because the information is not specified for the event type. DATA("SEQUENCE") is automatically defined in the Event SSVN for all events, so the assignment is ignored. If an application specifies Event Information Attributes that cannot be included for the event, the attributes are ignored and no error occurs.

Event Information Attributes

Event Information Attributes are keywords assigned to the Event SSVN to describe characteristics of MWAPI events during callback processing. The ANSI standard for the MWAPI defines fifteen Event Information Attributes and also permits implementations to define their own. Attribute names that begin with the letter "Z" are reserved for implementation definitions. Implementation-defined attributes are not standard and may not be portable across implementations. Table 2.3 lists MWAPI-defined Event Information Attributes.

TABLE **2.3**: *MWAPI-Defined Event Information Attributes*

CHOICE	PPOS
CLASS	PRIORFOCUS
COL[1]	PSTATE
ELEMENT	ROW[1]
KEY	SEQUENCE
NEXTFOCUS	TYPE
OK	WINDOW
PBUTTON	Implementation Value

[1] These keywords were added by the version 1.1 specification for the MWAPI.

The syntax shown in Example 2.7 is how an Event Information Attribute appears in the Event SSVN. The keywords listed in Table 2.3 take the place of the *event information attribute*, and its *value* gives quality or quantity to the characteristic from a specified domain. The value domain is determined by the Event Information Attribute used.

```
^$E(event information attribute)= value
```

EXAMPLE **2.7**: *Event Information Attribute Syntax*

Table 2.4 shows which Event Information Attributes are defined for user-triggered event types. The attributes defined in ^$E depend on the event type that occurred and whether the event occurred due to the execution of an ETRIGGER command or by user action. If an ETRIGGER command triggers one of the event types listed, the corresponding Event Information Attribute may be undefined. The third column of the table specifies whether the Event Information Attribute is automatically included for an application triggered event. Table 2.5 shows the format used to describe each MWAPI defined Event Information Attribute.

TABLE 2.4: *Event Information Attributes by Event Type*

ATTRIBUTE	EVENT TYPE		AUTOMATICALLY PROVIDED FOR ETR in ^$E
CHOICE	DESELECT	SELECT	If the event occurs for a menu choice, this attribute is automatically provided.
CLASS	All event types		Yes
COL	CLICK	PDOWN	No
	DBLCLICK	PUP	
	DESELECT	SELECT	
ELEMENT	All element event types		If the event occurs for an element, this attribute is automatically provided.
KEY	CHAR	KEYDOWN	No
	FKEYDOWN	KEYUP	
	FKEYUP		
NEXTFOCUS	CHANGE	UNFOCUS	No
OK	CHANGE	UNFOCUS	Yes
PBUTTON	CLICK	PDRAG	No
	DBLCLICK	PMOVE	
	PDOWN	PUP	
PPOS	CLICK	PDRAG[1]	No
	DBLCLICK	PMOVE	
	PDOWN	PUP	
PRIORFOCUS	FOCUS		No
PSTATE	CLICK	PDRAG	No
	DBLCLICK	PMOVE	
	PDOWN	PUP	
ROW	CLICK	PDOWN	No
	DBLCLICK	PUP	
	DESELECT	SELECT	
SEQUENCE	All event types		Yes
TYPE	All event types		Yes
WINDOW	All event types		Yes

[1] The PPOS attribute is undefined for PDRAG events that occur for scroll gadgets. Scroll gadgets are covered in Chapter 5.

TABLE 2.5: *Attribute Description Format*

ATTRIBUTE NAME	
Description:	This section describes the attribute's function.
Syntax:	If this section exists, the attribute's value can consist of more than one parameter and the required syntax is shown here.
Domain:	This section describes the domain of valid values for the attribute.
Access:	This section describes the method of access to the attribute.
Default:	This section presents the default value of the attribute.
Events:	This section lists the event type(s) that will define the attribute. This section is in the context of user-triggered events. If the event is triggered by an ETRIGGER command for one of the event type(s) listed, the attribute may be defined.
Notes:	This section lists any pertinent notes about this attribute. If the attribute is automatically defined for an ETRIGGER event using one of the event types listed, it is noted here. This section will cover any modifications made to this attribute definition by the MDC's version 1.1 type A specification for the MWAPI. If there are no further notes to list, this section will not exist.

CHOICE

Description: This attribute specifies the subscript value of the choice selected or deselected. The value returned is the *item* subscript value of the choice.

Domain: The domain of values is a valid subscript reference.

Access: The attribute's value can be modified through the syntax of the ETRIGGER, otherwise it can only be referenced.

Default: There is no default value for this attribute.

Events: DESELECT   SELECT

Notes: Chapters 5 and 7 explain the *item* subscript for a choice.
    The attribute node is automatically defined for application triggered events for menu choices.

CLASS

Description: This attribute specifies the event's class.

Domain: The domain of values is a string of characters.

Access: The value of this attribute can only be referenced for its value.

Default: There is no default value for this attribute.

Events: This attribute is returned for every MWAPI defined event types.

Notes: For MWAPI defined event types, this attribute's value is "WINDOW." For implementation-defined event types, the value is determined by the implementation.
    This attribute is automatically provided during callback processing for all events regardless of how they were triggered.

COL

Description: This attribute specifies the subscript value of the column associated with the event. The value returned is the *citem* subscript defining a column in the gadget.

Domain: The domain of values is a valid subscript reference.

Access: The attribute's value can be modified through the syntax of the ETRIGGER, otherwise it can only be referenced.

Default: There is no default value for this attribute.

Events: CLICK   PDOWN
DBLCLICK   PUP
DESELECT   SELECT

Notes: The *citem* subscript is covered in Chapter 5.
    This attribute was added to the MWAPI by the MDC's version 1.1 specification.

ELEMENT

Description: This attribute specifies the type and name of the element for which the event occurred.

Syntax: `element type,element name`

Domain: The domain of values for the *element name* parameter is an element specified for the current window. The *element type* parameter is determined by the kind of element that received the callback as shown below:

18

Element Type	Element
G	Gadget
M	Menu
T	Timer

Access: The value of this attribute can only be referenced for its value.

Default: There is no default value for this attribute.

Events: This attribute is specified for all events that occur for elements.

Notes: This attribute's node is automatically defined for events triggered by the ETRIGGER command and directed to an element.

KEY

Description: This attribute specifies the key code(s) associated with a keyboard event.

Domain: The domain of values is a comma delineated string of keycodes, or the emptystring.

Access: The attribute's value can be modified through the syntax of the ETRIGGER, otherwise it can only be referenced.

Default: There is no default value for this attribute.

Events: CHAR   KEYUP
KEYDOWN

Notes If no keys were pressed during a pointer event, the value is the emptystring.[4] Keycodes are listed in Appendix A.

NEXTFOCUS

Description: This attribute specifies the name of the window or gadget that will receive a related FOCUS event.

Syntax: wname[,gname]

Domain: The domain of values is the name of a window name (*wname*), window name and gadget (*gname*), or the emptystring.

Access: The attribute's value can be modified through the syntax of the ETRIGGER, otherwise it can only be referenced.

Default: There is no default value for this attribute.

Events: CHANGE   UNFOCUS

Notes: If the window or gadget cannot receive a related FOCUS event, the value of this attribute is the emptystring.

 If the event is triggered by an ETRIGGER command, no related FOCUS event will occur.

OK

Description: This attribute specifies whether processing for the event will be completed normally.

Domain: If the attribute's node is defined, the value is the emptystring.

Access: The value of this attribute can only be modified using the M KILL command, or referenced for its value.

Default:	The default value is the emptystring.
Events:	CHANGE UNFOCUS
Notes:	If this attribute is defined, event processing will continue in the manner specified in the Event Processing section.

If this attribute is killed, event processing will terminate, a request to change focus is denied, a focus event will not trigger, and any normal actions of the underlying interface will not occur for the event.

This attribute is automatically defined during callback processing for a CHANGE or UNFOCUS event triggered by the ETRIGGER command.

If an application attempts to assign a value to this attribute, an error is generated with a code equal to "M47." |

PBUTTON

Description:	This attribute identifies the pointer button code associated with a pointer event.
Domain:	The domain of values is a pointer button code.
Access:	The attribute's value can be modified through the syntax of the ETRIGGER, otherwise it can only be referenced.
Default:	There is no default value for this attribute.
Events:	CLICK PDRAG
DBLCLICK   PMOVE
PDOWN   PUP
Notes:	If no pointer buttons are pressed when the event is triggered, the value of this attribute is the emptystring. Pointer button codes are listed in Appendix A.

PPOS

Description:	This attribute identifies the pointer position of a pointer event.
Syntax:	*hpos,vpos,unitspec*
Domain:	The domain of values for the *hpos* and *vpos* parameters are numeric literals. Version 1.1 of the MDC type A specification modified these parameters to include negative values. The *unitspec* parameter is the unit of measurement used by the window or element for which the event occurred.
Access:	The attribute's value can be modified through the syntax of the ETRIGGER, otherwise it can only be referenced.
Default:	There is no default value for this attribute.
Events:	CLICK PDRAG
DBLCLICK   PMOVE
PDOWN   PUP
Notes:	The parameters *hpos* and *vpos* are measured from the origin of the object for which the event occurred.

If the target of the callback is a scroll gadget, this attribute is not defined. |

PRIORFOCUS

Description:	This attribute specifies the name of the window, or gadget, that will receive a related CHANGE or UNFOCUS event.

Syntax:	`wname[,gname]`
Domain:	The domain of values is the name of a window (*wname*), window name and gadget (*gname*), or the emptystring.
Access:	The attribute's value can be modified through the syntax of the ETRIGGER, otherwise it can only be referenced.
Default:	There is no default value for this attribute.
Events:	This attribute is only defined for FOCUS events.
Notes:	If the previous window or gadget cannot receive callback processing for a CHANGE or UNFOCUS event, the value of this attribute is the emptystring.
	If the event is triggered by an ETRIGGER command, no related CHANGE or UNFOCUS event will occur.

PSTATE

Description:	This attribute identifies the pointer button codes associated with a pointer event.
Domain:	The domain of values is a comma delineated string of pointer button codes or the emptystring.
Access:	The attribute's value can be modified through the syntax of the ETRIGGER, otherwise it can only be referenced.
Default:	There is no default value for this attribute.
Events:	CLICK PDRAG DBLCLICK PMOVE PDOWN PUP
Notes:	Multiple pointer button codes are delineated by the comma character.
	If no pointer buttons were pushed for the event, the value of this attribute is the emptystring. Pointer button codes are listed in Appendix A.

ROW

Description:	This attribute identifies the row associated with the event. The value returned is the *ritem* subscript defining a row in the gadget.
Domain:	The domain of values is a valid subscript reference.
Access:	The attribute's value can be modified through the syntax of the ETRIGGER, otherwise it can only be referenced.
Default:	There is no default value for this attribute.
Events:	CLICK PDOWN DBLCLICK PUP DESELECT SELECT
Notes:	The *ritem* subscript is covered in Chapter 5.
	This attribute was added to the MWAPI by the MDC's version 1.1 specification.

SEQUENCE

Description:	This attribute uniquely identifies a unique number for each callback received in a process.

Domain:	The domain of values is a numeric literal.
Access:	The value of this attribute can only be referenced.
Default:	There is no default value for this attribute.
Events:	This attribute is defined for every MWAPI defined event type.
Notes:	The MWAPI keeps a running counter of the number of events for which callback processing occurs. The value of this attribute shows in this sequence where a valid event occurred.
	This attribute is automatically defined during callback processing for events triggered by the ETRIGGER command.

TYPE

Description:	This attribute identifies the type of event that occurred.
Domain:	The domain of values is a valid event type keyword as shown in Table 2.1.
Access:	The value of this attribute can only be referenced.
Default:	There is no default value for this attribute.
Events:	This attribute is defined for every MWAPI defined event.
Notes:	This attribute is automatically defined during callback processing for events triggered by the ETRIGGER command.

WINDOW

Description:	This attribute identifies the name of the window where the event occurred.
Domain:	The domain of values is a window name defined for the current logical display.
Access:	The value of this attribute can only be referenced.
Default:	There is no default value for this attribute.
Events:	This attribute is defined for every MWAPI defined event.
Notes:	This attribute is automatically defined during callback processing for events triggered by the ETRIGGER command.

Implementation

This section presents a few event processing techniques a programmer can use to process events in an MWAPI application. Each of these techniques has their advantages and disadvantages, so the situation and the programming style will dictate the method used to process events. These situations are demonstrated in the Implementation sections of later chapters.

Use one callback routine for each event node. This is a rather simplistic method for determining what event occurred and for what entity. The programmer will know exactly what event occurred for which window or element. This method has the advantage of simplicity, but will probably require duplication of code and source code larger than necessary.

Use one callback for all entities, similar entities, or similar event types. This method is a bit more complicated than the method above. It requires application code to reference the Event SSVN to determine the event that occurred, and for which object. This method can have the advantage of reducing overall source code size required to process events, but it can be more time intensive and complicated to design.

Events can be stacked for processing at a later time. This method can prevent the user from having to wait for an event to process completely before another interaction, but the stacking of events, and the subsequent processing, is more complicated than the processing techniques mentioned above. All windows in the same M process are disabled while events are being stacked.

Highlights

The ESTART command is used to activate event processing for a stack level. The ESTOP command explicitly deactivates event processing for the current stack level. Control resumes with the code following the most recently executed ESTART command.

Event type keywords permit the programmer to define the events that can be processed. User-triggered events occur for the entity with focus at the time of event occurrence, as defined by ^$DI($PD,"FOCUS"). Events triggered by ETRIGGER execution can occur for any event node, regardless of focus. During callback processing, characteristics of events are available to processing routines in the form of Event Information Attribute node values that are assigned to the Event SSVN (^$E). ENABLE and FILTERIN Event Specification Attributes enable and restrict, respectively, the processing for the event type keyword from which they are descended. When the processing routine terminates, control is returned to the event loop to await another callback.

If an ESTART command is executed during callback processing, event processing can be stacked and ^$E becomes undefined. The window with focus must indicate a window with its MODAL attribute equal to "APPLICATION." If processing is terminated at the stack level, the stack is popped, ^$E is defined with the previously stacked values, and the program continues execution with the code following the terminated ESTART.

This chapter has built a foundation for working with MWAPI entities. The concepts discussed here are demonstrated and referred to in the chapters that follow.

Exercises

1. What is the name of the Event SSVN?
2. How does an application determine the entity for which callback processing occurs?
3. How do events occur?
4. Does the modification of a SSVN cause an MWAPI event to occur?
5. How is the method the MWAPI uses to notify and process events different from the polling technique?
6. What commands activate and deactivate event processing?

7. How can a programmer control the processing of an event once event processing has been activated?

8. If an ESTOP command is executed, does program execution continue after the most recently executed ESTART command?

9. How is the processing for events stacked?

10. Once event processing is activated, how can it be deactivated?

11. What is the ETRIGGER command used for?

12. When can ^$E event attribute values be assigned by application code?

Endnotes

[1] The MDC's version 1.1 specification changed the error code from "M?10."

[2] The MDC's version 1.1 specification changed the error code from "M?3."

[3] The MDC's version 1.1 specification changed the error code from "M?2."

[4] The MDC's version 1.1 specification for the MWAPI made a few modifications to the ANSI MWAPI standard for this attribute:

A. This attribute is no longer available for pointer events.

B. The FKEYDOWN and FKEYUP event types have been removed.

C. The CHAR event type was added.

Logical Displays

3

This chapter focuses on the environments where entities are displayed and function. *Logical displays* are conceptual objects that describe the operating environments to (and provide the frameworks for) the containment of their descendants. Descendant objects may be conceptual or physical, and provide the front end and interaction to the application. Multiple logical displays can exist for each M process, and each can describe the characteristics of different environments. Each display is a separate operating envelope for its descendants; their defined areas can overlap, but they cannot share information.

The characteristics of logical displays are described by attribute node values assigned to the Display SSVN (^$DI[SPLAY]), which contain the following information about their environments:

1. hardware capabilities including the presence of a keyboard, mouse, and pen device;
2. the contents of the clipboard;
3. the default characteristics to pass down to its descendants; and
4. the object where user actions are directed.

The characteristics of logical displays that are defined for different processes, and even in the same process, can have dissimilar properties.

The discussion of the logical display is broken down into several sections. The Creation and Modification section discusses how a logical display is created, how it interacts with its descendants, and how an application can modify it. The Display Attributes section presents the attributes available to define the characteristics of logical displays. The Implementation section shows an example of ^$DI and discusses its settings. After reading this chapter, the reader will know how to ascertain environmental characteristics of a logical display and use them for the creation and function of entities.

Creation and Modification

The method of creation of logical displays is not specifically stated in the MWAPI specification; it is left up to the determination of the MWAPI implementation. Regardless of the method of creation, a logical display must exist prior to the existence of any of its descendants. When a logical display is created, the initial values are assigned to the M process's Display SSVN, which is determined either by the underlying windowing platform or the MWAPI implementation to describe the environment, using the syntax shown in Example 3.1.

```
^$DI(display name,attribute name)
```

EXAMPLE 3.1: *Display Attribute Reference Syntax*

The *display name* subscript is the name of a logical display to uniquely define each logical display in the M process. Its maximum stringlength is thirty-one characters. Characteristics are identified by the *attribute name* subscript, and are one of the keywords identified in the Display Attributes section. The value of a display attribute node defines the quality, or quantity, of the characteristic the attribute describes, and must fall within a specified range of values. The range of values that can be assigned to an attribute is referred to as the *attribute's domain*.

One of the goals of the MWAPI is to maintain the same look and feel of the underlying windowing platform. In an effort to accomplish this, the windowing platform's current color, font, and unit-of-measurement characteristics are inherited as default values by the color, font, and unit-of-measurement attributes of each logical display. These default attribute values are passed down to the display's descendant entities to define attributes with the same name. They may be modified at any time, and the new values are inherited by those descendants created after the modification.

After a logical display is created, many of its attribute node values can be modified using the syntax shown in Example 3.2. The M SET command is used in this example, but the M MERGE command will work as well. The special variable $PD returns the name of the current logical display, and can be used in place of a display's name. A few rules must be followed to avoid errors making such modifications:

- The name of the logical display subscript must specify a logical display created for the current process or an error will occur with a code equal to "M48."[1]
- The attribute name must be specified in Table 3.1 or an error will occur with its code equal to "M46."[2]
- If the assignment of an attributes value is not within the domain of values for the attribute, an error will occur with a code equal to "M47."[3]

```
S ^$DI(display name,display attribute)=value
```

EXAMPLE 3.2: *Display Attribute Syntax*

Display Attributes

Display attributes are special keywords assigned to Display SSVNs. They are used to define the characteristics that make up logical displays. Attributes are assigned as upper-case subscripts descended from a logical display's name in the Display SSVN (^$DI[SPLAY]). The MWAPI defines twenty attribute keywords and permits application- and implementation-defined attributes to describe the logical display. Application attributes are assigned by an application and cannot exceed a maximum stringlength of thirty-one characters. The data stored in ^$DI should logically pertain to the logical display; however, this is not a requirement. Keywords starting with "Y" are reserved for application attributes, and keywords starting with "Z" are reserved for implementation-defined attributes. Implementation attributes are defined by the vendor's implementation and may not be portable. Attributes defined by the MWAPI are standard and portable across vendor implementations of the MWAPI. Table 3.1 lists MWAPI defined attributes available to logical displays grouped by functional category:

Appearance: Keywords in this category define default color and pointer appearance characteristics for child windows.

Hardware: Hardware capabilities of environments are described by attributes in this category.

Input Focus: This category indicates where user actions are directed.

Properties: These attributes define properties of the logical display.

System: Capabilities of the windowing platform are defined by the system category.

Text: This category defines text capabilities for descendant entities.

TABLE 3.1: *MWAPI-Defined Display Attributes*

APPEARANCE	BCOLOR	PROPERTIES	SIZE
	COLOR		UNITS
	COLORTYPE	SYSTEM	CLIPBOARD
	FCOLOR		PLATFORM
	PTYPE[1]	TEXT	FFACE[1]
	SPECTRUM		FSIZE[1]
HARDWARE	KEYBOARD		FSTYLE[1]
	PEN		TBCOLOR[1]
	PTR		TFCOLOR[1]
INPUT FOCUS	FOCUS		TYPEFACE

[1] These keywords were added by the version 1.1 specification for the MWAPI.

27

In an effort to maintain the look and feel of the underlying windowing platform (if there is one), attribute values that describe color, font, and unit-of-measurement characteristics that exist when a logical display is created are inherited by the logical display. These values are inherited as default values by the children of the display. If an application modifies any of these values, all children of the logical display created after the modification will inherit the new values. Even though ^$DI contains attribute values that define visual characteristics, a logical display has no visual effects of its own. Table 3.2 lists the attributes that provide default values to descendants of a logical display.

TABLE 3.2: *Inherited Attributes*

BCOLOR	FSTYLE
COLOR	TBCOLOR
FCOLOR	TFCOLOR
FFACE	UNITS
FSIZE	

The values of the attributes listed in Table 3.2 can be modified using the syntax shown in Example 3.2. If an application seeks to restore the value of an attribute with a default, it must use the attribute node reference, as shown in Example 3.3, as the argument to an M KILL command. An M KILL command that is used on an attribute that has no default will leave the attribute's value undefined. Attributes are described below using the format presented in Table 3.3.

```
K ^$DI($PD,display attribute)
```

EXAMPLE 3.3: *Display Attribute Kill Syntax*

TABLE 3.3: *Attribute Description Format*

ATTRIBUTE NAME	
Description:	This section describes the attribute's function.
Syntax:	If this section exists, the attributes value can consist of more than one parameter. The required syntax is shown here.
Domain:	This section lists the domain of allowable values for the attribute.
Access:	This section lists the method(s) of usage for this attribute.
Default:	This section specifies the default value for this attribute.
Notes:	This section lists any pertinent notes about this attribute. This section will cover any modifications made to this attribute definition by the MDC's version 1.1 specification for the MWAPI. If there are no further notes to list, this section will not exist.

BCOLOR

Description: This attribute indicates the default value for the BCOLOR Window Attribute for child windows of the logical display.

Syntax: `rcolor,gcolor,bcolor`

Domain: The domain of values are color definitions specified by the amount of red, green, and blue (RGB). Black="0,0,0" and white="65535,65535,65535." Appropriate color values lie between 0 and 65535.

Access: The value of this attribute can be modified and referenced.

Default: The default value is the value for the background color defined for underlying windowing system. If there is no underlying windowing system, the value is defined by the MWAPI.

Notes: The value of this attribute serves as the default background for child windows of the display. Color values are listed in Appendix A.

CLIPBOARD

Description: This attribute specifies the data associated with the logical display's clipboard.

Domain: The domain of values consists of a string of characters. This attribute is not defined if there is no value present in the clipboard.

Access: The value of this attribute can be modified and referenced.

Default: A default value is not applicable for this attribute. Since the clipboard is defined and emptied by user interaction, there may be no value to assign to CLIPBOARD when ^$DI is created.

Notes: If the underlying windowing platform does not supply a clipboard function, the clipboard capability is supplied by the MWAPI implementation.

The M language specification for maximum stringlength has been modified for this attribute. The MWAPI extends the maximum stringlength limitation for the clipboard to a string long enough to hold the contents of the clipboard.

COLOR

Description: This attribute specifies the default COLOR Window Attribute value for child windows of the logical display.

Syntax: `rcolor,gcolor,bcolor`

Domain: The domain of values are color definitions specified by the amount of red, green, and blue (RGB). Black="0,0,0" and white="65535,65535,65535." Appropriate color values lie between 0 and 65535.

Access: The value of this attribute can be modified or referenced.

Default: The default value is the value for the application area color for windows as defined by the underlying windowing system. If there is no underlying windowing system, the value is defined by the MWAPI.

Notes: The value of this attribute serves as the default for the color of the application area of child windows. Color values are listed in Appendix A.

COLORTYPE

Description: This attribute indicates the color capabilities of the logical display.

Domain:	The domain of values are:	

Value	Description
COLOR	The logical display can display colors.
GREY	The logical display can display multiple shades of grey.
MONO	The logical display can display only two colors.
Implementation Value	The value is defined by the implementation. Values beginning with "Z" are reserved for implementation values.

Access: The value of this attribute can only be referenced.

Default: This attribute has no default value. The value of this attribute is derived from the color capability of the physical display device.

Notes: If the value of this attribute is GREY, the color attributes will display shades of grey determined by their color values.

If the value of this attribute is MONO, color attributes are displayed using the capabilities of the physical display.

FCOLOR

Description: This attribute indicates the default FCOLOR Window Attribute for child windows of the logical display.

Syntax: `rcolor,gcolor,bcolor`

Domain: The domain of values are color definitions as specified by the amount of red, green, and blue (RGB). Black="0,0,0" and white="65535,65535,65535." Appropriate color values lie between 0 and 65535.

Access: The value of this attribute can be modified and referenced.

Default: The default value is the foreground color determined for the underlying windowing platform.

Notes: The value of this attribute serves as the default foreground for child windows of the display. Color values are listed in Appendix A.

FFACE

Description: This attribute specifies the default FFACE Window Attribute for child windows of the logical display.

Domain: The domain is one of the *fontface* values defined by the third level subscript of the logical display's TYPEFACE attribute node or one of the fontfaces listed below.

Fontface	Description
M,DEFAULT	This is the default typeface as defined for the underlying windowing system. If there is no underlying windowing platform, the MWAPI will define it.
M,FIXED	This is a nonproportional typeface.
M,SANS	This is a proportional typeface from the sans-serif family.
M,SERIF	This is a proportional typeface from the serif family.

Implementation Value   The value is defined by the implementation. Values beginning with "Z" are reserved for implementation values.

Access: The value of this attribute can be modified and referenced.

Default: The default value of this attribute is M,DEFAULT.

Notes: The value of this attribute serves as the default value for the fontface used by text in child windows of the logical display.

Modification of the value of this attribute will not effect descendants already created.

If the value requested cannot be provided, an alternative value is assigned by the underlying windowing interface. In any case, any reference to this attribute will reflect the actual value.

FOCUS

Description: This attribute is used to define the object that will receive focus in the logical display.

Syntax: *window name[gadget name]* or the emptystring.

Domain: The domain of values for the *window name* parameter is the name of a window defined in ^$W. The domain for the *gadget name* parameter, if specified, is the name of a gadget defined for the window. If input focus is not directed to a window in the logical display, the value is the emptystring.

Access: The value of this attribute can be modified and referenced.

Default: If there is a default value for this attribute, it is determined by the underlying windowing platform.

Notes: If a window or gadget has focus, keyboard and pointer inputs associated with the logical display are sent to the window or gadget.

The MWAPI dynamically updates this attribute as the user changes the object of focus.

Focus can be modified by application code or a user action such as clicking on an object. An application can influence which object receives focus by assigning the appropriate value(s) to this attribute. If application code makes the modification, an event will not occur.

If an application sets focus to a window that is in its iconic state (the window's MIN attribute node equals true), the window is restored to its open state (MIN is false). Window attributes are covered in Chapter 4.

An error, with a code of "M49"[4] will occur if an application attempts to assign focus to: (1) an invisible window (the window's VISIBLE attribute node equals false); (2) an inactive window (the window's ACTIVE attribute node equals false); (3) a gadget that is not capable of receiving focus; (4) a window that is disabled because of a modal window (the other window's MODAL attribute is defined); or (5) a window defined for a logical display of another process (the window's DISPLAY attribute does not equal the value of $PD).

31

FSIZE

Description: This attribute specifies the default FSIZE Window Attribute value for child windows of the logical display.

Domain: The domain is a positive numeric value that specifies point size (1/72 inch). If the FFACE attribute value is found in the logical display's TYPEFACE attribute node, the possible values are indicated by its descendant subscripts (see the TYPEFACE attribute).

Access: The value of this attribute can be modified and referenced.

Default: The default value is 12.

Notes: The value of this attribute serves as the default size of text in child windows of display.

Modification of the value of this attribute will not affect descendants already created.

If the value requested cannot be provided, an alternative value is assigned by the underlying windowing interface. In any case, any reference to this attribute will reflect the actual value.

FSTYLE

Description: This attribute specifies the default FSTYLE Window Attribute value for child windows of the logical display.

Domain: The domain of values are:

Value	Description
NORMAL	The text is displayed in a normal style.
BOLD	The text is displayed in bold.
ITALIC	The text is displayed in italics.
ULINE	The text is displayed underlined.
Implementation Value	The text is displayed in an implementation-defined manner. Values beginning with "Z" are reserved for implementation values.

Access: The value of this attribute can be modified and referenced.

Default: The default value is NORMAL.

Notes: The values listed may be combined using the comma character as a delineator: BOLD,ULINE. The value NORMAL cannot be combined with other values.

The value of this attribute serves as the default style for text used in child windows of the display.

Modification of the value of this attribute will not affect descendants already created.

If the value requested cannot be provided, an alternative value is assigned by the underlying windowing interface. In any case, any reference to this attribute will reflect the actual value.

KEYBOARD

Description: This attribute indicates if a keyboard is connected and available to the logical display.

Domain: If this attribute is defined, the value is the emptystring.

Access: This attribute can only be referenced.

Default: A default value is not applicable to this attribute. A logical display does not have to have a keyboard.

Notes: If this attribute is defined, the logical display has a keyboard.
   If this attribute is not defined, the logical display does not have a keyboard.

PEN

Description: This attribute indicates if a pen is connected and available to the logical display.

Domain: If this attribute is defined, the value is the emptystring.

Access: This attribute can only be referenced.

Default: A default value is not applicable to this attribute. A logical display does not have to have a pen.

Notes: If this attribute is defined, the logical display has a pen.
   If this attribute is not defined, the logical display does not have a pen.

PLATFORM

Description: This attribute identifies the name and version of the underlying windowing platform.

Syntax: `[platform name, version id]`

Domain: The domain of values for the *platform name* parameter is one of the values listed below.

Value	Description
MAC	Apple Macintosh
MSWIN	Microsoft Windows
PM	Presentation Manager
X/MTF	Xwindow/Motif
X/OPNLK	Xwindow/Open Look
Implementation Value	The value is defined by the implementation. Values beginning with "Z" are reserved for implementation values.

  The domain of values for the *version id* parameter are characters.

Access: This attribute can only be referenced for its value.

Default: A default value is not applicable to this attribute. The platform name value may not be indicated for the underlying windowing platform.

Notes: If there is no underlying windowing platform, the value of this attribute is implementation-defined.

PTR

Description: This attribute indicates if a pointer device is connected and available to the logical display.

Domain: If this attribute is defined, the value is the emptystring.

Access: This attribute can only be referenced.

Default: A default value is not applicable to this attribute. A logical display does not have to have a pointer device.

Notes: If this attribute is defined, the logical display has a pointer device.

    If this attribute is not defined, the logical display does not have a pointer device.

PTYPE

Description: This attribute specifies the appearance of the pointer when it is over the view-port of a child window defined for the logical display.

Domain: The domain of values are:

Value	Description
M,CROSS	Indicates cross-hair appearance.
M,IBEAM	Indicates I-beam appearance.
M,WAIT	Indicates wait appearance.

External Resource	
R,*resourceid*	A resource ID specifies a valid resource to be included.
F,*fileid*	A file ID indicates the path to a valid file identifier to be included.
Implementation Value	The value is defined by the implementation. Values beginning with "Z" are reserved for implementation values.

Access: The value of this attribute can be modified and referenced.

Default: This attribute has no default value.

Notes: Windows and gadgets can also specify the appearance of the pointer, but the value of the PTYPE Display Attribute takes precedence.

    If this attribute is not defined and the pointer is not over an entity with its PTYPE attribute defined, the appearance of the pointer is determined by the windowing platform.

    If the logical display does not have a pointer device attached to it (the PTR attribute is not defined), the value of this attribute is ignored.

SIZE

Description: This attribute specifies the size of the logical display.

Syntax: `hsize,vsize,unitspec`

Domain: The value of this attribute consists of three parameters: the horizontal size (*hsize*), the vertical size (*vsize*), and the unit of measurement (*unitspec*). The domain of values for the *hsize* and *vsize* parameters are positive numeric literals, including zero. The domain of values for the *unitspec* component are:

Value	Description
CHAR[,*chars*]	This unit of measurement is based upon the current font. The value domain for the *chars* parameter is one or more characters.

PIXEL	This unit of measurement is based upon the size of a pixel.
POINT	This unit of measurement is based upon the point (1/72 inches).
REL[,hscale,vscale]	This unit of measurement is based upon a scale relative to the size of the physical display. The parameters *hscale* and *vscale* have the domain of numeric literal values.
Implementation Value	This unit of measurement is defined by the implementation. Values beginning with "Z" are reserved for implementation values.

Access: The value of this attribute can only be referenced.

Default: The default value, if any, is platform dependent.

Notes: The basis font for a unit of measurement of CHAR is specified by the values of the FFACE, FSIZE, and FSTYLE Display Attributes. If the *chars* parameter is specified, and not equal to the emptystring, the average width of all characters specified is used to determine the unit of measurement.

The *hscale* and *vscale* parameters of the REL unit of measurement specify the degree the horizontal and vertical coordinates match the same coordinates of the physical display. If *hscale*, *vscale*, or both are unspecified, the default for the missing parameter is 100.

SPECTRUM

Description: This attribute specifies the number of distinct colors or greytones the logical display supports.

Domain: The domain of values are numeric literals determined by the value of the logical displays COLORTYPE attribute. The values can are determined in the manner specified below.

COLORTYPE

Attribute Value	Description
COLOR	The value of this attribute is the number of distinct color values (number of RGB combinations) the logical display supports.
GREY	The value of this attribute is the number of distinct greytones the logical display supports.
MONO	The value of this attribute is 2.
Implementation Value	The value is defined by the implementation. Values beginning with "Z" are reserved for implementation values.

Access: The value of this attribute can only be referenced.

Default: There is no default value for this attribute.

Notes: The value of this attribute is determined by the capabilities of the physical display. These capabilities can differ between displays.

TBCOLOR

Description: This attribute specifies the default TBCOLOR Window Attribute value for child windows of the logical display.

Syntax: `rcolor,gcolor,bcolor`

Domain: The domain of values are color definitions specified by the amount of red, green, and blue (RGB). Black="0,0,0" and white="65535,65535,65535." Appropriate color values lie between 0 and 65535.

Access: The value of this attribute can be modified and referenced.

Default: There is no specified default value for this attribute.

Notes: The value of this attribute serves as the default background color for the title of child windows. Color values are listed in Appendix A.

TFCOLOR

Description: This attribute specifies the default TFCOLOR Window Attribute value for child windows of the logical display.

Syntax: `rcolor,gcolor,bcolor`

Domain: The domain of values are color definitions specified by the amount of red, green, and blue (RGB). Black="0,0,0" and white="65535,65535,65535." Appropriate color values lie between 0 and 65535.

Access: The value of this attribute can be modified and referenced.

Default: The MWAPI does not specify a default value for this attribute.

Notes: The value of this attribute serves as the default value for the foreground color for the title of child windows of the display. Color values are listed in Appendix A.

TYPEFACE

Description: This attribute provides information, via descendant nodes, about the typeface (*fontface*) capabilities of the logical display.

Syntax: The syntax for this attribute's node varies from the syntax shown in Example 3.2. The syntax for this node is:

`^$DI(display name,"TYPEFACE",fontface,fontsize)=""`

Domain: The subscript *fontface* is the name of a fontface available to the logical display by the underlying windowing platform, and provides a domain of values for the FFACE attribute. The subscript *fontsize* indicates the fontsizes available for the *fontface* specified. The domain of values for *fontsize* are positive numeric values that indicate a measurement in points (1/72 of an inch) and define a value domain for the FSIZE attribute. A fontsize value of zero indicates a scaleable fontface. The value of this attribute and all nodes descended from it is the emptystring.

Access: This node can only be referenced.

Default: There is no default value for this attribute.

Notes: If an application attempts to assign value to a font attribute that does not exist as a descendant node to the TYPEFACE attribute, or is not one of the MWAPI

keywords (see the domain for the FFACE display attribute), the MWAPI implementation will make an appropriate substitution.

Since there is no requirement for an underlying windowing interface, this
node may not exist.

UNITS

Description: This attribute defines the unit of measurement of the logical display.

Domain: The domain values are as follows:

Value	Description
CHAR[,*chars*]	The unit of measurement is based upon the current font. The value domain for the *chars* parameter is one or more characters.
PIXEL	The unit of measurement is based upon the size of a pixel.
POINT	The unit of measurement is based upon the point (1/72 inches).
REL[,*hscale*,*vscale*]	This unit of measurement is based upon a scale relative to the size of the physical display.
Implementation Value	The value is defined by the implementation. Values beginning with "Z" are reserved for implementation values.

Access: The value of this attribute can be modified and referenced.

Default: The default value is PIXEL.

Notes: The basis font for a unit of measurement of CHAR is specified by the values of
the FFACE, FSIZE, and FSTYLE Display Attributes. If the *chars* parameter is
specified, and not equal to the emptystring, the average width of all characters
specified is used to determine the unit of measure.

The *hscale* and *vscale* parameters of the REL unit of measurement specify
the degree the horizontal and vertical coordinates match the same coordinates
of the physical display. If *hscale, vscale,* or both are not specified, the default for
the missing parameter is 100.

The value of this attribute serves as the default UNITS attribute value of all
application child windows of the logical display.

Implementation

Below is an example of the SSVN ^$DISPLAY. The information contained in this SSVN
tells the characteristics, or capabilities, of the logical display CONSOLE.

The existence of the KEYBOARD and PTR attribute nodes indicate both a keyboard and pointer device, such as a mouse, are connected to the logical display
"CONSOLE." The value of the COLORTYPE attribute shows that the windowing system is capable of displaying the number of color combinations defined by SPEC-
TRUM. The background, foreground, and application color area settings in the

windowing system's control panel are reflected in the assignments to BCOLOR, FCOLOR, and COLOR respectively. PLATFORM tells the host it is Microsoft Windows, and TYPEFACE lists the font capabilities of "MSWIN." All descendants will default to use the style of type defined as normal for the windowing platform in 12 points with no formatting. The size of the logical display is 640,480 measured in the units of measurement defined by the UNITS attribute.

```
^$DI("CONSOLE","BCOLOR") <65535,65535,65535>
^$DI("CONSOLE","COLOR") <65535,65535,65535>
^$DI("CONSOLE","COLORTYPE") <COLOR>
^$DI("CONSOLE","FCOLOR") <0,0,0>
^$DI("CONSOLE","FFACE") <M,DEFAULT>
^$DI("CONSOLE","FOCUS") <>
^$DI("CONSOLE","FSIZE") <12>
^$DI("CONSOLE","FSTYLE") <NORMAL>
^$DI("CONSOLE","KEYBOARD") <>
^$DI("CONSOLE","PLATFORM") <MSWIN>
^$DI("CONSOLE","PTR") <>
^$DI("CONSOLE","SIZE") <640,480>
^$DI("CONSOLE","SPECTRUM") <256>
^$DI("CONSOLE","TYPEFACE","Algerian",35) <>
^$DI("CONSOLE","TYPEFACE","Arial",36) <>
^$DI("CONSOLE","TYPEFACE","Arial Rounded MT Bold",37) <>
^$DI("CONSOLE","TYPEFACE","Bookman Old Style",37) <>
^$DI("CONSOLE","TYPEFACE","Braggadocio",39) <>
^$DI("CONSOLE","TYPEFACE","Britannic Bold",36) <>
^$DI("CONSOLE","TYPEFACE","Brush Script MT",39) <>
^$DI("CONSOLE","TYPEFACE","Century Gothic",38) <>
^$DI("CONSOLE","TYPEFACE","Colonna MT",34) <>
^$DI("CONSOLE","TYPEFACE","Courier",13) <>
^$DI("CONSOLE","TYPEFACE","Courier",16) <>
^$DI("CONSOLE","TYPEFACE","Courier",20) <>
^$DI("CONSOLE","TYPEFACE","Courier New",37) <>
^$DI("CONSOLE","TYPEFACE","Desdemona",36) <>
^$DI("CONSOLE","TYPEFACE","Fences",33) <>
^$DI("CONSOLE","TYPEFACE","Fixedsys",15) <>
^$DI("CONSOLE","TYPEFACE","Footlight MT Light",34) <>
^$DI("CONSOLE","TYPEFACE","Impact",39) <>
^$DI("CONSOLE","TYPEFACE","Kino MT",37) <>
^$DI("CONSOLE","TYPEFACE","MS Dialog",10) <>
^$DI("CONSOLE","TYPEFACE","MS Dialog",13) <>
^$DI("CONSOLE","TYPEFACE","MS Dialog",16) <>
^$DI("CONSOLE","TYPEFACE","MS Dialog Light",10) <>
^$DI("CONSOLE","TYPEFACE","MS Dialog Light",13) <>
^$DI("CONSOLE","TYPEFACE","MS Dialog Light",16) <>
^$DI("CONSOLE","TYPEFACE","MS LineDraw",16) <>
^$DI("CONSOLE","TYPEFACE","MS LineDraw",37) <>
^$DI("CONSOLE","TYPEFACE","MS Sans Serif",13) <>
^$DI("CONSOLE","TYPEFACE","MS Sans Serif",16) <>
^$DI("CONSOLE","TYPEFACE","MS Sans Serif",20) <>
^$DI("CONSOLE","TYPEFACE","MS Sans Serif",24) <>
```

```
^$DI("CONSOLE","TYPEFACE","MS Sans Serif",29) <>
^$DI("CONSOLE","TYPEFACE","MS Sans Serif",37) <>
^$DI("CONSOLE","TYPEFACE","MS Serif",10) <>
^$DI("CONSOLE","TYPEFACE","MS Serif",11) <>
^$DI("CONSOLE","TYPEFACE","MS Serif",13) <>
^$DI("CONSOLE","TYPEFACE","MS Serif",16) <>
^$DI("CONSOLE","TYPEFACE","MS Serif",19) <>
^$DI("CONSOLE","TYPEFACE","MS Serif",21) <>
^$DI("CONSOLE","TYPEFACE","MS Serif",27) <>
^$DI("CONSOLE","TYPEFACE","MS Serif",35) <>
^$DI("CONSOLE","TYPEFACE","MS SystemEx",12) <>
^$DI("CONSOLE","TYPEFACE","MS Serif",16) <>
^$DI("CONSOLE","TYPEFACE","MS Serif",20) <>
^$DI("CONSOLE","TYPEFACE","MT Extra",33) <>
^$DI("CONSOLE","TYPEFACE","Matura MT Script Capitals",42) <>
^$DI("CONSOLE","TYPEFACE","Modern",32) <>
^$DI("CONSOLE","TYPEFACE","Playbill",33) <>
^$DI("CONSOLE","TYPEFACE","Roman",32) <>
^$DI("CONSOLE","TYPEFACE","Script",37) <>
^$DI("CONSOLE","TYPEFACE","Small Fonts",3) <>
^$DI("CONSOLE","TYPEFACE","Small Fonts",5) <>
^$DI("CONSOLE","TYPEFACE","Small Fonts",6) <>
^$DI("CONSOLE","TYPEFACE","Small Fonts",8) <>
^$DI("CONSOLE","TYPEFACE","Small Fonts",10) <>
^$DI("CONSOLE","TYPEFACE","Small Fonts",11) <>
^$DI("CONSOLE","TYPEFACE","Symbol",13) <>
^$DI("CONSOLE","TYPEFACE","Symbol",16) <>
^$DI("CONSOLE","TYPEFACE","Symbol",19) <>
^$DI("CONSOLE","TYPEFACE","Symbol",21) <>
^$DI("CONSOLE","TYPEFACE","Symbol",27) <>
^$DI("CONSOLE","TYPEFACE","Symbol",35) <>
^$DI("CONSOLE","TYPEFACE","Symbol",39) <>
^$DI("CONSOLE","TYPEFACE","System",16) <>
^$DI("CONSOLE","TYPEFACE","Terminal",12) <>
^$DI("CONSOLE","TYPEFACE","Times New Roman",36) <>
^$DI("CONSOLE","TYPEFACE","Wide Latin",40) <>
^$DI("CONSOLE","TYPEFACE","Wingdings",36) <>
^$DI("CONSOLE","UNITS") <PIXEL>
```

Highlights

A logical display is an environment where entities can exist and function and events can occur. An M process can consist of a multiple number of logical displays. These environments can overlap, but cannot be shared. The Display SSVN (^$DI[SPLAY]) describes the characteristics of logical displays through attribute node values.

When event processing is active, users can interact with the entities of a logical display and trigger events. If user action causes an event to occur, callback processing can occur for the entity with focus. The entity of focus is determined by the value of

^$DI($PD,"FOCUS"). The value of ^$DI($PD,"FOCUS") is automatically updated by user action to indicate the entity to receive input and events. $PD is an intrinsic variable that returns the name of the current logical display.

The next several chapters cover the entities that can be assigned to logical displays. The creation of entities and the detail coverage of their attributes will show how characteristics of a logical display are used in their creation and function.

Exercises

1. Can a physical device have more than one logical display?

2. What role does the Display SSVN play in the MWAPI system?

3. How does an M process separate the characteristics of one logical display from another?

4. Can logical displays be shared among M processes?

5. What is $PD?

6. Are all windows contained within a logical display the children of the display?

7. Where do inherited color and font attributes get their initial value?

8. Does a change to the value of an inherited attribute cause a modification to entities already created for the logical display?

9. Does an application need to modify the value of ^$DI($PD,"FOCUS") when user action indicates focus should be directed to another object?

Endnotes

[1] The MDC's version 1.1 specification changed the error code from "M?3."

[2] The MDC's version 1.1 specification changed the error code from "M?1."

[3] The MDC's version 1.1 specification changed the error code from "M?2."

[4] The MDC's version 1.1 specification changed the error code from "M?4."

Windows 4

Windows create a basis for the MWAPI system to communicate with users, and is the focus of this chapter. The MWAPI standard defines two different types of windows: *application* and *MTERM*. Application windows, which are GUI windows, provide the basic mechanisms for eliciting user input and displaying output. MTERM windows, which provide terminal emulation, are used to allow older, non-MWAPI code to run in a window. An MTERM window is similar to a MS Window's "DOS box." The MWAPI specification also permits developers to define window types in addition to the standard types for their implementations, but since they are nonstandard they may not be portable.

The definitions that describe windows are stored as values to attribute nodes assigned to the Window SSVN (^$W). Each M process running an implementation of the MWAPI can have its own copy of ^$W to define the entities in the process. An M process can contain a maximum of thirty-one windows, with the parent of each window either a logical display or another window defined for the same process. The parent of all MTERM windows is a logical display, but the parents of application windows may not be logical displays.

A window is created upon the successful conclusion of the assignment of at least one of its attributes. The attribute values not explicitly defined when the window is being created can be implicitly defined using default values supplied by the parent, the windowing platform, or the MWAPI specification. Window creation is covered in detail in the Creation and Modification section, and the Window Attributes section covers all the attributes specified for describing windows.

This chapter instructs the reader on how to create and modify windows, process their events, and work with the environment defined by their logical display. Window types and descriptions of their parts are found in the Window Types section. Creating and modifying application and MTERM windows are discussed and demonstrated in the Creation and Modification section. The Window Attributes section presents an in-depth coverage of the attributes available to application and MTERM windows.

Besides being the parent to other windows and elements, application windows can receive and process events. The Event Processing section extends the subject of Chapter 2 by focusing on detecting and processing of window related events. The creation of both application and MTERM windows is demonstrated, along with sample code, in the Implementation section.

After reading this chapter you will know how to create an application around application windows and how to run existing non-MWAPI applications in a windowing environment.

Window Types

The MWAPI defines application windows and MTERM windows, and permits implementation-defined window types.

Application: An application window is the basic input/output mechanism of the MWAPI. Application windows can contain elements.

MTERM: This type of window is for terminal emulation. Use this kind of a window when using legacy M code that does not use MWAPI syntax. The creation of elements for MTERM windows is not defined by the MWAPI standard, and is reserved to vendor implementations. Its appearance is similar to that of an MS Window's "DOS box."

Implementation: An implementation window type is defined by a vendor's implementation and is neither standard nor portable. Names beginning with the character "Z" are reserved for the implementation values.

Only application and MTERM windows are guaranteed portable.

Window Parts

The definition that follows describes the application window in Figure 4.1. The MWAPI system was designed to maintain the look and feel of the underlying windowing interface. Depending on the underlying platform, the window created on your system can appear different based on its look-and-feel characteristics. The window shown for this definition was created in a MS Windows 3.1 environment, and the descriptions are appropriate to windows created with other windowing systems.

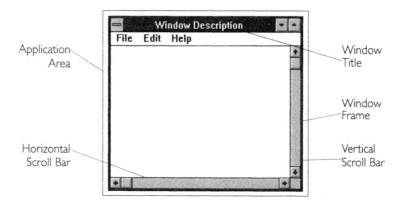

Figure 4.1: *Window Description*

Application area: The application area is a virtual space for the placement of the window's elements; it is the same size or larger than the viewport; and it may provide the basis for determining the position of child elements. The size of the application area is dynamically adjusted to be large enough to contain all of its elements and designated child windows whose VISIBLE attributes equal true. The origin of a window's application area is at the same coordinates as the window's position when the window is first created. After creation, the origin can move with each scroll movement of the application area.

Window viewport: The viewport is an area of the window that allows the user to view some portion of the application area. The amount of the application area that can be viewed at one time is dependent on the size of the viewport and the application area. Depending upon the values given to a window's SCROLL and RESIZE attributes, the user may be able to scroll the application area within the viewport or resize the viewport in order to view more (or less) of the application area.

Window frame: A frame can surround a window's viewport and can contain a menubar, a title bar with the window's title, and window controls. The window controls can include an iconify and/or resize button and a control menu box for a platform supplied system menu. The actual appearance and controls of a window's frame are determined by the underlying windowing platform.

Creation and Modification

Windows are defined by their characteristics. These attributes are defined by values assigned to window attribute nodes assigned to the Window SSVN (^$W). Each M process can contain a maximum of thirty-one windows in its copy of ^$W. Example 4.1 uses the M SET command to show the syntax for the assignment of an attribute to a window.

```
S ^$W(window name,window attribute)=value
```

EXAMPLE 4.1: *Window Attribute Syntax*

The first subscript is the name of the window, either in quotes or assigned as a variable name. The MWAPI standard specifies a maximum stringlength of thirty-one alphanumeric characters for a window name, and the first letter may be a percent sign. The window name subscript is very important for identifying a window, and the name must be unique. When focus is given to the window, or an element defined to it, the first piece of ^$DI($PD,"FOCUS") is the window's name. If an event occurs for a window, or one of its elements, the value of ^$E("WINDOW") is the name of the window. The name is an important identifier, and there is no data at this subscript level.

The second subscript must be the name of an attribute specified for the type of window. If the attribute is not specified for the window type, an error will occur with a code of "M46."[1] All window attributes are available for application windows, but not for MTERM windows. The Window Attributes section identifies attributes that are available to application and MTERM windows.

The *value* argument specifies a certain value for the window characteristic specified by the attribute. The value assigned to an attribute must fall within a specified value domain determined by the keyword. The Window Attributes section specifies the domain of values for each window attribute. If the value consists of multiple parameters or a string, it must be enclosed in quotes or assigned as a variable. If the assignment is not within the domain of values for the attribute, an error will occur with a code of "M47."[2]

A window is created when one or more attributes is assigned to ^$W. Window attribute nodes can be assigned to ^$W using the M SET command, shown in Example 4.1, or the M MERGE command. The result of the assignment does not affect the window until the successful conclusion of the merge. Using this command to modify attributes of a window will appear to change the characteristics all at the same time.

An assignment made with the M MERGE command entails first assigning the subscript(s) and value(s) into either a global or local array, then merging the array of attributes into ^$W. The merge is made by including the array reference as the argument to the MERGE command. Example 4.2 illustrates an assignment to ^$W using the MERGE command.

```
S ARR("WIN","BCOLOR")="0,0,0"
S ARR("WIN","TITLE")="WINDOW TITLE"
M ^$W=ARR
```

EXAMPLE 4.2: *Attribute Assignment Using M MERGE Command*

Application code can specify the characteristics desired for a window by explicitly assigning various values to its attributes in their value domains. Many window attributes, if not explicitly defined, are implicitly defined using default values. Default values come from the window's parent, the underlying windowing platform, or the MWAPI specification. The position, size, and type of a window must be known during the creation process. Unless otherwise specified, these three attributes are known at creation time due to the default values they receive. This defaulting of attribute values is what makes it possible to create a window by the assignment of at least one of its attributes.

When one or more attributes are assigned to a window, the MWAPI searches the current process's copy of ^$W for an existing window of the same name. If one exists, the attributes are assigned or modified for the existing window. If the window does not exist, a new window (whose type is defined by its TYPE attribute) is created using the window name, the attribute values specified in the assignment, and those attributes not specified that have default values. If an attribute with a default value is explicitly defined, then the explicit value is used for the attribute.

The information just covered is relatively generic to either type of window. The following two sections detail the differences in the creation of the two window types.

Application Windows

When a window is created, the MWAPI creates an application window unless told otherwise by its TYPE attribute value. Application windows can be created either by (1) the explicit assignment of an attribute for the window, or (2) the creation of an element for the window.

The first method was previously discussed. An application window can also be created, as the latter statement describes, when window attributes are implicitly defined by the MWAPI implementation using default values.

An application window is destroyed by specifying the window's name as the first-level subscript of ^$W in the argument to a M KILL command. Example 4.3 shows how to destroy an application window. If the *window name* subscript is omitted, all windows defined in ^$W for the current process are destroyed; if the window name specified does not exist, the request for destruction is ignored.

```
K ^$W(window name)
```

EXAMPLE 4.3: *Window Destruction Syntax*

MTERM Windows

The MWAPI does not prohibit the creation of an MTERM window using the methods explained in Examples 4.2 and 4.3. If the window's TYPE attribute is not assigned the value "MTERM," the MWAPI assumes it is an application window and creates one. The value of the window's TYPE attribute must be "MTERM" to create an MTERM window in this manner. The assignment is made to ^$W, but the window does not have visibility. MTERM windows do not have a VISIBLE attribute, so they will not be visible until opened. Even if the window is created as previously mentioned, the MTERM window will still have to be opened before it can be used. Opening an MTERM window gives it visibility.

MTERM windows are opened by specifying "MTERM" in the syntax of an M OPEN command. Example 4.4 shows an example of the syntax required to open an MTERM window.

```
O[:post conditional] device identifier:[parameters]:[timeout]:"MTERM"
```

EXAMPLE 4.4: *MTERM Open Syntax*

The *device identifier* parameter in Example 4.4 specifies the name of the MTERM window. The MWAPI standard does not specify the effect of the *parameters* component of the OPEN command's syntax on an MTERM window. However, the size of the window can be determined based on these parameters. Use of these parameters prevents portability. The *post conditional* and *timeout* parameters have the same effect on the OPEN command as they do in the standard M language.

When the OPEN command is executed to open an MTERM window, the MWAPI will search the current process's copy of ^$W for a window whose name matches the string specified by the device identifier. If a matching window name is found with a TYPE attribute value other than MTERM, an error will occur with a code of "M50."[3] If the window name specified in the OPEN command does not exist in ^$W, an MTERM window is created and its TYPE attribute is assigned the value of MTERM. The OPEN command causes the window to become visible, provided it is not obscured by another window.

Once the MTERM window is opened, the SET or MERGE commands may be used to change any of its modifiable attribute values. You cannot modify the value of the TYPE attribute. The OPEN command gives the current process ownership of the MTERM device. Execution of the M USE command with the MTERM window's name as its argument redirects input and output to the window. While the MTERM device is the current device, all input and output is directed to it.

The way an MTERM window is destroyed is directly related to the method of the window's creation. An MTERM window created via the OPEN command is destroyed by using the window's name as the argument to an M CLOSE command. Example 4.5 shows the syntax required for closing an MTERM window.

```
C device identifier
```

EXAMPLE 4.5: *MTERM Close Syntax*

If the MTERM window was created via explicit assignment to ^$W, the CLOSE command will not destroy the window, but will cause it to become invisible. Using the name of the window in the argument of an M KILL command does destroy the window, but the window must be closed first using the syntax shown in Example 4.5. If the MTERM window is not closed prior to the execution of the KILL command, an error will occur with a code of "M51."[4]

The next section explains the attributes available to both application and MTERM windows. Examples of MTERM and application windows are shown with explanations, sample code, and event processing, in the implementation section of this chapter.

Window Attributes

Window attributes are case-sensitive special keywords used in uppercase characters to define the characteristics that make up windows. Attributes are stored as subscripts descended from the window they modify in the Window SSVN. The MWAPI defines thirty-three Window attributes and permits application- and implementation-specified attributes. Keywords starting with "Y" are reserved for application attributes. Application attributes are limited to a maximum stringlength of thirty-one characters, and are defined by the applications to hold data in ^$W that logically pertain to the window, though this is not a requirement. Keywords starting with "Z" are reserved for implementation-defined attributes. Both attributes defined by the MWAPI and application are portable across vendor implementations of the MWAPI. Implementation attributes are defined by the vendor's implementation, are not standard, and may not be portable.

Table 4.1 lists the attributes available to MWAPI windows by their functional categories. All attributes listed are available to application windows. Attributes available to MTERM windows are shown in Table 4.2. Application- and implementation-specified attributes are permitted for both window types.

Actions: This category defines actions that can be performed on windows.

Appearance: Color characteristics are defined by this category, and define defaults for children.

Properties: This category of attributes describe the qualities of a window.

Text: This category defines the font characteristics and text used in the window, and defines defaults values for children.

State: These attributes define the window's state.

TABLE 4.1: *MWAPI-Defined Window Attributes*

Category	Attribute	Category	Attribute
ACTIONS	DEFBUTTON	PROPERTIES	SIZE
	EVENT	(Continued)	SIZEMIN
	ICONIFY		SIZEWIN
	MODAL		UNITS
	NEXTG		TYPE
	RESIZE	STATE	ACTIVE
	SCROLL		MIN
APPEARANCE	BCOLOR		TIED
	COLOR		VISIBLE
	FCOLOR	TEXT	FFACE
	PTYPE[1]		FSIZE
PROPERTIES	DISPLAY		FSTYLE
	PARENT		ITITLE
	ICON		TBCOLOR[1]
	ID		TFCOLOR[1]
	MENUBAR		TITLE
	POS		

[1] These keywords were added by the version 1.1 specification for the MWAPI.

47

TABLE **4.2**: *MTERM Window Attributes*

DISPLAY	SIZE
MODAL	TITLE
POS	TYPE
RESIZE	UNITS

Many of the attributes available to application and MTERM windows inherit default values, which are derived from the underlying windowing interface, the MWAPI specification, and the window's parent, according to the following process. The parent of a window is determined by the existence or value of its PARENT attribute. If the window's PARENT attribute is not defined, its parent is the logical display specified by the value of the DISPLAY window attribute. If the PARENT attribute exists, the parent is the window specified by the attribute's value. This relationship does not hold for MTERM windows, because their parents are logical displays. Table 4.3 lists the attributes whose values are passed down to the child from the parent to act as defaults for attributes with the same name.

TABLE **4.3**: *Inherited Attributes*

BCOLOR	FSTYLE
COLOR	TBCOLOR
FCOLOR	TFCOLOR
FFACE	UNITS
FSIZE	

The values of the attributes listed in Table 4.3 are modifiable using the syntax shown in Examples 4.1 and 4.2. Once an attribute with a default value is modified, the new value is inherited by subsequently created descendants and the default value can be restored using the attribute node reference as the argument to an M KILL command. Example 4.6 shows the KILL command syntax for an attribute node. Modification of these attributes will not affect entities that already exist. If the KILL command specifies an attribute without a default value, it becomes undefined.

```
K ^$W(window name,window attribute)
```

EXAMPLE **4.6**: *Window Attribute Kill Syntax*

There are a few errors that can be encountered when making window attribute assignments.

If an application attempts to assign a value to an attribute not specified for the window type, an error will occur with a code of "M46."[5]

If the value of the assignment is not within the domain for the attribute, an error will occur with a code of "M47."[6]

Attributes are described below in the format shown in Table 4.4. If any of the section(s) are not necessary to the description of the attribute, the section(s) will not be shown.

TABLE 4.4: *Attribute Description Format*

ATTRIBUTE NAME	
Description:	This section describes the attribute's function.
Syntax:	If this section exists, the attributes value can consist of more than one parameter. The required syntax is shown here.
Domain:	This section lists the domain of allowable values for this attribute.
Access:	This section lists the method(s) of usage for this attribute.
Default:	This section specifies the default value for this attribute.
Notes:	This section lists any pertinent notes about this attribute. This section covers any modifications made to this attribute definition by the MDC's version 1.1 specification for the MWAPI. If there are no further notes to list, this section will not exist.

ACTIVE

Description:	This attribute specifies whether a user can interact with the window.
Domain:	The domain of values is an expression that evaluates to true or false.
Access:	The value can be assigned when the window is being created, modified after creation, and referenced.
Default:	The default is true.
Notes:	If the value is true, the window, its elements, and its child windows can be active. Users can interact with active windows and events can occur for them. If the value is false, the window, its elements, and its child windows are disabled. When a window is inactive, the user cannot interact with it, and no user-triggered events can occur for it. Events triggered by an ETRIGGER command can occur both for inactive and active windows and their elements.

BCOLOR

Description:	This attribute specifies the default background color for gadgets created for the window.
Syntax:	`rcolor,gcolor,bcolor`
Domain:	The domain of values are color definitions as specified by amounts of red, green, and blue (RGB). Black="0,0,0" and white="65535,65535,65535." Appropriate color values lie between 0 and 65535.
Access:	The value of this attribute can be assigned when the window is being created, modified after creation, and referenced.
Default:	The default value is the value of the parent's BCOLOR attribute.
Notes:	Change in the value of this attribute will not affect gadgets already created. The value of this attribute provides the child's BCOLOR default. Color values are listed in Appendix A.

COLOR

Description:	The value of this attribute specifies the color of the application area of the window.
Syntax:	`rcolor,gcolor,bcolor`
Domain:	The domain of values are color definitions as specified by amounts of red, green, and blue (RGB). Black="0,0,0" and white="65535,65535,65535." Appropriate color values lie between 0 and 65535.
Access:	The value of this attribute can be assigned when the window is being created, modified after creation, and referenced.
Default:	The default value is the value of the parent's COLOR attribute.
Notes:	Change in the value of this attribute will not affect the color of the application areas of child windows already created.
	Color codes are listed in Appendix A.

DEFBUTTON

Description:	This attribute specifies a gadget to be selected when the user presses the selector key while the window has focus.
Domain:	The domain of values is the name of a Push Button gadget defined for the window.
Access:	The value of this attribute can be assigned when the window is being created, modified after creation, and referenced.
Default:	The default value is established by the underlying windowing platform, if there is one, and by the MWAPI otherwise.
Notes:	The selector key is determined by the underlying windowing platform. MS Windows designates the return key as the selector key.
	An attempt to assign the name of a gadget that is not a child to the window, or a button gadget, will result in an error code of "M52."[7]

DISPLAY

Description:	The value of this attribute specifies the logical display where the window is displayed when it is visible and function.
Domain:	The domain of values is a string of characters that name a logical display created for the current M process.
Access:	The value of this attribute can be assigned when the window is being created and referenced.
Default:	The default value is the value of $PD.
Notes:	This attribute is specified for application and MTERM windows.

EVENT

Description:	This attribute specifies via descendant node(s) callback routine(s) for defined event types.
Syntax:	`^$W(window name,"EVENT",event type)=value`
Domain:	There is no value at the subscript level of this attribute. The arguments of descendant nodes define callback routines. The Event Processing section of

this chapter describes the *event types* that can be assigned as subscript nodes. The *value* parameter is a valid M routine reference to process the event.

Access: Descendant nodes of this attribute can be assigned when the window is being created, modified after creation, and referenced.

Default: There is no default value for this attribute.

Notes: The MWAPI standard specifies EVENT attribute nodes for application windows, but reserves specifying EVENT attribute nodes for MTERM windows to implementers. Implementation-specified nodes are not standard and may not be portable.

FCOLOR

Description: This attribute specifies the default foreground color used for gadgets subsequently created for the window.

Syntax: `rcolor,gcolor,bcolor`

Domain: The domain of values are color definitions as specified by amounts of red, green, and blue (RGB). Black="0,0,0" and white="65535,65535,65535." Appropriate color values lie between 0 and 65535.

Access: The value of this attribute can be assigned when the window is being created, modified after creation, and referenced.

Default: The default value is the value of the parent's FCOLOR attribute.

Notes: Change in the value of this attribute will not affect gadgets already created.
　　　The value of this attribute is the default value for the FCOLOR attribute of its children.
　　　Color values are listed in Appendix A.

FFACE

Description: This attribute specifies the default value for the FFACE attribute of the window's children.

Domain: The domain is one of the fontface values defined as subscripts in the parent logical display's TYPEFACE attribute. One of the fontfaces listed below can also be used:

Font Face	Description
M,DEFAULT	This is the default typeface as defined for the underlying windowing system. If there is no underlying windowing platform, the MWAPI defines this fontface.
M,FIXED	This value assigns a nonproportional typeface for text in the window.
M,SANS	This value defines a proportional typeface from the sans-serif family.
M,SERIF	This is a proportional typeface from the serif family.
Implementation Value	This value begins with a "Z," and be defined by the M implementation.

Access: The value of this attribute can be assigned when the window is being created, modified after creation, and referenced.

51

Default:	The default is the current value of the parent's FFACE attribute.[8]
Notes:	Changing the value of this attribute does not affect gadgets already created for the window.
	If a requested font cannot be supported by the underlying windowing platform, a substitute is used. In any case, any reference reflects the actual value.

FSIZE

Description:	This attribute specifies the default FSIZE attribute value for the window's children.
Domain:	The domain of values is a positive numeric value that specifies point size (1/72 inch) for the fontface in use.
Access:	The value of this attribute can be assigned when the window is being created, modified after creation, and referenced.
Default:	The default is the current value of the parent's FFACE attribute.[9]
Notes:	If the fontface value is derived from the parent logical display's TYPEFACE attribute, use one of its subscripted values for this attribute.
	Changing the value of this attribute does not affect entities already created.
	If a requested font cannot be supported by the underlying windowing platform, a substitute is used. In any case, any reference reflects the actual value.

FSTYLE

Description:	This attribute specifies the default type style to be used by subsequently created gadgets of the window.
Syntax:	`fstyle[,fstyle]...`
Domain:	The domain of values are:

Value	Description
NORMAL	The text is displayed in a normal style.
BOLD	The text is displayed in bold.
ITALIC	The text is displayed in italics.
ULINE	The text is displayed underlined
Implementation Value	The text is displayed in an implementation-defined manner. Values beginning with "Z" are reserved for implementation values and may not be portable.

Access:	The value of this attribute can be assigned when the window is being created, modified after creation, and referenced.
Default:	The default is the current value of the parent's FFACE attribute.[10]
Notes:	Changing the value of this attribute does not affect gadgets already created.
	The value of this attribute is the default value for the FSTYLE attribute of gadgets created for the window.
	The values listed can be combined using the comma as a delineator: BOLD,ULINE. The value NORMAL cannot be combined with other values.
	If the value requested cannot be provided, an alternative value is assigned by the underlying windowing interface. In any case, any reference reflects the actual value.

ICON

Description: This attribute specifies the icon to display if the window is changed from its open state to its iconic state.

Domain: The domain of values are:

Value	Description
F,*fileid*	This is for a file specifier. The path to the file is specified by *fileid*.
R,*resourceid*	This is for a resource identifier. The resource is specified by *resourceid*.
Implementation Value	This value is determined by the vendor's implementation of the MWAPI and is not standard.

Access: The value of this attribute can be assigned when the window is being created, modified after creation, and referenced.

Default: The default value is determined by the underlying windowing platform.

Notes: The values for *fileid* and *resourceid* are platform or hardware dependent and may not be portable.

ICONIFY

Description: This attribute specifies whether the window can be iconified.

Domain: The domain of values are expressions that evaluate to true or false.

Access: The value of this attribute can be assigned when the window is being created and referenced.

Default: The default value is established by the underlying windowing platform.

Notes: If the value of this attribute is true, the underlying windowing platform will provide a means for the user to iconify the window. If the value of this attribute is false, the user cannot cause the window to be iconified. The windowing platform may display a means to iconify the window even though the user cannot cause the windows to be iconified. Figure 4.1 shows a window with a means to be iconified.

    If a parent window is iconified, then all its visible child windows will be made invisible. When the parent window is returned to its open state, all its child windows defined to be visible are again visible.

ID

Description: This attribute specifies an internal identifier that assists the windowing platform in identifying the window.

Domain: The MWAPI standard does not specify a value domain for this attribute. The domain of values is determined by the underlying windowing platform.

Access: The value of this attribute can only be referenced.

Default: There is no default value for this attribute.

Notes: The value given to this attribute differs from the unique name given to each window. The MWAPI uses the window name to reference windows.

ITITLE

Description: This attribute specifies the text to display with the icon when the window is in its iconic state.

Domain: The domain of values is one or more characters.

Access: The value of this attribute can be assigned when the window is being created, modified after creation, and referenced.

Default: The default value is the title assigned to the window.

Notes: The title of a window is specified by the value of its TITLE attribute.

MENUBAR

Description: This attribute specifies the menubar for the window.

Domain: The domain of values is the name of a menu defined for the window or the empty string.

Access: The value of this attribute can be assigned when the window is being created, modified after creation, and referenced.

Default: There is no default value for this attribute.

Notes: If this attribute is not defined when the window is created, the window is not created with a menu bar.

Even though the MWAPI standard allows the menu bar to be modified after the window has been created, the underlying windowing platform may not allow it. In such a case any modification attempt is ignored.

An empty menubar is used if:

The value of this attribute specifies the name of a menu that is not defined for the window.
The value of this attribute is the emptystring.

Placement of the menubar is determined by the underlying windowing platform. Figure 4.1 shows the menubar in the window frame.

Chapter 7 covers menus in detail.

MIN

Description: This attribute specifies whether the window is in its iconic state.

Domain: The domain of values is an expression that evaluates to true or false.

Access: The value of this attribute can be assigned when the window is being created, modified after creation, and referenced.

Default: The default value is false.

Notes: If the value of this attribute evaluates to true, the window is in its iconic state. If the value evaluates to false, the window is in its open state.

The programmer can manipulate the state of the window by the value assigned to this attribute. If the assigned value evaluates to true, the window may be iconified. If the assigned value evaluates to false, and the window is iconified, the window is restored to its open state.

Iconification of a window ultimately depends on whether the underlying windowing platform allows it or not (see the window's ICONIFY attribute).

MODAL

Description: If this attribute is defined and the window is visible, the value specifies how the window disables all other windows.

Domain: The domain of values are:

Value	Description
ANCESTORS	The window disables all of its ancestor windows.
APPLICATION	The window disables all other active windows defined in ^$W.
PARENT	The window disables only its parent's window.
Implementation Value	This value is determined by the vendor's implementation of the MWAPI and is not standard.

Access: The method of access depends upon the window type. The value of this attribute can only be referenced by a MTERM window. For an application window, the value can be assigned when the window is being created and referenced.

Default: The default value depends on the window type. For a MTERM window the default is APPLICATION and there is no default for application windows.

Notes: If an application attempts to create a nonmodal child window for a modal parent window an error will occur with an code equal to "M54."[11] The restrictions a modal window places on other windows is removed when the modal window is invisible (see the VISIBLE attribute) or destroyed.

    Stacking events can only occur for windows, or their child elements, when this attribute equals "APPLICATION."

NEXTG

Description: This attribute specifies the gadget that will, by default, receive focus if the window receives focus and no gadget defined for the window receives focus.

Domain: The domain of values is the name of a gadget defined for the window.

Access: The value of this attribute can be assigned when the window is being created, modified after creation, and referenced.

Default: There is no default value for this attribute.

Notes: The MDC's version 1.1 type A standard states that the effect of the NEXTG attribute occurs only the first time a window receives focus after it is created or the value its VISIBLE attribute changes from false to true.

    If an application attempts to assign a value to this attribute that is not the name of a gadget defined for the window, an error will occur with a code equal to "M49."[12]

    If this attribute specifies a gadget that cannot receive focus, the MWAPI will search the NEXTG attributes of each gadget until one is found that can receive focus. If the search does not find a gadget to receive focus, it will remain with the window.

PARENT

Description: This attribute specifies the parent of the window.

Domain:	If this attribute is defined, the domain of values is the name of a window defined for the current logical display
Access:	The value of this attribute can be assigned when the window is being created and referenced.
Default:	There is no default value for this attribute.
Notes:	If the parent is a logical display, this attribute is undefined.

The value of this attribute has the effect of linking the two windows together for the following purposes:

If the parent becomes invisible or is iconified, the child window will also become invisible.

If the parent becomes visible, all its children with true VISIBLE attributes values also become visible.

If the parent is killed, the child will also be killed.

A windows child can be destroyed independent of its parent.

POS

Description:	This attribute defines the origin (0,0) of the window frame with respect to the origin of the parent expressed in the unit of measure specified by the *unitspec* component of this attribute.
Syntax:	*hpos[,[vpos][,unitspec]]* or *,vpos[,unitspec]*
Domain:	The domain of values for the *hpos* and *vpos* parameters are numeric literals.[13] The domain of values for the *unitspec* component are:

Value	Description
CHAR[,*chars*]	This value specifies that the position is measured relative to the size of a character in the basis font. The *chars* parameter has the domain of one or more characters.
PIXEL	This value specifies that the position measurement is measured in pixels.
POINT	This value specifies that the position is measured in points. The size of a point is 1/72 of an inch.
REL[,*hscale*,*vscale*]	This value specifies a relative measurement with respect to a basis size. The parameters *hscale* and *vscale* have the domain of numeric literal values.
Implementation Value	This value is determined by the vendor's implementation of the MWAPI is not standard and may not be portable.

Access:	The value of this attribute can be assigned when the window is being created, modified after creation, and referenced.
Default:	The default value is determined by the windowing platform.
Notes:	The position of a window is normally measured relative to the origin (0,0) of its logical display. If the parent is another window and its TIED attribute is true, the origin of the application area is used.

If the assignment, after the window has been created, does not include either *hpos* or *vpos* , the current value for the unspecified parameter is used.

If an *hpos* or *vpos* value is assigned that cannot be provided by the windowing platform, a substitute is used.

If the *unitspec* parameter is not explicitly specified when a value is assigned to this attribute, unitspec will default to the current value of the window's UNITS attribute.

If the unit of measure is CHAR, the vertical unit of measure is equal to the line spacing of the basis font. If *chars* is specified and not the emptystring, the horizontal unit of measure equals the width of the average character in the string. If chars is the emptystring or not specified, the horizontal unit of measure equals the maximum character width in the basis font. If the window's TIED attribute evaluates to true, the basis font is determined by its parent's font attributes, otherwise the window's logical display font attributes are used.

If the unit of measure is REL and the window's TIED attribute evaluates to true, the basis size is the size of the parent window's application area when it was created. If the window's TIED attribute evaluates to false, the basis size is the size of the window's logical display. If *hscale* and *vscale* are not specified, both parameters default to 100.

Any reference to this attribute will yield the syntax above, specifying the actual size of *hpos*, *vpos,* and the *unitspec* used.

PTYPE

Description: This attribute specifies the pointer appearance when the pointer is in the window's viewport.

Domain: The domain of values is one of the following values:

Value	Description
M,CROSS	This value specifies a pointer appearance of cross-hairs.
M,IBEAM	This value specifies a pointer appearance of an I-beam.
M,WAIT	This value specifies a pointer appearance of a waiting state.
F,*fileid*	This is for a file specifier. The path to the file is specified by *fileid*.
R,*resourceid*	This is for a resource identifier. The resource is specified by *resourceid*.
Implementation Value	This value is determined by the vendor's implementation of the MWAPI and is not standard.

Access: The value of this attribute can be assigned when the window is being created, modified after creation, and referenced.

Default: This attribute has no default value.

Notes: If the pointer is over a gadget with a defined PTYPE attribute, its value will dictate the appearance.

If the PTYPE attribute of the window's logical display is defined, its value has precedence over the appearance of the pointer in the window's viewport.

If the window's logical display does not have a pointer device connected (^$DI($PD,"PTR") is undefined), the value of this attribute is ignored.

The values for F,*fileid* and R,*resourceid* are platform or hardware dependent and may not be portable.

RESIZE

Description: This attribute specifies whether the user can change the size of the window.

Domain: The domain of values is an expression that evaluates to true or false.

Access: The value of this attribute can be assigned when the window is being created and referenced.

Default: The default value is determined by the windowing platform.

Notes: If the value of this attribute evaluates to true the window can be resized. If the value evaluates to false, the window cannot be resized.

SCROLL

Description: This attribute specifies whether the window will include scroll bars for viewing the portion of the application area that is out of view of the window's viewport.

Domain: The domain of values is an expression that evaluates to true or false.

Access: The value of this attribute can be assigned when the window is being created and referenced.

Default: The default value is true.[14]

Notes: If this attribute evaluates to true, scroll bars are present when the window's application area cannot be fully viewed by the viewport.

If this attribute evaluates to false, scroll bars will not be present if the underlying interface allows them to be omitted.

The display of scroll bars when the size of the window's application area can be viewed by the viewport without scrolling is a look-and-feel issue and is determined by the windowing platform.

Scroll bar controls do not require application intervention to move the application area.

SIZE

Description: This attribute specifies the size of the window's viewport (height and width) in the unit of measure specified by the value of the *unitspec* parameter.

Syntax: *hsize[,[vsize][,unitspec]]* or *,vsize[,unitspec]*

Domain: The domain of values for the *hsize* and *vsize* parameters are positive numeric literals. The domain of values for the *unitspec* component are:

Value	Description
CHAR[,*chars*]	This value specifies that the position is measured relative to the size of a character in the basis font. The domain of values for the *chars* parameter is one or more characters.

PIXEL	This value specifies that the position measurement is measured in pixels.
POINT	This value specifies that the position is measured in points. The size of a point is 1/72 of an inch.
REL[,*hscale*,*vscale*]	This value specifies a relative measurement with respect to a basis size. The parameters *hscale* and *vscale* have the domain of numeric literal values.
Implementation Value	This value is determined by the vendor's implementation of the MWAPI and is not standard.

Access: The value of this attribute can be assigned when the window is being created, modified after creation, and referenced.

Default: The default values for *hsize* and *vsize* depends upon the window type. The MWAPI attempts to make the window large enough to encompass all gadgets, assigned to it at the time it is created, with nonnegative POS attribute values. If the POS or SIZE attribute of one of the gadgets is measured using a REL unit of measure, the window's *hsize*, *vsize*, or both default to 75 percent the respective parameters of the window's logical display.

The default for an MTERM window can be determined by arguments in the OPEN command. If a size cannot be determined by the open arguments, the default is equivalent to 80,24,CHAR.

Notes: The size of a window's viewport is measured in a positive direction from the window's origin.

If the *unitspec* parameter is not explicitly specified when a value is assigned to this attribute, unitspec will default to the current value of the window's UNITS attribute.

If the unit of measure is CHAR, the vertical unit of measure is equal to the line spacing of the basis font. The basis font is determined from the values of the window's FFACE, FSIZE, and FSTYLE attributes. If *chars* is specified and not the emptystring, the horizontal unit of measure equals the width of the average character in the string. If *chars* is the emptystring or not specified, the horizontal unit of measure equals the maximum character width in the basis font.

If the unit of measure is REL and the window's TIED attribute evaluates to true, the basis size is the size of the parent window's viewport when it was created. If the window's TIED attribute evaluates to false, the basis size is the size of the window's logical display. If *hscale* and *vscale* are not specified, both parameters default to 100.

If the assignment of a *hsize* or *vsize*, but not both, is not specified, after the window is created, the default for the parameter is the current assigned value for the parameter.

If an *hsize* or *vsize* value is assigned that cannot be provided by the windowing platform, the value is determined by the underlying windowing platform.

Any reference to this attribute will yield the syntax above specifying the actual size of *hsize*, *vsize*, and the current value specified by the window's UNITS attribute for the *unitspec* parameter.

SIZEMIN

Description: This attribute specifies the minimum size a user can resize the window's viewport, expressed in the unit of measure specified by the *unitspec* parameter.

Syntax: The syntax is the same syntax used for the SIZE attribute.

Domain: The domain of values is the same as stated for the SIZE attribute.

Access: The value of this attribute can be assigned when the window is being created, modified after creation, and referenced.

Default: The default value is determined by the windowing platform.

Notes: The notes are the same as those for the SIZE attribute.

SIZEWIN

Description: This attribute specifies the overall size for a window expressed in a unit of measure specified by the *unitspec* parameter. The size value of this attribute includes the window's frame, if any.

Syntax: The syntax is the same syntax used for the SIZE attribute.

Domain: The domain of values is the same as stated for the SIZE attribute.

Access: The value of this attribute can be assigned when the window is being created, modified after creation, and referenced.

Default: The default value is not defined.

Notes: The notes are the same as those for the SIZE attribute.

TBCOLOR

Description: This attribute specifies the default background color for child gadgets title.

Syntax: `rcolor,gcolor,bcolor`

Domain: The domain of values are color definitions as specified by amounts of red, green, and blue (RGB). Black="0,0,0" and white="65535,65535,65535." Appropriate color values lie between 0 and 65535.

Access: The value of this attribute can be assigned when the window is being created, modified after creation, and referenced.

Default: The default value is the value of the TBCOLOR attribute of the window's parent. If the parent's TBCOLOR attribute is undefined, there is no default value for this attribute.

Notes: Modification of this attribute's value will have no effect on gadgets already created for the window.

The value at this attribute node is the default value for the TBCOLOR attribute of gadgets defined for the window. If this attribute is undefined, the value of the window's COLOR attribute value will act as the default.

Color values are listed in Appendix A.

TFCOLOR

Description: This attribute specifies the default foreground title of gadgets defined for the window.

Syntax: `rcolor,gcolor,bcolor`

Domain: The domain of values are color definition as specified by amounts of red, green, and blue (RGB). Black="0,0,0" and white="65535,65535,65535." Appropriate color values lie between 0 and 65535.

Access: The value of this attribute can be assigned when the window is being created, modified after creation, and referenced.

Default: The default value is the value of the TFCOLOR attribute of the parent. If the parent's TFCOLOR attribute is undefined, there is no default value.

Notes: Modification of this attribute's value will have no effect on gadgets already created for the window.

The value at this attribute node is the default value of the TFCOLOR attribute of gadgets defined for the window. If this attribute is undefined, the value of the gadget's FCOLOR attribute will act as the default.

Color values are listed in Appendix A.

TIED

Description: This attribute determines whether the window maintains its position relative to, and overlapping, its parent window.

Domain: The domain of values is an expression that evaluates to true or false.

Access: The value of this attribute can be assigned when the window is being created and referenced.

Default: The default value is false.

Notes: If an application attempts to assign a value to this attribute that evaluates to true, and the value of the window's PARENT attribute identifies a logical display, an error will occur with a code equal to "M47."[15]

The value of this attribute can affect the determination of the unit of measure for the window, and the relationship between the parent and child windows (see the POS and UNITS attributes).

TITLE

Description: This attribute specifies the title of the window.

Domain: The domain of values is a string of characters.

Access: The value of this attribute can be assigned when the window is being created, modified, and referenced.

Default: The default value is determined by the type of window. If the window is an application window, there is no default value. If the window is an MTERM window, the default value is *window name* specified when the window was opened.

Notes: The maximum stringlength is 255 characters.

If this attribute is not defined when the window is created, an assignment of a title to the window may not be allowed by the windowing platform. In this case the assignment is ignored.

If the underlying windowing platform does not permit a title to be displayed for a window, the value of this attribute is ignored.

TYPE

Description: This attribute specifies the window's type.

Domain: The domain of values are listed below:

Value	Description
APPLICATION	This value specifies the window is an application window.
MTERM	This value specifies the window is a MTERM window.
Implementation Value	This value is reserved for an implementation-defined window. Implementation windows are not standard.

Access: The value of this attribute can be assigned when the window is being created and referenced.

Default: The default value is determined by the method of creation as defined in the Creation and Modification section. If the window was created by the OPEN command, the default is MTERM. The default for any other creation method is APPLICATION.

Notes: If an application attempts to OPEN an MTERM window with its TYPE attributes value equal to APPLICATION, an error will occur with an error code equal to "M50."[16]

UNITS

Description: This attribute defines the unit of measure for the window.

Domain: The domain of values are shown below:

Value	Description
CHAR[,*chars*]	This value specifies that the position is measured relative to the size of a character in the basis font. The value domain for the *chars* attribute is one or more characters.
PIXEL	This value specifies that the position measurement is measured in pixels.
POINT	This value specifies that the position is measured in points. The size of a point is 1/72 of an inch.
REL[,*hscale*,*vscale*]	This value specifies a relative measurement with respect to a basis size. The parameters *hscale* and *vscale* have the domain of numeric literal values.
Implementation Value	This value is determined by the vendor's implementation of the MWAPI and is not standard.

Access: The value of this attribute can be assigned when the window is being created, modified after creation, and referenced.

Default: The default value is dependent upon the window type it is defined for. The default value for an application window is the value of the parent's UNITS attribute. The default value for an MTERM window is CHAR. An MTERM window is not defined to have FFACE, FSIZE, and FSTYLE attributes, therefore the values of M,FIXED, 12, and NORMAL are used for these attributes respectively.

Notes: The value of this attribute serves as the default *unitspec* values of POS, SIZE, SIZEMIN, and SIZEWIN attributes of the window.

62

The basis font for a unit of measure of CHAR is specified by the window's FFACE, FSIZE, and FSTYLE attributes, if the window's TYPE attribute's value equals APPLICATION. If the TYPE attribute specifies an MTERM window, the basis font is determined as if the FACE, FSIZE, and FSTYLE attributes were assigned values of M,DEFAULT, 12, and NORMAL respectively. If the *chars* parameter is specified, and not equal to the emptystring, the average width of all characters specified is used to determine the unit of measure.

If the unit of measure is REL and the window's TIED attribute evaluates to true, the basis size is the size of the parent window's viewport. The basis for measurement is the size of the display specified in the window's DISPLAY attribute, if the TIED attribute evaluates to false. The basis for an MTERM window is the size of its logical display. If *hscale* and *vscale* are not specified they will default to 100.

VISIBLE

Description: This attribute specifies whether the window is visible or not.

Domain: The domain of values is an expression that evaluates to true or false.

Access: The value of this attribute can be assigned when the window is being created, modified after creation, and referenced.

Default: The default value is true.

Notes: The window is visible, if the value of this attribute evaluates to true. The window is invisible, if the value of this attribute evaluates to false.

If the assigned value evaluates to false, and the window is visible, the window is invisible. The effect may not be seen if the window is obscured by another window.

Event Processing

This section covers the processing of callbacks received by windows, and uses as its foundation the Event processing discussed in Chapter 2. The MWAPI standard specifies that events can occur for application windows but not for MTERM windows. An implementation of the MWAPI may include implementation-specific features to allow event occurrence for MTERM windows. Features not specified by the MWAPI standard are not guaranteed portability with conforming implementations.

Once event processing has been activated, events can occur for a window as the result of user interaction with it or the execution of an ETRIGGER that references one of the entity's EVENT attribute nodes. Focus must be directed to an active window (the value of ^$DI($PD,"FOCUS") is equal to the window's name) before a user can trigger an event for it. An event triggered by an ETRIGGER command can occur for any application window regardless of focus.

A developer can define the events that can send callbacks to a window for processing by assigning matching-event-type keywords as subscripts to the window's EVENT attribute node. An application can trigger a particular event through the execution of an ETRIGGER command with the desired EVENT attribute node specified in its argument.

Example 4.7 shows an EVENT attribute node and assignment can be made using the SET or MERGE commands.

```
^$W(window name,"EVENT",event type)=value
```

EXAMPLE 4.7: *Window Event Node*

Window name uniquely identifies the window, and EVENT identifies the characteristic as describing an event. The event that can cause the node to receive a callback is determined by *event type*. A window's EVENT attribute node can have several descended event types, and the argument, or *value*, of each specify one or more comma delineated routine references to process the event.

Event Types

The MWAPI specification defines eighteen keywords describing events that can cause callback processing to occur for a window. Vendors can define event types for their implementations beginning with the character "Z." Unlike standard even types, implementation-defined keywords are not guaranteed portability across conforming MWAPI implementations.

The keywords can be divided into the three categories shown in Table 4.5. The descriptions are discussed from the point of view of the applications user. All events listed can be triggered by an application.

Keyboard: The keywords in this category are initiated from the keyboard.

Pointer: Events described by this category are triggered from the pointer device.

State: This category are from events to the state or properties of the window.

TABLE 4.5: *MWAPI-Defined Event Types*

Category	Attribute	Category	Attribute
KEYBOARD[1]	CHAR[2]	STATE	CLOSE
	KEYDOWN		FOCUS
	KEYUP		MAX
	HELP		MIN
POINTER	CLICK		MOVE
	DBLCLICK		RESIZE
	PDOWN		RESTORE
	PDRAG		UNFOCUS
	PMOVE		
	PUP		

[1] FKEYDOWN and FKEYUP were deleted by version 1.1. The KEYDOWN and KEYUP keywords describe the events these event types did.

[2] This keyword was added by the version 1.1 specification for the MWAPI.

If an event occurs for a window with an enabled *event type* node defined to process the event, reference ^$E("WINDOW") to determine the window for which the event occurred as well as ^$E("TYPE"), which contains the *event type* that triggered the event. If the event is for keyboard action, ^$E("KEY") contains the key or character codes that triggered the callback. If the event is for a pointer event ^$E("PBUTTON"), ^$E("PSTATE") references the associated pointer button codes and ^$E("PPOS") identifies the position of the pointer when the event occurred. Table 4.6 presents the format to used to describe event types available for windows.

TABLE 4.6: *Event Type Description Format*

EVENT TYPE	
Description:	This section indicates when callback processing may occur for the event type. The descriptions for user-triggered events assume the window alone has focus. ^$DI($PD,"FOCUS") contains only the name of the window.
Event Information Attributes:	This section lists the Event Information attributes available to describe the event object.
Notes:	Where appropriate, this section will provide notes on the attribute.

CHAR

Description:	Callback processing can occur for a CHAR event type when a user presses one or more keyboard keys, or the event node is referenced in the argument of an executed ETRIGGER command.

Event Information Attributes:

CLASS	TYPE
KEY	WINDOW
SEQUENCE	

Notes:	Reference ^$E("KEY") to determine the keyboard code(s) that triggered this event.
	Keycodes are listed in Appendix A.

CLICK

Description:	Callback processing can occur for a CLICK event type as the result of either:

The user pressing and releasing a pointer button without a change in its position.
Callback processing for a user-triggered DBLCLICK event.
The execution of an ETRIGGER command that references the event node in its argument.

Event Information Attributes:

CLASS	PPOS	SEQUENCE
COL	PSTATE	TYPE
PBUTTON	ROW	WINDOW

65

Notes: Reference ^$E("PBUTTON") to determine the pointer button and any modifier keys depressed when this event type was triggered. The position of the pointer is determined by referencing ^$E("PPOS"), and ^$E("PSTATE") lists pointer buttons depressed when the event occurred. Pointer button codes are listed in Appendix A.

     If the event is triggered by the user, the sequence of events is: PDOWN, CLICK, and PUP.[17] An event triggered by ETRIGGER execution will not cause a sequence to occur.

CLOSE

Description: Callback processing can occur for this event type for a request to destroy the window.

Event Information Attributes:

CLASS	TYPE
SEQUENCE	WINDOW

Notes: The request to destroy the window can come from the window's system control menu box, if there is one.

DBLCLICK

Description: Callback processing can occur for this event type when a pointer button is pressed and released twice without changing the pointer position, or by the execution of an ETRIGGER command with a reference to the event node.

Event Information Attributes:

CLASS	PPOS	SEQUENCE
COL	PSTATE	TYPE
PBUTTON	ROW	WINDOW

Notes: The second depression and release of the pointer button must occur during a period of time defined by the underlying windowing platform.

     Reference ^$E("PBUTTON") to determine the pointer button and any modifier keys pressed when this event type was triggered. The position of the pointer is determined by referencing ^$E("PPOS"), and ^$E("PSTATE") lists pointer buttons pressed when the event occurred. Pointer button codes are listed in Appendix A.

     If the user triggers this event type, the following sequence of event will occur: PDOWN, CLICK, PUP, PDOWN, DBLCLICK, and PUP.

     If this event type is triggered by the execution of an ETRIGGER command, no additional events are triggered.

FOCUS

Description: Callback processing can occur for this event type when the user causes the window to receive focus or upon the execution of an ETRIGGER command that references the event node in its argument.

Event Information Attributes:

CLASS	TYPE
PRIORFOCUS	WINDOW
SEQUENCE	

Notes: A window also receives focus even when one of its elements receives focus.

When focus is directed to another window in the process, the window loosing focus may receive a callback for an UNFOCUS event. During the processing for the FOCUS event ^$E("PRIORFOCUS") is referenced to determine the name of the window losing focus. If an UNFOCUS event cannot occur, the value is the emptystring.

HELP

Description: Callback processing can occur for this event type when the user presses the help key, or an ETRIGGER command is executed with reference to the event node in its argument.

Event Information Attributes:

CLASS	TYPE
SEQUENCE	WINDOW

Notes: The help key is determined by the underlying windowing platform.

KEYDOWN

Description: Callback processing can occur for the event type when the user presses a key on the keyboard or an executed ETRIGGER command references the event node in its argument.

Event Information Attributes:

CLASS	TYPE
KEY	WINDOW
SEQUENCE	

Notes: Reference ^$E("KEY") to determine the keycode that caused the event. Keycodes are listed in Appendix A.

Use this keyword vs. FKEYDOWN.

KEYUP

Description: Callback processing can occur for the event type when the user releases a key on the keyboard or an executed ETRIGGER command references the event node in its argument.

Event Information Attributes:

CLASS	TYPE
KEY	WINDOW
SEQUENCE	

Notes: Reference ^$E("KEY") to determine the keycode that caused the event. Keycodes are listed in Appendix A.

Use this keyword vs. FKEYUP.

MAX

Description: Callback processing can occur for this event type when the user causes the window to be expanded to its maximum size or the execution of an ETRIGGER command that references the event node in its argument.

Event Information Attributes:

CLASS	TYPE
SEQUENCE	WINDOW

Notes: A user initiated request to maximize a window can be made through the window's system control menu box or the window's resize button.

MIN

Description: Callback processing can occur for this event type when the user causes the window to be iconified, or an ETRIGGER command is executed with the event node referenced in its argument.

Event Information Attributes:

CLASS	TYPE
SEQUENCE	WINDOW

Notes: A user initiated request to minimize a window can be made through the window's system control menu box or the window's resize button.

MOVE

Callback processing can occur when the user causes the window's position to change or an ETRIGGER command is executed with reference to the event node in its argument.

Event Information Attributes:

CLASS	TYPE
SEQUENCE	WINDOW

Notes: The underlying windowing platform will provide a means to move a window. An application modification to the POS Window Attribute will not trigger an event.

PDOWN

Description: Callback processing can occur for this event type as a result of:

The user depressing a pointer button.
User-triggered callback processing for a CLICK or DBLCLICK event type triggered by the user.
Execution of an ETRIGGER command with reference to the event node in its argument.

Event Information Attributes:

CLASS	PPOS	SEQUENCE
COL	PSTATE	TYPE
PBUTTON	ROW	WINDOW

Notes: Reference ^$E("PBUTTON") to determine the pointer button and any modifier keys depressed when the event type was triggered. The position of the pointer is determined by referencing ^$E("PPOS"), ^$E("PSTATE") lists pointer buttons depressed when the event occurred. Pointer button codes are listed in Appendix A.

PDRAG

Description: Callback processing can occur for this event type when the user moves the pointer device with at least one pointer button depressed or an ETRIGGER command is executed with the event node referenced in its argument.

Event Information Attributes:

CLASS	PPOS	TYPE
PBUTTON	PSTATE	WINDOW
PPOS	SEQUENCE	

Notes: Reference ^$E("PBUTTON") to determine the pointer button and any modifier keys depressed when the event was triggered. The position of the pointer is determined by referencing ^$E("PPOS"), and ^$E("PSTATE") lists pointer buttons depressed when the event occurred. Pointer button codes are listed in Appendix A.

PMOVE

Description: Callback processing can occur for this event type when the user moves the pointer device with no pointer buttons depressed or an ETRIGGER command is executed with the event node referenced in its argument.

Event Information Attributes:

CLASS	PPOS	TYPE
PBUTTON	PSTATE	WINDOW
PPOS	SEQUENCE	

Notes: Reference ^$E("PPOS") to determine the position of the pointer as PMOVE events occur.

PUP

Description: Callback processing can occur for this event type as a result of:

> The user releasing a pointer button.
> User-triggered callback processing for a CLICK or DBLCLICK event type triggered by user action.
> Execution of an ETRIGGER command with reference to the event node in its argument.

Event Information Attributes:

CLASS	PPOS	SEQUENCE
COL	PSTATE	TYPE
PBUTTON	ROW	WINDOW

Notes: Reference ^$E("PBUTTON") to determine the pointer button and any modifier keys depressed when this event type was triggered. The position of the pointer is determined by referencing ^$E("PPOS"), and ^$E("PSTATE") lists pointer buttons depressed when the event occurred. Pointer button codes are listed in Appendix A.

RESIZE

Description: Callback processing can occur for this event type when the user changes the size of the window by dragging its frame or the ETRIGGER command is executed with a reference to the event node in its argument.

Event Information Attributes:

CLASS	TYPE
SEQUENCE	WINDOW

Notes: This event type will not occur when the window is iconified, restored from its iconic state, or maximized.

A MAX event will occur instead of a RESIZE event when the window is resized to its maximum size with the window's system control menu or resize button.

A MIN event will occur instead of a RESIZE event when the window is iconified.

A RESTORE event will occur instead of a RESIZE event when the window is restored from its iconic state.

RESTORE

Description: Callback processing can occur for this event type when the user causes the window to change from its iconic state to its open state or the execution of an ETRIGGER command with the event node referenced in its argument.

Event Information Attributes:

CLASS	TYPE
SEQUENCE	WINDOW

Notes: The underlying windowing interface will allow for a means to restore a window from its iconic state.

UNFOCUS

Description: Callback processing can occur for this event type when user action causes focus to pass from the window to another in the same M process, or as the result of the execution of an ETRIGGER command with a reference to the event node in its argument.

Event Information Attributes:

CLASS	SEQUENCE
NEXTFOCUS	TYPE
OK	WINDOW

Notes: If input focus is moved to a window not defined in the same process, an UNFOCUS event will wait until focus is brought to another window in the process.

If during callback processing for the UNFOCUS event, the window receiving focus can receive a FOCUS event, ^$E("NEXTFOCUS") contains its name.

Event types can be assigned to ^$W using either the SET or MERGE commands. The syntax shown in Example 4.8 shows an assignment made with the SET command.

```
S ^$W("WIN","EVENT","CLOSE")="CLOSE^WINDOW"
```

EXAMPLE 4.8: *Event Type Assignment Using SET Command*

Event Specification Attributes

Each EVENT node is, by default, enabled to receive callback processing. Event Specification Attributes can be used to restrict a node's ability to respond to an event. The MWAPI defines the keywords ENABLE and FILTERIN, and permits vendors to define their own keywords. These attributes are maintained as subscripts of the event types they modify. Example 4.9 details the syntax required for inclusion of these modifiers. Event Specification Attributes are uppercase keywords that must be enclosed in quotes or assigned as a variable.

```
^$W(window name,"EVENT",event type,event specification attribute)=value
```

EXAMPLE 4.9: *Event Specification Node Syntax*

The ENABLE attribute node is implicitly created with a true value for each event node. If the value of the node evaluates to true and event processing is active for the process, callback processing can occur for the event type specified. If the value is false, a callback will not occur for the event type. An application can be designed to use this attribute to toggle an event node's ability to receive a callback. Example 4.10 shows how this looks for the assignment made in Example 4.8.

```
^$W("WIN","EVENT","CLOSE")="CLOSE^WINDOW"
^$W("WIN","EVENT","CLOSE","ENABLE")=1
```

EXAMPLE 4.10: *Event Node Assignment*

Events in the keyboard and pointer categories (Tables 2.2 and 4.6 categorize event types) can have restrictions placed on their ability to process callbacks when callback processing is enabled for the event type. The Event Specification Attribute FILTERIN restricts an event to one or more characters, pointers, or keycodes. Example 4.11 shows an assignment of the FILTERIN attribute to restrict the window's click event to either the user click on the window with the left pointer button depressed or the execution of an ETRIGGER with the event node referenced in its *SSVN node reference* and "PBUTTON=PB1" referenced as a subscript of its *data structure name*. Example 4.12 shows the syntax required for an ETRIGGER to meet the FILTERIN requirement.

```
S ^$W("WIN","EVENT","CLICK","FILTERIN")="PB1"
```

EXAMPLE 4.11: *Event Specification Attribute Assignment Using Set Command*

```
S ARRAY("PBUTTON")="PB1"
ETRIGGER ^$W("WIN","EVENT","CLICK"):ARRAY
```

EXAMPLE 4.12: *ETRIGGER with Simulated Left Pointer Button Depressed*

A detailed explanation of Event Information Attribute is found in Chapter 2.

Implementation

This section presents a demonstration of window creation, destruction, relationships, and use. The presentation of the windows will include some of the ideas and concepts learned up to this point.

Application Window

This implementation demonstrates the creation and interaction with three application windows. The windows used are titled and named "PARENT", "CHILDA," and "CHILDB" where window "PARENT" is the parent window of the other two. Each window will demonstrate the use of different attributes and event types. The code in Example 4.13 is used for this demonstration.

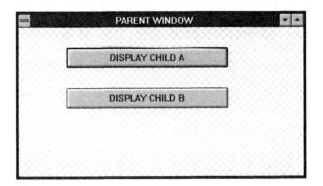

FIGURE **4.2**: *Window Parent*

```
PARENT  K ^$W,W
+1      ; build parent window
+2      S W("PARENT","TITLE")="PARENT WINDOW"
+3      S W("PARENT","POS")="100,50"
+4      S W("PARENT","SIZE")="400,200"
+5      S W("PARENT","SIZEMIN")="350,100"
+6      S W("PARENT","SIZEWIN")="450,250"
+7      S W("PARENT","DEFBUTTON")="CHILDABUTTON"
+8      S W("PARENT","NEXTG")="CHILDBBUTTON"
+9      S W("PARENT","EVENT","CLOSE")="CLOSE^APPWIN"
+10     S W("PARENT","EVENT","FOCUS")="FOCUS^APPWIN"
+11     S W("PARENT","EVENT","UNFOCUS")="UNFOCUS^APPWIN"
+12     ; button for child window a
+13     S W("PARENT","G","CHILDABUTTON","TYPE")="BUTTON"
+14     S W("PARENT","G","CHILDABUTTON","POS")="75,30"
+15     S W("PARENT","G","CHILDABUTTON","SIZE")="250,30"
+16     S W("PARENT","G","CHILDABUTTON","TITLE")="DISPLAY CHILD A"
```

```
+17     S W("PARENT","G","CHILDABUTTON","EVENT","SELECT")="SELECT^APPWIN"
+18     ; button for child window b
+19     S W("PARENT","G","CHILDBBUTTON","TYPE")="BUTTON"
+20     S W("PARENT","G","CHILDBBUTTON","POS")="75,90"
+21     S W("PARENT","G","CHILDBBUTTON","SIZE")="250,30"
+22     S W("PARENT","G","CHILDBBUTTON","TITLE")="DISPLAY CHILD B"
+23     S W("PARENT","G","CHILDBBUTTON","EVENT","SELECT")="SELECT^APPWIN"
+24     ; child window A
+25     S W("CHILDA","TITLE")="CHILD WINDOW A"
+26     S W("CHILDA","POS")="100,50"
+27     S W("CHILDA","SIZE")="200,100"
+28     S W("CHILDA","PTYPE")="M,CROSS"
+29     S W("CHILDA","TIED")=1
+30     S W("CHILDA","PARENT")="PARENT"
+31     S W("CHILDA","EVENT","CLICK")="ETRIGG^APPWIN"
+32     S W("CHILDA","EVENT","CLOSE")="CLOSE^APPWIN"
+33     S W("CHILDA","VISIBLE")=0
+34     S W("CHILDA","MODAL")="ANCESTORS"
+35     ; child window B
+36     S W("CHILDB","TITLE")="CHILD WINDOW B"
+37     S W("CHILDB","POS")="350,50"
+38     S W("CHILDB","SIZE")="200,100"
+39     S W("CHILDB","VISIBLE")=0
+40     S W("CHILDB","PARENT")="PARENT"
+41     S W("CHILDB","EVENT","CLOSE")="CLOSE^APPWIN"
+42     M ^$W=W
+43     S ^$DI($PD,"FOCUS")="PARENT"
+44     ESTA
+45     W !,"THIS LINE OF CODE IS EXECUTED AFTER THE ESTOP"
+46     Q
        ;
CLOSE   S WINDOW=^$E("WINDOW")
+1      S ^$W(WINDOW,"VISIBLE")=0
+2      K ^$E("OK")
+3      I WINDOW["PARENT" K ^$W(WINDOW) ESTO
        Q
        ;
FOCUS   W !,"WINDOW "_^$E("WINDOW")_" HAS FOCUS",! Q
        ;
UNFOCUS W !,"THE FOCUS WAS ON ",^$E("PRIORFOCUS")
+1      W !,"THE FOCUS IS NOW ON ",^$E("NEXTFOCUS")
+2      Q
        ;
SELECT  S ELEMENT=^$E("ELEMENT")
+1      S WINDOW=$E(ELEMENT,3,8)
+2      S ^$W(WINDOW,"VISIBLE")=1
+3      S ^$DI($PD,"FOCUS")=WINDOW
+4      Q
        ;
ETRIGG  ETR ^$W("CHILDA","EVENT","CLOSE") Q
```

EXAMPLE 4.13: *Application Window Demonstration Code*

Attributes are assigned to the local array "W" prior to their merge into the Window SSVN (^$W). The merge assigns the nodes and values contained in the array along with default values to those attributes not explicitly defined. The stated objects are created upon the conclusion of the MERGE command and window "PARENT" is visible. Child windows A and B are not visible because their VISIBLE attributes have zero values. The ESTART (ESTA) command activates event processing and causes program execution to loop awaiting events to process. The ESTOP (ESTO) command (tag CLOSE+3) termi- nates event processing when a close event occurs for window "PARENT," and execution will continue with the code following the activating ESTART command. The parent window uses two push button gadgets named "CHILDABUTTON" and "CHILDBBUT- TON" to display each child window. Gadgets are covered in detail in the next chapter.

Child window A is invisible when array W is merged into ^$W, but the depression of the push button entitled "DISPLAY CHILD A" will cause it to become visible. This but- ton can be depressed by a click on the gadget by a pointer device or by the depression of the windowing interface's designated select button. This is possible because the value of the parent window's DEFBUTTON attribute designates this push button's name. The button depression causes the event loop to send a callback for a select event to the but- ton gadget named "CHILDABUTTON." The callback is received by the button's event attribute, and an implicit M DO is executed to direct program execution to tag SELECT of routine APPWIN for processing. Tag SELECT references the Event SSVN (^$E) to determine the element that is making the call. The first six characters of the element name, by design, defines the name of the window to make visible. Since the first two characters returned as the value of ^$E("ELEMENT") define the element type and include a comma delineator, the third to eighth characters must be extracted to get the first six characters of the element name. Once the window has been made visible, focus is directed to the window. Figure 4.3 illustrates the appearance of child window A.

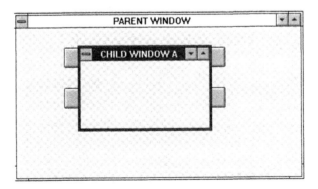

FIGURE 4.3: *Child Window A*

Child window A has its TIED attribute defined with the value of true, so when it is made visible its position relates to window PARENT. When focus is directed back to the parent window, child A will always be atop its parent window. Child window A has a

MODAL attribute equal to ANCESTORS and implicitly disables all visible ancestor windows when it is visible. Child window A must either be made invisible or destroyed in order to re-enable its parent. This example provides two methods of making child window A invisible: (1) a close event generated from a request to close the window from the system control menu box, or (2) a click of the mouse anywhere in the area of the window.

The first method will cause callback processing to be directed to the value of the window's close EVENT attribute node and the tag CLOSE of routine APPWIN to be called to make the window invisible. Prior to exiting the tag, ^$E("OK") is killed, discontinuing callback processing and returning focus to its parent. The second method causes a callback to the value of the window's click EVENT attribute node. Tag ETRIGG executes an ETRIGGER command to cause a close event to occur and thus call tag CLOSE to make the window invisible. The cursor appears as a cross when it is over this window, otherwise it will appear as determined by the underlying windowing interface.

Child window B is made visible in a manner similar to that of child window A, but its push button is not designated as the value of a DEFBUTTON attribute. Figure 4.4 illustrates the appearance of child window B.

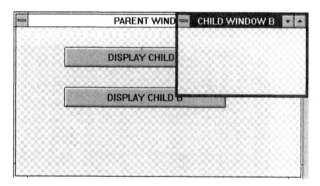

FIGURE 4.4: *Child Window B*

Child window B is not a tied window. Therefore, it does not maintain its position relative to its parent. If focus is redirected to the parent window, the parent window is not required to overlap the child when it is visible. This window is made invisible in a manner similar to child window A. Since this is not a modal window, user interaction with the parent window is possible while the child is visible.

Since child window A and child window B are children of window Parent, both child windows are iconified when the parent is iconified. All descendant windows are destroyed when the parent is destroyed, and when the user selects "close" from the system control menu box, processing is directed to tag CLOSE to kill the parent window. After the parent is destroyed, the ESTOP command is executed and execution will continue after the related ESTART command. This program will conclude by writing the line, "THIS LINE OF CODE IS EXECUTED AFTER THE ESTOP."

MTERM Window

This subsection demonstrates the creation and use of a MTERM window. The window was created by merging attributes for the window into the Window SSVN:

```
S W("MTWIN","TYPE")="MTERM"
S W("MTWIN","TITLE")="TOP 5 MORTGAGE RATES"
M ^$W("MTWIN")=W("MTWIN")
```

When attributes are merged into ^$W for a nonexistent window, an application window is created by default. The window must be explicitly defined as an MTERM to avoid the default. After the attributes have been merged, the window will need to be opened to become visible:

```
O "MTWIN":::"MTERM"
```

Once the window has been opened, input and output can be redirected to produce Figure 4.5.

```
U "MTWIN" D ^TOP5MOR
```

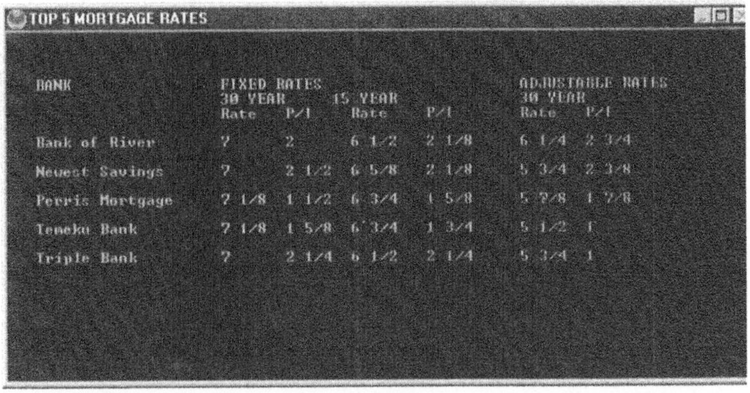

FIGURE 4.5: *MTERM Window*

After the window's use, closing it will make the window invisible. Since the window was created via merging attributes into the Window SSVN, closing the device will still leave the object defined. K ^$W("MTWIN") will destroy the window's definitions.

Highlights

Each M process running the MWAPI will have its own Window SSVN (^$W) to maintain the characteristics that define its windows and elements. Each window in the M process can be assigned to any one of the process's logical displays. A window is created by assigning value to at least one of its attribute nodes into ^$W

The MWAPI standard defines two types of windows, and permits implementers to define their own. The standard defines application and MTERM windows. Application windows, the basic input/output mechanisms for the MWAPI, can contain elements and receive events. MTERM windows are used to run older code, and their use of elements and events is reserved to implementers of the MWAPI.

In the MWAPI hierarchy mentioned in Chapter 1, windows are descended from logical displays, and can be the ancestors of windows. A window's PARENT attribute specifies whether its parent is a logical display or another window defined in the same Window SSVN. The parent of an MTERM window is always a logical display.

The kinds of events for which a window can receive callbacks are determined by specifying the event type in the first-level subscript descended from the entity's EVENT attribute node. The value at this subscript level specifies the argument to an M DO command to process the event. The processing of an event can be further modified by two additional subscripts: ENABLE and FILTERIN.

The next chapter discusses gadgets in-detail. Gadgets are a type of element that can be assigned to application windows to perform specialized tasks.

Exercises

1. Who can be the parent of a window, and what attribute specifies this?
2. Describe the types of windows specified by the MWAPI.
3. Describe the parts of a window.
4. How is a window created?
5. Why can a window be created by an assignment of one of its attribute nodes?
6. How can callback processing for a certain event be modified?
7. Create an application window with the following characteristics:
   (a) position the window in the center of its logical display;
   (b) the window's dimensions should be 450 X 250 points;
   (c) the application area of the window is blue;
   (d) assign callback nodes and routines to process click and close events;
   (e) the close event should only destroy the calling window;
   (f) the click event is restricted to the left pointer button only;
   (g) the title of the window should be "Window Exercise;"
   (h) the callback routine for a click event will write the pointer position to an MTERM window and await the press of a key before closing; and
   (i) the MTERM window will use the Window SSVN to assign "Pointer Position" to its title.

Endnotes

[1] The MDC's version 1.1 specification for the MWAPI changed the error code from "M?1."

[2] The MDC's version 1.1 specification for the MWAPI changed the error code from "M?2."

[3] The MDC's version 1.1 specification for the MWAPI changed the error code from "M?5."

[4] The MDC's version 1.1 specification for the MWAPI changed the error code from "M?6."

[5] The MDC's version 1.1 specification for the MWAPI changed the error code from "M?1."

[6] The MDC's version 1.1 specification for the MWAPI changed the error code from "M?2."

[7] The MDC's version 1.1 specification for the MWAPI changed the error code from "M?7."

[8] Version 1.1 of the MWAPI changed it from M,DEFAULT.

[9] Version 1.1 of the MWAPI changed the default from 12.

[10] Version 1.1 of the MWAPI changed it from M,DEFAULT.

[11] Version 1.1 of the MWAPI changed the error code from "M?9."

[12] Version 1.1 of the MWAPI changed the error code from "M?4."

[13] Version 1.1 of the MDC type A specification modified the domain to include negative values.

[14] Version 1.1 of the MWAPI specification changed the default from defined by the windowing platform.

[15] Version 1.1 of the MWAPI specification changed the error code from "M?2."

[16] The MDC's version 1.1 specification for the MWAPI changed the error code from "M?5."

[17] Version 1.1 of the MWAPI specification changed the sequence from PDOWN, PUP, and CLICK.

Gadgets

5

A gadget is a type of element used for specialized tasks, such as input and output of text, presenting choices, and drawing graphical objects. This chapter takes a detailed look at fourteen of the fifteen gadgets specified for the MWAPI. (The final gadget type is introduced in this chapter, but due to its unique properties, the details of its characteristics are deferred to Chapter 6.) Although gadgets are a special type of window, they may not exist by themselves or be the parent to any entity.

The Gadget Types section describes each gadget type, points out some uses for the elements, and puts them into categories for ease of identification. A generic description for creating gadgets and their characterizing properties is found in the Creation and Modification and Gadget Attributes sections respectively. The attributes available for displaying a list of choices within a specified gadget are described in the Choice Attributes section. The Row and Column Attributes section discusses some of the unique characterizations available to one of the gadgets described in this chapter. The Event Processing section takes a look at event processing as it relates to gadgets. Demonstrations of sample applications, complete with code, build a platform for clear and concise discussions for the use of each gadget type in an application.

Gadgets are defined by the values assigned to their attribute nodes in the window SSVN. If not explicitly specified, some of these attributes receive default values from the MWAPI specification, the underlying windowing system, and the gadget's parent. The syntax for the specification of a gadget is descended from the parent's name in the Window SSVN (^$W). If the parent does not exist when a gadget's attributes are merged into the Window SSVN, it is created using default values. This is seen in Example 5.1 and Figure 5.2 and the call to tag "HELP" in Chapter 9.

The MWAPI standard specifies that only application windows may contain gadgets. The creation of gadgets for a MTERM window is reserved to the MWAPI implementation, and may not be portable. A single window can contain a maximum of 255 gad-

TABLE 5.1: *Gadget Types*

Gadget	Type	Description
Check Box	CHECK	The Check Box gadget enables the user to turn an indicator on or off, such as to indicate yes or no.
Document	DOCUMENT	The Document gadget gives the user editing capabilities of more than one line of text, such as a text processor.
Generic Box	GENERIC	A Generic Box is an area where the user can draw graphical objects, is introduced in this chapter, and detailed in Chapter 6.
Group Frame	FRAME	A Group Frame is an outline used to group related gadgets or to draw horizontal and vertical lines on a window.
Label	LABEL	A Label gadget is used to display text.
List Box	LIST	A List Box gadget is used to display a list of choices to the user.
List Button	LISTBUTTON	A List Button gadget is a combination of a List Box gadget and a Push Button gadget used to display choices, but the list is not visible until the Push Button is selected.
List Entry Box	LISTENTRY	A List Entry Box gadget combines a text area with an area to display choices.
Long List Box	LONGLIST	A Long List Box gadget is much like the List gadget. It is for displaying a list of choices, but gives the programmer much more control than the List Box gadget does.
Push Button	BUTTON	The Push Button gadget displays a button for selection.
Radio Button Set	RADIO	The Radio Button Set lists a set of choices in a matrix format permitting selection of only one choice at a time. If a choice is selected when another one is selected, the first choice is deselected.
Scroll	SCROLL	The Scroll gadget is a scroll bar with horizontal or vertical orientation.
Symbol	SYMBOL	The Symbol gadget is used to display an image within a window.
Table[1]	TABLE	A Table gadget is used to display a list of choices or images in a table format.
Text	TEXT	A Text gadget allows the user to view and edit a single line of text.
Implementation-specific Value	Z...	A gadget of this type is for an implementation-specific definition.

[1] The MDC's version 1.1 specification added the Table gadget to the list.

gets, and the total of all elements in an M process cannot exceed 2,047 (gadgets, menus, and timers).

Gadget Types

The ANSI standard for the MWAPI defines fifteen different types of gadgets. Additional gadgets can be defined by the vendor of an implementation, but they are not guaranteed the level of portability of standard ones. Gadget types beginning with the letter "Z" are reserved for implementation-defined gadgets, are not standard, and may not be portable. Table 5.1 lists the MWAPI gadgets along with a brief description of each.

Gadgets can be grouped by the function they perform. Text gadgets are used to display and accept text. Choice gadgets are used to display a list of selectable choices. Table 5.2 shows the different gadgets categorized by function.

TABLE 5.2: *Gadgets Categorized*

Category	Gadget	
Choice	List Box	Long List Box
	List Button	Radio Button Set
	List Entry Box	Table
Text	Document	Text
	Label	
Miscellaneous	Check Box	Push Button
	Generic Box	Scroll
	Group Frame	Symbol

Creation and Modification

This section shows how to create a gadget and modify its characteristics. The characteristics that make up a gadget are stored as values assigned to attribute nodes in ^$W. Example 5.1 shows the syntax of a gadget's attribute node as assigned to ^$W.

```
^$W(window name,"G",gadget name,gadget attribute)=value
```

EXAMPLE 5.1: *Gadget Attribute Syntax*

The *window name* subscript is the name of the gadget's parent. The window's name must be unique among all the other windows in the current process; its maximum allowable stringlength is thirty-one alphanumeric characters; its first character must be either an alphabetic character or a percent sign; and it must be enclosed in quotes or assigned as a variable.

The second subscript identifies the type of element being referenced. The character "G" is used to indicate that the node is for a gadget. Chapter 7 discusses key letters for other element types.

The *gadget name* subscript specifies the name of the gadget and must be unique among all the gadget names specified for the parent window. The name given to a gadget is the identifier used when it receives focus or when an event occurs for it. Like window names, gadget names must not exceed a maximum stringlength of thirty-one alphanumeric characters, the first character can be a percent, and the name must be enclosed in quotes or assigned as a variable.

The fourth subscript, *gadget attribute*, is the name of an attribute for describing a characteristic of the gadget, which are covered in the Gadget Attributes section. Note that not all attributes can be assigned to all gadget types: if an attribute is used that is not specified for the gadget type, an error will occur with a code of "M46."[1] Gadget attributes must be contained in quotes or assigned as a variable.

The node's argument (*value*) quantifies, or qualifies, the gadget's attribute. The value assigned to each Gadget attribute node must fall within a certain domain of values determined by the keyword. If the value of an attribute has one or more parameters, they must be delineated by a comma character and enclosed in quotes or assigned as a variable. If the value assigned to an attribute node, or any of its parameters, is beyond the domain of values for the attribute, an error will occur with a code of "M47."[2]

The requirements for creating a gadget are quite different from that of creating a window. Unlike a window, gadgets have minimum numbers of attributes that must be specified prior to merging into ^$W. The required attributes normally include type, position, and size, and are determined based upon a gadget's type. If any of the required attributes are not specified when a gadget is being created, an error will occur with code of "M52."[3]

The M MERGE command must be used to create gadgets. The M SET command will *not* work in the creation of a gadget, because the gadget has multiple attribute values that must be explicitly defined during the creation process. Example 5.2 demonstrates the method required to create a Push Button gadget by merging a local array defined with attribute modes for the element into the window SSVN; Figure 5.1 shows the result.

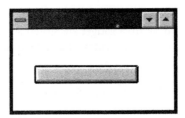

FIGURE 5.1: *Sample Gadget*

```
S W("WIN","G","BUTTON","TYPE")="BUTTON"
S W("WIN","G","BUTTON","POS")="20,40"
S W("WIN","G","BUTTON","SIZE")="60,20"
M ^$W=W
```

EXAMPLE 5.2: *Gadget Creation*

Once a gadget has been created, application code may use either the SET or MERGE commands to add and modify new and existing attributes, unless otherwise specified by the keyword. The value of the TYPE attribute identifies the type of gadget (see Table 5.1) and cannot be assigned a new value after the object is created. The gadget created from the code shown in Example 5.2 will remain a push button gadget until either it, or its parent window, is destroyed.

When the required attributes for gadget are merged into ^$W, as shown in Example 5.2, the MWAPI searches the current process's copy of the window SSVN for an existing window whose name matches the string specified by *window name*. If the window exists with the same name, the MWAPI searches the window for a gadget name that matches the string specified by *gadget name*. If the gadget exists, the specified attribute(s) that can be modified will take on the new valid value(s). If the gadget does not exist, it is created.

If the search fails to find a matching *window name*, the gadget's parent will be created, using default window attribute values. The MWAPI attempts to make the window's viewport large enough to encompass all visible gadgets, defined at the time of creation, whose position (POS) attributes do not contain negative values. If the size or position of any of the gadgets is determined based on the unit of measurement of its parent, the unspecified horizontal and vertical dimensions of the parent will default to 75 percent of the respective dimension of its logical display.

Gadget Attributes

Gadget attributes are case-sensitive keywords used to define characteristics of gadgets. They are stored as the fourth-level subscript descended from the parent window's name (see Example 5.1 for the syntax). The MWAPI specification defines fifty attributes available for use by gadgets, and permits the use of application- and implementation-defined keywords. Application attributes, which provide the programmer with a means to store additional information within the definition of a gadget, must begin with the letter "Y."

Implementation attributes are keywords defined by the vendor of an MWAPI implementation. The character "Z" is reserved for the first letter in the name of implementation-defined attributes. A hierarchy exists in the scope and portability of attributes: those defined in applications have the scope of (and are portable to the extent of) the application where they are specified. Implementation attributes have the scope of the entire implementation and may not be portable. Those attributes specified by the MWAPI standard are guaranteed portable among all conforming implementations and platforms. Table 5.3 list the attributes available to gadgets categorized by function.

Actions: This category defines actions that can be performed on gadgets.

Appearance: Characteristics defining a gadget's appearance are listed in this category.

Drawing: Attributes in this category are for drawing objects in a Generic Box gadget.

Properties: This category of attributes describe the qualities of a gadget.

Selection:	This category describes choices and their capabilities in the gadget.
State:	These attributes define state and general capabilities.
Text:	Text and font used in the gadget are defined by these attributes.
Value:	These attributes are used for describing a gadget's value.

TABLE 5.3: *Gadget Attributes Categorized*

Category	Attribute	Category	Attribute
ACTIONS	CANCEL	PROPERTIES	TYPE
	EVENT	(Continued)	UNITS
	NEXTG	SELECTION	CHOICE
	SCROLL		HCOLID[1]
APPEARANCE	BCOLOR		HROWID[1]
	FCOLOR		LEFTSHOW
	FRAMED		SELECTMAX
	GRID[1]		TOPSHOW
	PTYPE[1]	STATE	ACTIVE
	TBCOLOR		SCROLLDIR
	TFCOLOR		VISIBLE
DRAWING	DRAW	TEXT	FFACE
	DRAWTYPE		FSIZE
PROPERTIES	COL[1]		FSTYLE
	COLWIDTH[1]		TFFACE
	ID		TFSIZE
	POS		TFSTYLE
	RESOURCE		TITLE
	ROW[1]		TPOS
	ROWCOL	VALUE	CANCHANGE
	ROWHEIGHT		CHANGED
	SCROLLBY		CHARMAX
	SCROLLPOS		INSELECT
	SCROLLRANGE		SELECTVAL
	SIZE		VALUE

[1] These attributes were added to the MWAPI specification by the MDC's version 1.1 extension for the MWAPI.

TABLE 5.4: *Inherited Attributes*

BCOLOR	FSTYLE
COLOR	TBCOLOR
FCOLOR	TFCOLOR
FFACE	UNITS
FSIZE	

TABLE 5.5: *Gadgets Attributes*

ATTRIBUTE	Check Box	Document	Generic Box	Group Frame	Label	List Box	List Button	List Entry Box	Long List Box	Push Button	Radio Button Set	Scroll	Symbol	Table	Text
ACTIVE	X	X	X			X	X	X	X	X	X	X		X	X
BCOLOR	X	X	X			X	X	X	X		X	X		X	X
CANCEL	X	X	X	X		X	X	X	X	X	X			X	X
CANCHANGE	X	X				X	X	X	X		X	X		X	X
CHANGED	X	X						X				X			X
CHARMAX															
CHOICE						X	X	X	X		X				
COL														X	
COLWIDTH														X	
DRAW			X												
DRAWTYPE			X												
EVENT	X	X	X			X	X	X	X		X			X	X
FCOLOR	X	X	X	X	X	X	X	X	X	X	X	X		X	X
FFACE		X	X			X	X	X	X			X		X	X
FRAMED		X	X		X										
FSIZE	X	X	X			X	X	X	X			X		X	X
FSTYLE	X	X	X			X	X	X	X			X		X	X
GRID														X	
HCOLID														X	
HROWID														X	
ID	X	X	X	X	X	X	X	X	X	X	X	X		X	X
INSELECT		X						X					X	X	X
LEFTSHOW															
NEXTG	X	X	X	X	X	X	X	X	X	X	X	X	X	X	X
POS	X	X	X	X	X	X	X	X	X	X	X	X	X	X	X
PTYPE	X	X	X	X	X	X	X	X	X	X	X	X	X	X	X
RESOURCE										X			X		
ROW														X	
ROWCOL											X				
ROWHEIGHT														X	
SCROLL		X													
SCROLLBY									X			X			
SCROLLDIR									X			X			
SCROLLPOS									X						
SCROLLRANGE												X			
SELECTMAX						X									
SELECTVAL															
SIZE	X	X	X	X	X	X	X	X	X	X	X	X	X	X	X
TBCOLOR		X				X	X	X	X			X		X	X
TFCOLOR		X				X	X	X	X			X		X	X
TFFACE	X	X		X	X	X	X	X	X	X	X	X		X	X
TFSIZE	X	X		X	X	X	X	X	X	X	X	X		X	X
TFSTYLE	X	X		X	X	X	X	X	X	X	X	X		X	X
TITLE	X	X		X		X	X	X	X	X	X	X		X	X
TOPSHOW															
TPOS	X	X		X		X	X	X	X		X	X		X	X
TYPE	X	X	X	X	X	X	X	X	X	X	X	X	X	X	X
UNITS	X	X	X		X	X	X	X	X	X	X	X	X	X	X
VALUE	X	X				X	X	X	X		X	X		X	X
VISIBLE	X	X	X	X	X	X	X	X	X	X	X	X	X	X	X

Some gadget attributes receive default values to define characteristics that are not explicitly defined. The values for these attributes come from the underlying windowing interface, the MWAPI specification, and the gadget's parent. The parent of a gadget is determined by the *window name* subscript in its syntax (see Example 5.1). Table 5.4 shows the attributes with default values derived from the parent's attributes with the same name.

The values of the attributes listed in Table 5.4 are modified from their defaults by using the syntax shown in Example 5.1 as the argument to an M SET command, or by using the M MERGE command as shown in Example 5.2. Once modified, the default values are restored using the attribute node reference, as shown in Example 5.1, as the argument to a M KILL command. Using the KILL command on an attribute that has no default leaves the attribute's node undefined.

Table 5.5 identifies the attributes available for use by gadget type.

Attributes are listed below using the format presented in Table 5.6. If any of the sections shown in Table 5.6 are not necessary to the description of the attribute, the section(s) is/are not shown.

TABLE **5.6**: *Gadget Attribute Description Format*

ATTRIBUTE NAME	
Description:	This section describes the attribute's function.
Syntax:	If the attributes value can consist of more than one parameter this section will exist to show the syntax.
Domain:	This section lists the domain of allowable values for this attribute.
Access:	This section lists the method(s) of usage for this attribute.
Default:	This section specifies the default value for this attribute.
Notes:	This section may contain notes on this attribute.

ACTIVE

Description:	This attribute specifies whether a user may interact with the gadget.
Domain:	The domain of values is an expression that evaluates to true or false.
Access:	The value of this attribute can be assigned when the window is being created, modified after creation, and referenced.
Default:	The default value of this attribute is true.
Notes:	If the value of this attribute is true, users may interact with the gadget and user-triggered events may occur for it. If the value is false, the gadget is disabled and user-triggered events may not occur for it.
	Events triggered by an ETRIGGER command may occur for inactive, as well as active, gadgets.
	When a gadget is not active, the gadget text appears gray to indicate its inactive status.

BCOLOR

Description: The value of this attribute specifies the background color of the gadget.

Syntax: `rcolor,gcolor,bcolor`

Domain: The domain of values is a color definition as specified by the amount of red, green, and blue (RGB). Black="0,0,0" and white="65535,65535,65535." Appropriate color values lie between 0 and 65535.

Access: The value of this attribute can be assigned when the gadget is being created, modified after creation, and referenced.

Default: The default value is the value of the parent's BCOLOR attribute.

Notes: Color codes are listed in Appendix A.

CANCEL

Description: This attribute determines whether an enabled CHANGE or UNFOCUS event may occur for the gadget that previously had focus.

Domain: The value domain is an expression that evaluates to true or false.

Access: The value of this attribute can be assigned when the gadget is being created, modified after creation, and referenced.

Default: The default value is false.

Notes: If user action causes focus to be directed to a gadget with a false CANCEL attribute, any enabled UNFOCUS or CHANGE events may occur for the gadget that previously had focus.

If user action causes focus to be directed to a gadget with a true CANCEL attribute, the change in focus will not trigger any UNFOCUS or CHANGE event.

CANCHANGE

Description: This attribute determines whether the gadget's VALUE attribute can be changed by user action.

Domain: The value domain is an expression that evaluates to true or false.

Access: The value of this attribute can be assigned when the gadget is being created, modified after creation, and referenced.

Default: The default value is true.

Notes: If the value of this attribute is true, user actions may cause the gadget's VALUE attribute to be changed.

If the value of this attribute is false, user action may not cause the VALUE attribute to be modified.

If the application assigns a value to the VALUE attribute, the value of this attribute is not affected.[4]

CHANGED

Description: This attribute specifies whether the user has caused the gadget's VALUE attribute to change.

Domain: The domain of values are values that evaluates to true or false.

Access:	The value of this attribute can be assigned when the gadget is being created, modified after creation, and referenced.
Default:	The default value is false.
Notes:	If the value of a gadget's CHANGED attribute is true, user interaction with the gadget has caused the value of the gadget's VALUE attribute to change. The value of the CHANGED attribute will remain true even if the original value is restored to the VALUE attribute.
	If the value of this attribute is false, user interaction did not cause any change in the value of the attribute's VALUE attribute.

CHARMAX

Description:	The value of this attribute specifies the maximum number of characters a user may assign to the gadget.
Domain:	The domain of values are integers including zero.
Access:	The value of this attribute can be assigned when the gadget is being created and referenced.
Default:	The default value is zero.
Notes:	The value of zero indicates no explicit limit to the number of characters a user can enter into the gadget.
	The value of this attribute includes embedded line end characters.
	A Document gadget can contain a maximum of 32,767 characters.

CHOICE

Description:	This attribute specifies via descendant nodes choices to display in the gadget.
Syntax:	Nontable gadgets:
	`^$W(window name,"G",gadget name,"CHOICE",item)=choice`
	Table gadgets:
	`^$W(window name,"G",gadget name,"CHOICE",ritem,citem)= choice`
Domain:	There is no value at the subscript level of this attribute. Descendant nodes *item* or *ritem* and *citem* contain choice values (*choice*).
Access:	The value of this attribute can be assigned when the gadget is being created, modified after creation, and referenced.
Default:	There is no default value for this attribute.
Notes:	The *ritem* subscript identifies the row where the choice exists in the Table gadget, and the *citem* subscript specifies the column.
	The use of this attribute is described in more detail in the Choice Attributes section of this chapter.

COL

Description:	This attribute specifies the columns in a table gadget.
Syntax:	`^$W(window name,"G",gadget name,"COL",citem)=""`
Domain:	There is no value at the attribute level, but there is value at the lower subscript level (*citem*). The *citem* parameter specifies a column in the gadget and has the domain of characters.

Access:	The value of *citem* subscripts can be assigned when the gadget is being created, modified after creation, and referenced.
Default:	There is no default for this attribute, but descendants can be implicitly defined as choices are assigned to the table gadget.
Notes:	A *citem* subscript associated with this attribute does not have to exist as a *citem* subscript of the CHOICE attribute. If a column referenced in the syntax of the CHOICE attribute is not specified by the COL attribute, a COL attribute will be implicitly defined for the column. All columns have a COL attribute node. If the COL attribute specifies a column that does not exist in the syntax of the CHOICE attribute, the column will be empty.

COLWIDTH

Description:	The value of this attribute node specifies the default width for all columns in the gadget.
Syntax:	`hsize,[unitspec]`
Domain:	The domain of values for the *hsize* parameter is positive numeric literals including zero. The domain of values for the *unitspec* component is:

Value	Description
CHAR[,*chars*]	This value specifies that the position is measured relative to the size of a character in the basis font. The domain of values for the *chars* parameter is one or more characters.
PIXEL	This value specifies that the position measurement is measured in pixels.
POINT	This value specifies that the position is measured in points. The size of a point is 1/72 of an inch.
REL[,*hscale*,*vscale*]	This value specifies a relative measurement with respect to the parent window's size. The parameters *hscale* and *vscale* have the domain of numeric literal values.
Implementation Value	This value is determined by the vendor's implementation of the MWAPI, and is not standard.

Access:	The value of this attribute can be assigned when the gadget is being created, modified after creation, and referenced.
Default:	The default value is determined by the underlying windowing platform.
Notes:	If the *unitspec* parameter is not explicitly specified when value is assigned to this attribute, it will default to the current value of the gadget's UNITS attribute.

If the unit of measurement is CHAR, the vertical unit of measurement is equal to the line spacing of the basis font. The basis font is determined by the gadget's FFACE, FSIZE, and FSTYLE attribute values. The horizontal dimension is determined by the specification for the *chars* parameter. If *chars* is specified, and not the emptystring, the horizontal unit of measurement equals the width of the average character in the string. If *chars* is the emptystring, or not specified, the horizontal unit of measurement equals the maximum character width in the basis font. |

The basis size for a *unitspec* of REL is the size of the window's viewport. If *hscale* and *vscale* are not specified, both parameters default to 100.

If the assignment of *hsize* is not specified, after the gadget is created, the default for the parameter will be the current assigned value for the parameter.

If an *hsize* value is assigned that cannot be provided by the windowing platform, the value will be determined by the underlying windowing platform.

Any reference to this attribute will yield the syntax above specifying the actual size of *hsize*, and the current value specified by the gadget's UNITS attribute for the *unitspec* parameter.

DRAW

Description: The value of this attribute's node specifies the number of draw commands assigned to the gadget. Subscripts descended contain draw commands.

Domain: The domain of values are positive integers including zero.

Access: The value of this attribute is automatically updated, and the only access permitted to an application are to kill the attribute's node and to reference it.

Default: The default value is zero.

Notes: See Chapter 6 for more coverage of draw commands and drawing.

DRAWTYPE

Description: The value of this attribute's node identifies the type of draw commands listed in descendant subscripts of the gadget's DRAW attribute.

Domain: The allowable values are either MDRAW or an implementation-defined value.

Access: The value of this attribute can be assigned when the gadget is being created and referenced.

Default: The default value is MDRAW.

Notes: See Chapter 6 for more coverage of draw commands and drawing.

EVENT

Description: This attribute specifies via descendant node(s) callback routine(s) for defined event types.

Syntax: ^$W(*window name*,"G",*gadget name*,"EVENT",*event type*)=*value*

Domain: There is no value at the subscript level of this attribute. Descendant nodes specify event types, and their arguments define callback processing routines. The Event Processing section describes all the event types that can be assigned to gadgets.

Access: Descendant nodes of this attribute can be assigned when the gadget is being created, modified after creation, and referenced.

Default: There is no default value for this attribute.

Notes: The Event Processing section covers processing events for gadgets in detail.

FCOLOR

Description: This attribute specifies the foreground color of the gadget.

Syntax:	`rcolor,gcolor,bcolor`
Domain:	The domain of values are color definition as specified by amounts of red, green, and blue (RGB). Black="0,0,0" and white="65535,65535,65535." Appropriate color values lie between 0 and 65535.
Access:	The value of this attribute can be assigned when the gadget is being created, modified after creation, and referenced.
Default:	The default value is the value of the parent window's FCOLOR attribute.
Notes:	Text included in the gadget will be displayed in this color. Color codes are listed in Appendix A.

FFACE

Description:	This attribute specifies the typeface to be used for all the text in the gadget except the title.
Domain:	The domain is one of the *fontface* values defined by the TYPEFACE attribute in the gadget's logical display. One of the fontfaces listed below may also be used:

Font Name	Description
M,DEFAULT	This is the default typeface as defined for the underlying windowing system. If there is no underlying windowing platform, the MWAPI defines this fontface.
M,FIXED	This is a nonproportional typeface.
M,SANS	This is a proportional typeface from the sans-serif family.
M,SERIF	This is a proportional typeface from the serif family.
Implementation Value	This value will begin with a "Z," and be defined by the M implementation.

Access:	The value of this attribute can be assigned when the gadget is being created, and referenced.
Default:	The default value is the value of the parent window's FFACE attribute.
Notes:	If the specified value cannot be provided by the windowing platform, an alternate can be used.
	See the TFFACE attribute for the typeface used by the gadget's title.

FRAMED

Description:	This attribute specifies whether the gadget is encircled by a frame.
Domain:	The domain of allowable values is an expression that evaluates to true or false.
Access:	The value of this attribute can be assigned when the gadget is being created, and referenced.
Default:	The default value depends upon whether the gadget is of type Label or not. The default value for a Label is false, and for all other valid gadgets the default is true.
Notes:	If the windowing platform does not permit a frame, one will not exist.

FSIZE

Description: This attribute specifies the size of all text used within the gadget except for the title.

Domain: The domain of values is a positive numeric value that specifies point size (1/72 inch) in the fontface in use.

Access: The value of this attribute can be assigned when the gadget is being created, and referenced.

Default: The default value is the value of the parent window's FSIZE attribute.

Notes: If the value of the FFACE node names a *fontface* listed in the logical display's TYPEFACE attribute node, use one of its descendant subscript values.

    The TSIZE attribute specifies the size of the text used in the gadget's title.

    If the specified value cannot be provided by the windowing platform, an alternate can be used.

FSTYLE

Description: This attribute specifies the type style for all text used within a gadget except for the title.

Syntax: `fstyle[,fstyle]`

Domain: The domain of values are:

Value	Description
NORMAL	The text will be displayed in a normal style.
BOLD	The text will be displayed in bold.
ITALIC	The text will be displayed in italics.
ULINE	The text will be displayed underlined
Implementation Value	The text will be displayed in an implementation-defined manner. Values beginning with "Z" are reserved for implementation values.

Access: The value of this attribute can be assigned when the gadget is being created, and referenced.

Default: The default value is the value of the parent window's FSTYLE attribute.

Notes: The TSTYLE attribute specifies the type style for the text used in the gadget's title.

    The values listed can be combined using the comma as a delineator: BOLD,ULINE. The value NORMAL may not be combined with other values.

    If the value requested cannot be provided, an alternative value can be assigned by the underlying windowing interface. In any case, any reference to this attribute will reflect the actual value.

GRID

Description: This attribute specifies whether grid lines will be displayed between the columns and rows of the gadget.

Domain: The domain of allowable values is an expression that evaluates to true or false.

Access: The value of this attribute can be assigned when the gadget is being created, modified after creation, and referenced.

Default: The default value is true.

HCOLID

Description: This attribute specifies the header column, or columns, for the gadget.

Domain: The domain of values are *citem* subscripts (see the syntax of the COL and CHOICE attributes).

Access: The value of this attribute can be assigned when the gadget is being created, modified after creation, and referenced.

Default: This attribute has no default value.

Notes: All columns that do not follow the value of this attribute in collating sequence are used as headers and do not scroll. If modification to this attribute identifies a column with a selected choice, the choice will become deselected, and no event will occur.

HROWID

Description: This attribute specifies the header rows, or rows, for the gadget.

Domain: The domain of values are *ritem* subscripts (see the syntax of the ROW and CHOICE attributes).

Access: The value of this attribute can be assigned when the gadget is being created, modified after creation, and referenced.

Default: This attribute has no default value.

Notes: All rows that do not follow the value of this attribute in collating sequence are used as headers and do not scroll. If modification to this attribute identifies a row with a selected choice, the choice will become deselected, and no event will occur.

ID

Description: This attribute specifies an internal identifier to assists the underlying windowing interface in accessing the gadget.

Domain: The standard does not specify a domain of values for this attribute. The value is assigned by the windowing interface.

Access: The value may only be referenced for its value.

Default: There is no default value for this attribute.

INSELECT

Description: This attribute identifies a selection in a string of text.

Syntax: `insert,seloff`

Domain: The value of this attribute is made up of two parameters:

> The *insert* parameter identifies the insertion point in the text string and has the domain of positive numeric literals.

The *seloff* parameter indicates an offset (number of characters chosen) from the insertion point and the domain of values lie in the range of positive and negative numeric literals.

Access: The value of this attribute can be assigned when the gadget is being created, modified after creation, and referenced.

Default: The default value is platform dependent.

Notes: *Insert*

A value of zero indicates that the position before the first character in the string.

If the user selects characters to the left of the insertion point, *insert* will reflect that the position before the last character chosen.

An application can assign a value to *insert* less than zero, or greater than the stringlength of the text. If the value is less than zero, it will be zero. If the assignment is a number greater than the number of characters assigned to the gadget's VALUE attribute, the value reflects that the position of the last character.

Seloff

When the value of this attribute is referenced *seloff* indicates the number of characters selected, and is counted in a positive direction from the value of *insert*.

If an application assigns a positive value to *seloff*, characters to the right of *insert* are displayed selected. If an application assigns a negative value to *seloff*, characters to the left of *insert* are selected. If the value of *seloff* is zero, no characters are selected.

LEFTSHOW

Description: This attribute specifies the nonheader column to display to the far left in the scrolling region of a table gadget.

Domain: The domain of values are *citem* subscripts (see the syntax of the COL and CHOICE attributes) and the emptystring.

Access: The value of this attribute can be assigned when the gadget is being created, modified after creation, and referenced.

Default: The default value is the first nonheader column in the table.

Notes: If this attribute matches an existing citem subscript that is not a header, the column will display leftmost in the gadget. If the match is not exact, the nonheader column that follows in collating order will be used. The list may scroll so the selection will display as the first nonheader column. If no column follows, the last column will display leftmost.

The value of this attribute is automatically updated to indicate the column displayed leftmost in the gadget, and the columns may scroll appropriately.

NEXTG

Description: This attribute specifies the gadget focus is transferred to, if the user presses the key sequence that requests movement to the next gadget.

Domain:	The domain of values is the name of a gadget in the current window.
Access:	The value of this attribute can be assigned when the gadget is being created, modified after creation, and referenced.
Default:	There is no default value for this attribute.
Notes:	The key sequence that requests movement to the next gadget is defined by the underlying windowing platform. If there is no underlying windowing platform, the key sequence will be defined by the MWAPI system.

        If an application assigns a value to this attribute that identifies a gadget that is not assigned to the current window, an error will occur with a code of "M49."[5]

        If the gadget defined by this attribute is inactive or of a type unable to receive focus, executing the key sequence to transfer focus to the next gadget begins a search for a gadget that can receive focus. The process will look at the NEXTG attributes of each gadget, indicated by the previous gadget's NEXTG attribute, for a gadget that may receive focus. This process is continued until either a gadget is found that can receive focus or the search fails. If the search finds no gadget to receive focus, focus will remain with the original gadget.

POS

Description:	This attribute specifies the origin (0,0) of the gadget expressed in the unit of measurement specified by the *unitspec* component of this attribute.
Syntax:	`hpos[,[vpos][,unitspec]]` or `,vpos[,unitspec]`
Domain:	The domain of values for the *hpos* and *vpos* parameters are numeric literals. Version 1.1 of the MDC specification modified the domain to include negative values. The domain of values for the *unitspec* component is:

Value	Description
CHAR[,*chars*]	This value specifies that the position is measured relative to the size of a character in the basis font. The *chars* parameter has the domain of one or more characters.
PIXEL	This value specifies that the position measurement is measured in pixels.
POINT	This value specifies that the position is measured in points. The size of a point is 1/72 of an inch.
REL[,*hscale,vscale*]	This value specifies a relative measurement with respect to that the position of the parent window. The parameters *hscale* and *vscale* have the domain of numeric literal values.
Implementation Value	This value is determined by the vendor's implementation of the MWAPI and is not standard.

Access:	The value of this attribute can be assigned when the gadget is being created, modified after creation, and referenced.

Default: There is no default value for this attribute.

Notes: The position of a gadget is measured relative to the origin (0,0) of the its parent window's application area in the unit of measurement specified by the *unitspec* parameter.

If the *unitspec* parameter is not explicitly specified when value is assigned to this attribute, it will default to the current value of the gadget's UNITS attribute.

The value of this attribute does not include the title (if any) for the following gadgets:

Document	Long List Box
List Box	Radio Button Set
List Button	Text
List Entry Box	

The TPOS attribute, discussed later in this chapter, specifies the position of the title for these gadget types.

If after the gadget is created, the assignment of *hpos* or *vpos*, but not both, is not specified, after the gadget is created, the default for the parameter will be the current assigned value for the parameter.

If an *hpos* or *vpos* value is assigned that cannot be provided by the windowing platform, a substitute will be used.

If the unit of measurement is CHAR, the vertical unit of measurement is equal to the line spacing of the basis font. The basis font is determined by the FSTYLE, FSIZE, and FFACE attributes of the parent window. The horizontal dimension is determined by the specification for the *chars* parameter. If *chars* is specified, and not the emptystring, the horizontal unit of measurement equals the width of the average character in the string. If *chars* is the emptystring, or not specified, the horizontal unit of measurement equals the maximum character width in the basis font.

If the unit of measurement is REL, the basis size is the size of the parent window's viewport upon creation of the parent. If *hscale* and *vscale* are not specified, both parameters default to 100.

Any reference to this attribute will yield the syntax above specifying the actual size of *hpos, vpos,* and the current value specified by the gadget's UNITS attribute for the *unitspec* parameter.

If this attribute is not defined when the gadget is being created, an error will occur with a code of "M52."[6]

PTYPE

Description: This attribute specifies the pointer appearance when it is over area of the gadget.

Domain: The domain of values are:

Value	*Description*
M,CROSS	This value specifies a pointer appearance of cross-hairs.
M,IBEAM	This value specifies a pointer appearance of I-beam.

M,WAIT	This value specifies a pointer appearance of a waiting state.
F,*fileid*	This is for a file specifier. The path to the file is specified by *fileid*.
R,*resourceid*	This is for a resource identifier. The resource is specified by *resourceid*.
Implementation Value	This value is determined by the vendor's implementation of the MWAPI and is not standard.

Access: The value of this attribute can be assigned when the gadget is being created, modified after creation, and referenced.

Default: This attribute has no default value.

Notes: If the PTYPE attribute of the gadget's logical display is defined, its value has precedence over the pointer appearance. The value of a gadget's PTYPE attribute has precedence over the value of the parent window's PTYPE attribute.

    If the window's logical display does not have a pointer device connected (^$DI($PD,"PTR") is undefined), the value of this attribute will be ignored.

    The values for F,*fileid* and R,*resourceid* are platform or hardware dependent and may not be portable.

RESOURCE

Description: This attribute specifies an image to be displayed in the gadget.

Domain: The domain of values is dependent on the gadget type. The domain for a symbol gadget include the symbol and external resource lists below, and the domain of values for a push button gadget includes an entry in the external resource list only.

Identifier Symbol	*Description*
M,ERROR	This symbol indicates an error.
M,INFO	This symbol indicates information.
M,QUEST	This symbol indicates a question.
M,WARN	This symbol indicates a warning.

External Resource	
R,*resourceid*	A *resourceid* specifies a valid resource to be included.
F,*fileid*	A *fileid* indicates the path to a valid file identifier to be included.
Implementation Value	This identifier specifies a valid implementation value.

Access: The value of this attribute can be assigned when the gadget is being created, modified after creation, and referenced.

Default: This attribute has no default value.

Notes: The syntax for *resourceid* and *fileid* is platform dependent.

    Neither External Resource Identifiers nor Implementation Values are standard. Symbols are standard and defined for use by the MWAPI specification.

If this attribute is not defined at the time the symbol gadget is being created, an error will occur with a code of "M52."[7]

The MDC's version 1.1 makes this attribute modifiable.

ROW

Description:	This attribute specifies the rows in a table gadget.
Syntax:	`^$W(window name,"G",gadget name,"ROW",ritem)=""`
Domain:	There is no value at the attribute level, but there is at the lower subscript levels. The *ritem* parameter in the syntax listed has the domain of character values and uniquely identifies each row in the table gadget.
Access:	The value of *ritem* subscripts can be assigned when the gadget is being created, modified after creation, and referenced.
Default:	There is no default for this attribute, but descendants to this attribute can be implicitly defined as choices are assigned to the table gadget.
Notes:	A *ritem* subscript associated with this attribute does not have to exist as a *ritem* subscript of the CHOICE attribute. If a row referenced in the syntax of the CHOICE attribute is not specified by this attribute, a ROW attribute will be implicitly defined. All rows will have a ROW attribute node. If the attribute specifies a row that does not exist in the syntax of the CHOICE attribute, the row will be empty.

ROWCOL

Description:	This attribute specifies row/column format for displaying choices in a Radio Button Set gadget.
Syntax:	`rowcol[,rowcolsize[,filldir]]`
Domain:	The domain of values is as follows:

Parameter	Value
rowcol	The value for this parameter will be "ROW" (row) or "COL" (column).
rowcolsize	The value of this parameter is an integer greater than one.
filldir	The value of this parameter is either "H" (horizontal) or "V" (vertical).

Access:	This attribute can be assigned when the gadget is being created and referenced for its value.
Default:	If the value of this attribute is not explicitly assigned, the default value is "COL,1,V."
	If the *rowcolsize* parameter is not specified, the default value will be one.
	If the *filldir* parameter is not specified, the default is "V."
Notes:	If the value of the *rowcol* parameter is "ROW," the value assigned to the *rowcolsize* parameter determines the number of rows to use for the display of choices.
	If the value of the *rowcol* parameter is "COL," the value assigned to the *rowcolsize* parameter determines the number of columns to use for the display of choices.

The value of the *filldir* parameter determines how the matrix is loaded with choices. If the value is "H," the choices are filled in from left to right in row order. If the value is "V," the choices are filled in top to bottom in column order. Rows and columns are filled in from the origin of the matrix in a positive direction.

ROWHEIGHT

Description:	The value of this attribute node specifies the default height for rows in the table gadget.
Syntax:	`vsize,[unitspec]`
Domain:	The domain of values for the *vsize* parameter are positive numeric literals. The domain of values for the *unitspec* component is:

Value	Description
CHAR[,*chars*]	This value specifies the that position is measured relative to the size of a character in the basis font. The domain of values for the *chars* parameter is one or more characters.
PIXEL	This value specifies that the position measurement is measured in pixels.
POINT	This value specifies that the position is measured in points. The size of a point is 1/72 of an inch.
REL[,*hscale,vscale*]	This value specifies a relative measurement with respect to the parent window's size. The parameters *hscale* and *vscale* have the domain of numeric literal values.
Implementation Value	This value is determined by the vendor's implementation of the MWAPI and is not standard.

Access:	The value of this attribute can be assigned when the gadget is being created, modified after creation, and referenced.
Default:	The default value is determined by the underlying windowing platform.
Notes:	If the *unitspec* parameter is not explicitly specified when a value is assigned to this attribute, it will default to the current value of the gadget's UNITS attribute.

If the unit of measurement is CHAR, the vertical unit of measurement is equal to the line spacing of the basis font. The basis font is determined by the FSTYLE, FSIZE, and FFACE attributes of the parent window. The horizontal dimension is determined by the specification for the *chars* parameter. If *chars* is specified, and not the emptystring, the horizontal unit of measurement equals the width of the average character in the string. If *chars* is the emptystring, or not specified, the horizontal unit of measurement equals the maximum character width in the basis font.

If the unit of measurement is REL, the basis size is the size of the parent window's viewport upon creation of the parent. If *hscale* and *vscale* are not specified, both parameters default to 100.

If the assignment of a *vsize* is not specified, after the gadget is created, the default is the current assigned value for the parameter.

If a *vsize* value is assigned that cannot be provided by the windowing platform, an alternative will be used.

Any reference to this attribute will yield the syntax above specifying the actual size of *hsize, vsize,* and the current value specified by the gadget's UNITS attribute for the *unitspec* parameter.

SCROLL

Description:
: This attribute determines whether horizontal and/or vertical scrolling can occur and the range of movement.

Syntax:
: `hsize[,vsize][,unitspec]` or `,vsize[,unitspec]`

Domain:
: The value of this attribute may consist of three parameters: the horizontal size (*hsize*), the vertical size (*vsize*), and the unit of measurement (*unitspec*). The domain of values for the *hsize* and *vsize* parameters are positive numeric literals including zero. The domain of values for the *unitspec* component is:

Value	Description
CHAR[,*chars*]	This value specifies that the position is measured relative to the size of a character in the basis font. The domain of values for the *chars* parameter is one or more characters.
PIXEL	This value specifies that the position measurement is measured in pixels.
POINT	This value specifies that the position is measured in points. The size of a point is 1/72 of an inch.
REL[,*hscale,vscale*]	This value specifies a relative measurement with respect to a basis size. The parameters *hscale* and *vscale* have the domain of numeric literal values.
Implementation Value	This value is determined by the vendor's implementation of the MWAPI and is not standard.

Access:
: The value of this attribute can be assigned when the gadget is being created and referenced.

Default:
: If *hsize* or *vsize* is defined and the *unitspec* parameter is not specified, the default is the value of the gadget's UNITS attribute.

  The default value is the emptystring.

Notes:
: If *hsize* has a value of zero or greater, a vertical scroll bar can be used to scroll the gadget's text horizontally from zero to *hsize*. If *vsize* is zero or greater, a horizontal scrollbar can be used to scroll the text vertically from zero to *vsize*. If *hsize* or *vsize* equals the emptystring horizontal or vertical scrolling respectively will not occur.

  The use of scroll bars when the text can be viewed in the gadget's display area is dependent upon what the underlying windowing platform allows.

  The value of the *hsize* component determines the width for wrapping of text in a Document gadget.

If the unit of measurement is CHAR, the vertical unit of measurement is equal to the line spacing of the basis font. The basis font is determined by the FSTYLE, FSIZE, and FFACE attributes of the gadget. The horizontal dimension is determined by the specification for the *chars* parameter. If *chars* is specified, and not the emptystring, the horizontal unit of measurement equals the width of the average character in the string. If chars is the emptystring, or not specified, the horizontal unit of measurement equals the maximum character width in the basis font.

If the unit of measurement is REL, the basis size is the size of the parent window's viewport upon creation of the parent. If *hscale* and *vscale* are not specified, both parameters default to 100.

SCROLLBY

Description: This attribute specifies the amount of change to the Scroll gadget's VALUE attribute, when the user causes its position indicator to move.

Syntax: `scrollsmall` or `[scrollsmall],scrollbig`

Domain: The value domains for both *scrollsmall* and *scrollbig* are positive numeric integers including zero.

Access: The value of this attribute can be assigned when the gadget is being created, modified after creation, and referenced.

Default: The default value for the *scrollsmall* parameter is one.

The default value for the *scrollbig* parameter is determined by dividing the difference between the gadgets *scrollmax* and *scrollmin* parameters of the SCROLLRANGE attribute by five.

Notes: If the user requests a small movement, the gadget's VALUE attribute is either decreased or increased by the amount specified by the *scrollsmall* parameter. A small movement is indicated by clicking on one of the arrow movement controls on the gadget.

If the user requests a big movement, the gadget's VALUE attribute is either increased or decreased by the amount specified by the *scrollbig* parameter. A big movement is indicated by clicking within the gadget, not including dragging the movement indicator or clicking on an arrow movement control.

The gadget's VALUE attribute is increased by a variable amount, when the movement of the position indicator is towards the top of a vertical gadget, or to the right of a horizontal gadget.

SCROLLDIR

Description: This attribute specifies the orientation of a Scroll gadget.

Domain: The value domain is "H" (horizontal orientation) or "V" (vertical orientation).

Access: The value of this attribute can be merged into the Window SSVN for the gadget it will characterize at the time the gadget is created and referenced for its value.

Default: The default value is "H."

SCROLLPOS

Description: This attribute specifies that the position of the position indicator in the scroll bar of a Long List Box gadget relative to the scale is established by its SCROLLRANGE attribute.

Domain: The value domain is a numeric expression.

Access: The value of this attribute can be merged into the Window SSVN for the gadget it will characterize at the time the gadget is created, modified after creation, or referenced for its value.

Default: There is no default value for this attribute.

Notes: If this attribute is not defined, a position indicator will not be shown.
The value of this attribute returns the scroll value of the gadget.

SCROLLRANGE

Description: This attribute specifies the value range for scrolling in Scroll and Long List Box gadgets.

Syntax: *scrollmin* or [*scrollmin*],*scrollmax*

Domain: The value domains for *scrollmin* and *scrollmax* are numeric literals.

Access: The value of this attribute can be merged into the Window SSVN for the gadget it will characterize at the time the gadget is created, modified after creation, or referenced for its value.

Default: The default value for the *scrollmin* is zero, for *scrollmax,* 100.

Notes: *Scrollmin* and *scrollmax* define the range of values that can be assigned to the VALUE attribute of a Scroll gadget, and the SCROLLPOS attribute of a Long List Box gadget.
The position of a Scroll gadget's value indicator, is determined by the value of its VALUE attribute in relation to the range specified by this attribute.
The position of a Long List Box's position indicator is determined by the value of its SCROLLPOS attribute in relation to *scrollmin* and *scrollmax*.

SELECTMAX

Description: This attribute specifies the maximum number of choices that can be selected at the same time.

Domain: The value domain is a positive numeric integer including zero.

Access: The value of this attribute can be merged into the Window SSVN for the gadget it will characterize at the time the gadget is created or referenced for its value.

Default: The default value is one.

Notes: The value of zero indicates no maximum limit to the number of concurrent selections.

SELECTVAL

Description: This attribute contains the selected text in the gadget.

Domain: The domain of values are characters.

Access: The value of this attribute can be merged into the Window SSVN for the gadget it will characterize at the time the gadget is created or referenced for its value.

Default: There is no default value for this attribute.

Notes: If the gadget's INSELECT attribute is defined, this attribute indicates the characters selected. If the INSELECT attribute in not defined, this attribute will not exist for the gadget.

If the value of this attribute is modified, the selected value contained in the argument of the gadget's VALUE attribute will also be changed. If the selected value of "ABC" is changed to "XXX," "XXX" will replace "ABC" in the VALUE attribute's argument. If the selected value is killed, the result will be reflected by the VALUE attribute.

SIZE

Description: This attribute specifies the size of the gadget in the unit of measurement specified in its parameter list.

Syntax: `hsize[,[vsize][,unitspec]` or `,vsize[,unitspec]`

Domain: The domain of values for the *hsize* and *vsize* is positive numeric literals including zero. The domain of values for the *unitspec* component is:

CHAR[,*chars*]	This value specifies that the position is measured relative to the size of a character in the basis font. The domain of values for the *chars* parameter is one or more characters.
PIXEL	This value specifies that the position measurement is measured in pixels.
POINT	This value specifies that the position is measured in points. The size of a point is 1/72 of an inch.
REL[,*hscale,vscale*]	This value specifies a relative measurement with respect to the parent window's size. The parameters *hscale* and *vscale* have the domain of numeric literal values.
Implementation Value	This value is determined by the vendor's implementation of the MWAPI and is not standard.

Access: The value of this attribute can be assigned when the gadget is being created, modified after creation, and referenced.

Default: The defaults for *hsize* and *vsize* for a Symbol gadget are whatever is necessary to display its image. For the other gadget types the default values are platform dependent.

If *unitspec* is not specified, the default is the value of the gadgets UNITS attribute.

Notes: Horizontal and vertical coordinates are defined by *hsize* and *vsize*, and are measured in a positive direction from the gadget's position.

If a Group Frame gadget is assigned positive values for *hsize* and *vsize*, a rectangle will be produced. A zero vertical coordinate produces a horizontal line, and a zero horizontal coordinate produces a vertical line.

If this attribute is not defined when Generic Box or Group Frame gadgets are created, an error will occur with a code of "M52."[8]

If the assignment of *hpos* or *vpos*, but not both, is not specified, after the window is created, the default is the current assigned value for the parameter.

If an *hpos* or *vpos* value is assigned that cannot be provided by the windowing platform, a substitute will be used.

If the unit of measurement is CHAR, the vertical unit of measurement is equal to the line spacing of the basis font. The basis font is determined by the FSTYLE, FSIZE, and FFACE attributes of the gadget. If the gadget is not specified to use the FFACE attribute, the basis font is determined by its TFFACE, TFSIZE, and TFSTYLE attribute values. If the gadget is not specified to use these attributes, the basis font is determined by the FFACE, FSIZE, and FSTYLE attributes of the parent window. The horizontal dimension is determined by the specification for the *chars* parameter. If *chars* is specified, and not the emptystring, the horizontal unit of measurement equals the width of the average character in the string. If *chars* is the emptystring, or not specified, the horizontal unit of measurement equals the maximum character width in the basis font.

If the unit of measurement is REL, the basis size is the size of the parent window's viewport upon creation of the parent. If *hscale* and *vscale* are not specified, both parameters default to 100.

Any reference to this attribute will yield the syntax above specifying the actual size of *hpos*, *vpos,* and the current value specified by the gadget's UNITS attribute for the *unitspec* parameter.

TBCOLOR

Description:	This attribute specifies the background color for the gadget's title.
Syntax:	rcolor,gcolor,bcolor
Domain:	The domain of values are color definitions specified by amounts of red, green, and blue (RGB). Black="0,0,0" and white="65535,65535,65535." Appropriate color values lie between 0 and 65535.
Access:	The value of this attribute can be assigned when the gadget is being created, modified after creation, and referenced.
Default:	If the parent's TBCOLOR attribute is defined, its value is the default. If it is not defined, the value of the parent's COLOR attribute is used.[9]
Notes:	Color codes are listed in Appendix A.

TFCOLOR

Description:	This attribute specifies the color for the text in the gadget's title.
Syntax:	rcolor,gcolor,bcolor
Domain:	The domain of values are color definitions specified by amounts of red, green, and blue (RGB). Black="0,0,0" and white="65535,65535,65535." Appropriate color values lie between 0 and 65535.
Access:	The value of this attribute can be assigned when the gadget is being created, modified after creation, and referenced.
Default:	If the parent's TFCOLOR attribute is defined, its value is the default. If it is not defined, the value of the parent's FCOLOR attribute is used.[10]
Notes:	Color codes are listed in Appendix A.

TFFACE

Description: This attribute specifies the typeface used for the gadget's title.

Domain: The domain is one of the fontface values defined by the TYPEFACE attribute in the current logical display, and the fontfaces listed below:

Font Name	Description
M,DEFAULT	This is the default typeface as defined for the underlying windowing system. If there is no underlying windowing platform, The MWAPI defines this fontface.
M,FIXED	This is a nonproportional typeface.
M,SANS	This is a proportional typeface from the sans-serif family.
M,SERIF	This is a proportional typeface from the serif family.
Implementation Value	This value will begin with a "Z," and be defined by the M implementation.

Access: The value of this attribute can be assigned when the gadget is being created, modified after creation, and referenced.

Default: The default value is the value of the parent's FFACE attribute.

TFSIZE

Description: This attribute specifies the type size for the gadget's title.

Domain: The domain of values are positive numeric literals to specify a point size (1/72 inch) in the current font face.

Access: The value of this attribute can be assigned when the gadget is being created, modified after creation, and referenced.

Default: The default value is the value of the parent's FSIZE attribute.

TFSTYLE

Description: This attribute specifies the type style for the gadget's title.

Domain: The domain of values are:

Value	Description
NORMAL	The text will be displayed in a normal style.
BOLD	The text will be displayed in bold.
ITALIC	The text will be displayed in italics.
ULINE	The text will be displayed underlined
Implementation Value	The text will be displayed in an implementation-defined manner. Values beginning with "Z" are reserved for implementation values.

Access: The value of this attribute can be assigned when the gadget is being created, modified after creation, and referenced.

Default: The default value is the value of the parent's FSTYLE attribute.

Notes: The values listed can be combined using the comma as a delineator: BOLD,ULINE. The value NORMAL may not be combined with other values.

TITLE

Description: This attribute specifies the title that appears for the gadget.

Domain: The domain of values is one or more characters or the emptystring.

Access: The value of this attribute can be assigned when the gadget is being created, modified after creation, and referenced.

Default: The default value of this attribute for the Label gadget is the emptystring.
   There is no defined default for the other gadgets.

Notes: If the value of this attribute contains an ampersand character (&) followed by a character other than an ampersand, the choice can be selected by the depressing the following character on the keyboard. For instance: MS Windows displays an underscore under the character following the ampersand to indicate depressing the character on the keyboard will direct focus to the gadget. If the gadget cannot receive focus, its NEXTG attribute will be evaluated to determine where focus will go.
   If an ampersand character is to be displayed in the choice, precede it with one ampersand. Keyboard selection will not be occur by selecting the ampersand character on the keyboard.
   This attribute specifies text for a Label gadget. The Label gadget is for displaying text.
   Depending upon the gadget, the title may appear adjacent to, or within, the gadget. The title appears adjacent to all the gadget types permitted except Group Frame, Label, and Push Button.
   The title for a Group Frame appears within or overlaying the frame. The title of a Push Button appears in the button itself.

TOPSHOW

Description: This attribute specifies the choice to display at the top of the list of choices in the gadget.

Domain: The domain of values is either an emptystring or a choice (*item*) or row (*ritem* of a Table gadget) defined as a subscript of the gadget's CHOICE attribute.

Access: The value of this attribute can be assigned when the gadget is being created, modified after creation, and referenced.

Default: The default value is the first subscripted value (*item* or *ritem*) defined by the gadget's CHOICE attribute. If the gadget has no choices defined, the default is the emptystring.

Notes: A list of choices are values assigned to subscript nodes of the gadget's CHOICE attribute.
   The value of this attribute will change to reflect the choice, or row, at the top of the display area, as the user scrolls the list of choices.
   A subscript value can be assigned to this attribute and force a choice, or row, to display at the top of the list. If the value assigned does not exactly match a subscript in the list, the subscript that follows in collating will be assigned. If there is no match and no following subscript, the list of choices will scroll, if necessary, to display the last value.

TPOS

Description: This attribute specifies the position of the title relative to the gadget.

Domain: The domain of values are LEFT, RIGHT, TOP, and Implementation-defined values.

Access: The value of this attribute can be assigned when the gadget is being created, modified after creation, and referenced.

Default: The default value is TOP.

TYPE

Description: This attribute specifies the gadget type.

Domain: The domain of values are gadget types listed in Table 5.1 and those defined by the MWAPI implementation.

Access: The value of this attribute must be assigned when the gadget is being created and referenced.

Default: This attribute does not have a default value.

Notes: This is attribute is required of all gadgets.

UNITS

Description: This attribute defines the unit of measurement for the gadget.

Domain: The domain of values are shown below.

Value	*Description*
CHAR[,*chars*]	This value specifies that the position is measured relative to the size of a character in the basis font. The value domain for the *chars* attribute is one or more characters.
PIXEL	This value specifies that the position measurement is measured in pixels.
POINT	This value specifies that the position is measured in points. The size of a point is 1/72 of an inch.
REL[,*hscale*,*vscale*]	This value specifies a relative measurement with respect to a basis size. The parameters *hscale* and *vscale* have the domain of numeric literal values.
Implementation Value	This value is determined by the vendor's implementation of the MWAPI and is not standard.

Access: The value of this attribute can be assigned when the gadget is being created, modified after creation, and referenced.

Default: The default is the UNITS attribute value of the parent window.

Notes: If the unit of measurement is CHAR, the vertical unit of measurement is equal to the line spacing of the basis font. The basis font is determined by the FSTYLE, FSIZE, and FFACE attributes of the gadget. If the gadget is not specified to use the FFACE attribute, the basis font is determined by its TFFACE, TFSIZE, and TFSTYLE attribute values. If the gadget is not specified to use these attributes, the basis font is determined by the FFACE, FSIZE, and FSTYLE attributes of the parent window. The horizontal dimension is determined by the specification for the *chars* parameter. If *chars* is specified, and not the empty-string, the horizontal unit of measurement equals the width of the average character in the string. If chars is the emptystring, or not specified, the horizontal unit of measurement equals the maximum character width in the basis font.

If the unit of measurement is REL, the basis size is the size of the parent window's viewport upon creation of the parent. If *hscale* and *vscale* are not specified, both parameters default to 100.

VALUE

Description: This attribute specifies the value of the gadget.

Domain: The domain of values depends upon the gadget type:

If the gadget is a Check Box, the value will be an expression that evaluates to true or false.

If the gadget is a Document, List Entry Box, or a Text, characters make up the value domain.

If the gadget is a List Box, Long List Box, or Table, the value domain is integer. Descendant nodes have the value of emptystring.

If the gadget is a Radio Button or a List Button, the value will be either a subscript of one of its choices (*item*) or the emptystring.

If the gadget is a Scroll, the domain is a numeric value in the range defined by its SCROLLRANGE attribute.

Access: The value of this attribute can be assigned when the gadget is being created, modified after creation, and referenced.

Default: The defaults depend on the gadget type:

If a Text gadget, the default is zero.

If a Document, List Button, List Entry Box, Radio Button Set, or Text gadget, the default is the emptystring.

If a List Box, Long List Box, or Table gadget, no descendant exists and the default value is zero.

If a Scroll gadget, the *scrollmin* value of its SCROLLRANGE attribute is used.

Notes: The value of a Check Box gadget is either one (indicates selection) or zero (indicates either deselection or no selection).

The value of a Document, List Entry Box, and a Text gadget is the characters assigned. If the value of a Document gadget contains imbedded line end characters ($C(13,10)), the following character will begin a new line.

If a List Box, Long List Box, or a Table gadget, the value specifies the total number of choices selected. This value is automatically maintained, and may only be killed by an application. The subscripts of descendant nodes are *item*, or *ritem* and *citem*, subscripts of the choices selected. The value of subscript nodes is the emptystring.

The value of a Radio Button Set and a List Button gadget is the *item* subscript associated with the choice selected.

If an application assigns an *item* or *ritem* and *citem* values that correspond to one of the gadget's choices, it will indicate selection to the user. If the value does not exist as a subscript of the gadget's CHOICE attribute, or is defined as a header in a Table gadget, an error will occur with a code of "M48."[11]

VISIBLE

Description: This attribute specifies whether the gadget is visible or not.

Domain: The domain of values is an expression that evaluates to true or false.

Access: The value of this attribute can be assigned when the gadget is being created, modified after creation, and referenced.

Default: The default value is true.

Choice Attributes

This section focuses on the attributes available to describe characteristics of choices assigned to gadgets in the choice category. These attributes are maintained as descendants of *item* and *citem* and *ritem* subscripts of the CHOICE attribute. The CHOICE attribute described in the Gadget Attributes section and Table 5.2 list the gadget types that can use these attributes. Example 5.3 shows the syntax for a Choice attribute for nontable gadgets, and Example 5.4 shows the syntax for table gadgets.

`^$W(window name,"G",gadget name,"CHOICE",item,choice attribute)=value`

EXAMPLE 5.3: *Nontable Choice Attribute Syntax*

`^$W(window name,"G",gadget name,"CHOICE",ritem,citem,choice attribute)=value`

EXAMPLE 5.4: *Table Choice Attribute Syntax*

The first three subscripts in Examples 5.3 and 5.4 are as discussed in the Creation and Modification section. The fourth subscript is the CHOICE attribute keyword. The *item* subscript of Example 5.3 is the subscript of a choice assigned to the gadget. The *ritem* and *citem* subscripts in Example 5.4 are the row and column subscripts of a choice assigned to the Table gadget. The *choice attribute* subscript in both examples is a Choice attribute keyword from Table 5.7. The *value* argument must specify a valid value from the domain specified for the respective Choice attribute. If an application attempts to assign a value for a Choice attribute that is not specified by its domain of values, an error will occur with a code of "M47."[12]

The MWAPI standard specifies three keywords available to modify the behavior of choices in a gadget. The specification allows for the use of implementation- and application-defined Choice attributes, and implementation-defined keywords are not guaranteed portability. Implementation-defined Choice attributes must begin with the letter "Z" and application attributes must begin with the letter "Y." If an application attempts to specify a choice attribute that is not mentioned in Table 5.7, an error will occur with a code of "M46."[13] The RESOURCE keyword is only available to Table gadgets, and ACTIVE is not available to Tables. The format introduced in Table 5.5 is used to cover the detail explanation of each Choice attribute listed above. The Gadgets subsection lists gadgets that can use the respective attribute.

TABLE 5.7: *Choice Attributes*

ACTIVE	AID	RESOURCE[1]

[1]This attribute was added by version 1.1 of the MWAPI specification.

ACTIVE

Description:	This attribute specifies whether the choice is enabled or disabled for selection.
Domain:	The domain of allowable values is an expression that evaluates to true or false.
Access:	The value can be assigned when the window is being created, modified after creation, and referenced.
Default:	The default value is true.
Gadgets:	List Box Long List Box
	List Button Radio Button Set
	List Entry Box
Notes:	If the value evaluates to true, both user and application selections of the choice can occur.
	If the value evaluates to false: (1) the choice is displayed in reverse video, or some manner to indicate that it is disabled; (2) the user will not be able to select the choice; and (3) any previous selection of the choice is deselected.
	If an application attempts to select an inactive choice, an error will occur with a code of "M47."

AID

Description:	This attribute is provided so an application dependent value can be associated with the choice.
Domain:	The domain of allowable values is one or more characters.
Access:	The value can be assigned when the window is being created, modified after creation, and referenced.
Default:	There is no default value for this attribute.
Gadgets:	List Box Long List Box
	List Button Radio Button Set
	List Entry Box Table

RESOURCE

Description:	This attribute specifies an image to display in the cell.
Domain:	The domain of values is:

Value	*Description*
F,*fileid*	This is for a file specifier. The path to the file is specified by *fileid*.

	R,*resourceid*	This is for a resource identifier. The resource is specified by *resourceid*.
	Implementation Value	This value is determined by the vendor's implementation of the MWAPI and is not standard.
Access:		The value can be assigned when the window is being created, modified after creation, and referenced.
Default:		There is no default value for this attribute.
Gadgets:		This attribute is only specified for use by the Table gadget.
Notes:		The values for F,*fileid* and R,*resourceid* are platform or hardware dependent and may not be portable.
		If an image is assigned to a cell with text, an error will occur with a code of "M47."

Row and Column Attributes

This section focuses on Row and Column attributes, as specified for the MWAPI extension by the addition of version 1.1 of the MDC's MWAPI specification. Row and Column attributes are case-sensitive keywords added to define the characteristics of rows and columns of Table gadgets. Row attributes define the characteristics of rows, and Column attributes define the characteristics of columns. Examples 5.5 and 5.6 detail the syntax for Row and Column attributes, as they appear in ^$W.

`^$W(window name,"G",gadget name,"ROW",ritem,row attribute)=value`

EXAMPLE 5.5: *Row Attribute Syntax*

`^$W(window name,"G",gadget name,"COL",citem,column attribute)=value`

EXAMPLE 5.6: *Column Attribute Syntax*

The first three subscripts are as specified in the Creation and Modification section. The fourth-level subscript is a case-sensitive keyword to designate whether the object of the assignment is a row (ROW) or a column (COL). The fifth-level subscript specifies the row (*ritem*) or column (*citem*) is to receive the assignment. The *row attribute* and *column attribute* subscripts specify a row or column attribute from Table 5.8. The *value* argument must specify a valid value from a domain determined by the row or column attribute respectively. If an application attempts to assign a value to an attribute that is not specified by its domain of values, an error will occur with a code of "M47."[14]

The MDC's version 1.1 of the MWAPI specification defines one Row and one Column attributes. Implementers of the MWAPI can define attributes for both rows and columns. Implementation-defined keywords must begin with the letter "Z," and may not be portable. If an application attempts to specify a row or column attribute that is not mentioned in Table 5.7 , an error will occur with a code of "M46."[15]

TABLE **5.8**: *Row and Column Attributes*

TYPE:	
Row Attribute	ROWHEIGHT
Column Attribute	COLWIDTH

ROWHEIGHT and COLWIDTH keywords also exist as Gadget attributes, and specify default values for all row heights and column widths of the table gadget they are assigned. The attributes described here differ by defining characteristics of individual rows and columns. The format introduced in Table 5.5 is used to cover the detail explanation of each row and column attribute.

COLWIDTH

Description:	The value node specifies a column's width.
Syntax:	hsize,[unitspec]
Domain:	The domain of values for the *hsize* parameter is positive numeric literals including zero. The domain of values for the *unitspec* component is:

Value	Description
CHAR[,*chars*]	This value specifies that the position is measured relative to the size of a character in the basis font. The domain of values for the *chars* parameter is one or more characters.
PIXEL	This value specifies that the position measurement is measured in pixels.
POINT	This value specifies that the position is measured in points. The size of a point is 1/72 of an inch.
REL[,*hscale*,*vscale*]	This value specifies a relative measurement with respect to the parent window's size. The parameters *hscale* and *vscale* have the domain of numeric literal values.
Implementation Value	This value is determined by the vendor's implementation of the MWAPI and is not standard.

Access:	The value can be assigned when the gadget is being created, modified after creation, and referenced.
Default:	The default value is the value of the gadget's COLWIDTH attribute.
Notes:	If the *unitspec* parameter is not explicitly specified when value is assigned to this attribute, unitspec will default to the current value of the gadget's UNITS attribute.
	If the unit of measurement is CHAR, the vertical unit of measurement is equal to the line spacing of the basis font. The basis font is determined by the gadget's FFACE, FSIZE, and FSTYLE attribute values. The horizontal dimension is determined by the specification for the *chars* parameter. If *chars* is specified, and not the emptystring, the horizontal unit of measurement equals the width of the average character in the string. If *chars* is the emptystring, or not specified, the horizontal unit of measurement equals the maximum character width in the basis font.

The basis size for a *unitspec* of REL is the size of the window's viewport. If *hscale* and *vscale* are not specified, both parameters default to 100.

If the assignment of a *hsize* is not specified, after the gadget is created, the default is the current assigned value for the parameter.

If an *hsize* value is assigned that cannot be provided by the windowing platform, the value is determined by the underlying windowing platform.

Any reference to this attribute will yield the syntax above specifying the actual size of *hsize*, and the current value specified by the gadget's UNITS attribute for the *unitspec* parameter.

ROWHEIGHT

Description: The value node specifies the row's height.

Syntax: `vsize,[unitspec]`

Domain: The domain of values for the *vsize* parameter is positive numeric literals including zero. The domain of values for the *unitspec* component is:

Value	Description
CHAR[,*chars*]	This value specifies that the position is measured relative to the size of a character in the basis font. The domain of values for the *chars* parameter is one or more characters.
PIXEL	This value specifies that the position measurement is measured in pixels.
POINT	This value specifies that the position is measured in points. The size of a point is 1/72 of an inch.
REL[,*hscale*,*vscale*]	This value specifies a relative measurement with respect to the parent window's size. The parameters *hscale* and *vscale* have the domain of numeric literal values.
Implementation Value	This value is determined by the vendor's implementation of the MWAPI and is not standard.

Access: The value can be assigned when the gadget is being created, modified after creation, and referenced.

Default: The default value is the value of the gadget's ROWHEIGHT attribute.

Notes: If the *unitspec* parameter is not explicitly specified when value is assigned to this attribute, it will default to the current value of the gadget's UNITS attribute.

If the unit of measurement is CHAR, the vertical unit of measurement is equal to the line spacing of the basis font. The basis font is determined by the FSTYLE, FSIZE, and FFACE attributes of the gadget. The horizontal dimension is determined by the specification for the *chars* parameter. If *chars* is specified, and not the emptystring, the horizontal unit of measurement equals the width of the average character in the string. If *chars* is the emptystring, or not specified, the horizontal unit of measurement equals the maximum character width in the basis font.

If the unit of measurement is REL, the basis size is the size of the parent window's viewport upon creation of the parent. If *hscale* and *vscale* are not specified, both parameters default to 100.

If the assignment of a *vsize* is not specified, after the gadget is created, the default is the current assigned value for the parameter.

If a *vsize* value is assigned that cannot be provided by the windowing platform, an alternative is used determined by the windowing platform.

Any reference to this attribute will yield the syntax above specifying the actual size of *hsize*, *vsize*, and the current value specified by the gadget's UNITS attribute for the *unitspec* parameter.

Event Processing

This section extends the topic of event processing started in Chapter 2 with a look at the processing of gadget-related events. The events gadgets can respond to are specified by keywords assigned to the first-level subscript descended from their EVENT attribute nodes. Once event processing has been activated, events may occur for a gadget as the result of user interaction with them, or the execution of an ETRIGGER that references one of their EVENT attribute nodes. Focus must be directed to an active gadget (the value of ^$DI($PD,"FOCUS") contains the gadget's name) before a user can trigger an event for it. An event triggered by an ETRIGGER command can occur for any gadget regardless of focus, and the value of ^$DI($PD,"FOCUS") will remain unchanged.

The developer can define the events a gadget can receive callback processing for by assigning matching-event-type keywords as subscripts to its EVENT attribute node. An application can trigger a particular event through the execution of an ETRIGGER command with the desired EVENT attribute node specified in its argument. Example 5.7 shows an EVENT attribute node.

```
^$W(window name,"G",gadget name,"EVENT",event type)=value
```

EXAMPLE 5.7: *Gadget Event Node*

The first three subscripts follow the same requirements specified in the Creation and Modification section. The fourth subscript is the attribute keyword that describes the node for event processing. The event type keyword for the node to respond to is identified in the fifth subscript. The value of the node is a comma delineated list of routine(s) to process callbacks for the event. A gadget's EVENT attribute node can contain several subscripts, one for each *event type*.

Event Types

The MWAPI specification defines twenty-one event type keywords for indicating events that can cause callback processing to occur for gadgets. The MWAPI specification makes allowances for implementers to specify event types, but implementation values are not guaranteed the portability of standard values. The character "Z" is reserved for the first character in an implementation keyword. The gadget type determines the event types it can use and respond to. Table 5.9 lists the event type keywords available for gadgets. Event type keywords are uppercase keywords that must be enclosed in quotes or assigned as a variable. Table 5.10 identifies the event type keywords to the gadgets that can receive events.

The keywords can be divided into three categories. The descriptions are discussed from the point of view of the applications user. All events listed can be triggered by an application.

Keyboard: The keywords in this category are initiated from the keyboard.

Pointer: Events described by this category are triggered from the pointer device.

State: This category is from events to the state or properties of the window.

TABLE 5.9: *MWAPI-Defined Event Types*

Category	Attribute	Category	Attribute
KEYBOARD[1]	CHAR[2]	MOVEMENT	GOBOTTOM
	KEYDOWN		GODOWN
	KEYUP		GODOWNBIG
	HELP		GOTOP
			GOUP
			GOUPBIG
POINTER	CLICK	SELECTION	DESELECT
	DBLCLICK		SELECT
	PDOWN	STATE	FOCUS
	PDRAG	VALUE	UNFOCUS
	PMOVE		CHANGE
	PUP		

[1] FKEYDOWN and FKEYUP were deleted by version 1.1. The KEYDOWN and KEYUP keywords describe the events these event types dealt with.

[2] This keyword was added by the version 1.1 specification for the MWAPI.

Tables 5.10 identifies the event type keywords to gadgets that can use them.

If an event occurs for a gadget with an event type node defined to process the event, reference ^$E("WINDOW") to determine the window and gadget names and $P(^$E("ELEMENT"),",",2) to determine the element's name. ^$E("TYPE") indicates the event type that occurred. If the callback is for a select event for a gadget in the choice category, ^$E("CHOICE") identifies the *item* and ^$E("COL") and ^$E("ROW") identify the *citem* and *ritem* subscripts of the choice. Only some of the Event Information Attributes that are automatically returned in the Event SSVN for a user-triggered event are defined when the event is the result of ETRIGGER execution. Chapter 2 covers the ETRIGGER command and Event Information attributes in detail. Table 5.11 presents the format when detailing event types.

TABLE 5.10: *Gadget Event Types*

Event Type	Check Box	Document	Generic Box	List Box	List Button	List Entry Box	Long List Box	Push Button	Radio Button Set	Scroll	Table	Text
CHANGE	X	X		X	X	X	X		X		X	X
CHAR		X	X		X	X						X
CLICK			X								X	
DBLCLICK		X	X	X		X	X				X	
DESELECT	X			X	X	X	X		X		X	
FOCUS	X	X	X	X	X	X	X	X	X		X	X
GOBOTTOM							X					
GODOWN							X					
GODOWNBIG							X					
GOTOP							X					
GOUP							X					
GOUPBIG							X					
HELP	X	X	X	X	X	X	X	X	X	X	X	X
KEYDOWN		X	X			X						X
KEYUP		X	X			X						X
PDOWN			X								X	
PDRAG			X							X	X	
PMOVE			X								X	
PUP			X								X	
SELECT	X			X	X	X	X	X	X	X	X	
UNFOCUS	X	X	X	X	X	X	X	X	X		X	

TABLE 5.11: *Event Type Description Format*

EVENT TYPE	
Description:	This section indicates when callback processing can occur for the event type.
Event Information Attributes:	
	This section lists the Event Information attributes available to describe the event object.
Notes:	Where appropriate, this section will provide notes on the attribute.

CHANGE

Description: Callback processing can occur when user action causes focus to move from the gadget to another gadget defined to the same window and the value of the gadget's CHANGED attribute evaluates to true. Executing an ETRIGGER that references the event node in its argument can also cause the callback to occur.

Event Information Attributes:

CLASS	OK	WINDOW
ELEMENT	SEQUENCE	
NEXTFOCUS	TYPE	

Notes: If a change event occurs for a gadget with an enabled UNFOCUS event type node, callback processing is directed to the value of the CHANGE subscript only.

Use of this event type for Table gadgets was added by the MDC's version 1.1 specification for the MWAPI.

CHAR

Description: Callback processing can occur for a CHAR event type when a user presses one or more keyboard keys, or the execution of an ETRIGGER command with the event node referenced in its argument.

Event Information Attributes:

CLASS	SEQUENCE
ELEMENT	TYPE
KEY	WINDOW

Notes: Reference ^$E("KEY") to determine the keyboard code(s) that triggered this event.

Keycodes are found in Appendix A.

CLICK

Description: Callback processing can occur when a pointer button is pressed and released with no change in the pointer position, or the execution of an ETRIGGER command with the event node referenced in its argument.

Event Information Attributes:

CLASS	PBUTTON	ROW	WINDOW
COL	PPOS	SEQUENCE	
ELEMENT	PSTATE	TYPE	

Notes: Reference ^$E("PBUTTON") to determine the pointer button and any modifier keys depressed when this event type was triggered. The position of the pointer is determined by ^$E("PPOS"), and ^$E("PSTATE") lists pointer buttons depressed when the event occurred.

User triggering of this event will cause a sequence of events to occur. The sequence is PDOWN, CLICK, and PUP. (Version 1.1 of the MDC's MWAPI specification change the sequence from: PDOWN, PUP, and CLICK.)

If this event type is triggered by the execution of an ETRIGGER command, no additional event is triggered.

Pointer button codes are listed in Appendix A.

Use of this event type for Table gadgets was added by the MDC's version 1.1 specification.

DBLCLICK

Description: Callback processing can occur when a pointer button is pressed and released twice, within a platform-dependent time interval, with no change in the pointer position, or the execution of an ETRIGGER command with the event node referenced in its argument.

Event Information Attributes:

CLASS	PBUTTON	ROW	WINDOW
COL	PPOS	SEQUENCE	
ELEMENT	PSTATE	TYPE	

Notes: The second depression and release of the pointer button must occur during a period of time defined by the underlying windowing platform.

Reference ^$E("PBUTTON") to determine the pointer button and any modifier keys depressed when this event type was triggered. The position of the pointer is determined by ^$E("PPOS"), and ^$E("PSTATE") lists of pointer buttons depressed when the event occurred.

User triggering of this event by user action will cause a sequence of events to occur. The sequence is: PDOWN, CLICK, PUP, PDOWN, DBLCLICK, and PUP. (Version 1.1 of the MDC's MWAPI specification changed the sequence from: PDOWN, PUP, CLICK, PDOWN, DBLCLICK, and PUP.)

If this event type is triggered by the execution of an ETRIGGER command, no additional event is triggered.

Pointer button codes are listed in Appendix A.

Use of this event type for Table gadgets was added by the MDC's version 1.1 specification.

DESELECT

Description: Callback processing can occur when the user deselects a previously selected choice, or the execution of an ETRIGGER command with the event node referenced in its argument.

Event Information Attributes

CHOICE	ELEMENT	TYPE
CLASS	ROW	WINDOW
COL	SEQUENCE	

Notes: Reference ^$E("CHOICE"), or ^$E("COL") and ^$E("ROW") for Table gadgets, to determine the subscript, or subscripts, associated with the deselected choice.

Use of this event type for Table gadgets was added by the MDC's version 1.1 specification for the MWAPI.

FOCUS

Description: Callback processing can occur when the user makes a gadget the object of focus, or the execution of an ETRIGGER command with the event node referenced in its argument.

Event Information Attributes:

CLASS	SEQUENCE
ELEMENT	TYPE
PRIORFOCUS	WINDOW

GOBOTTOM

Description: Callback processing can occur when the user selects the gadget's "go bottom" movement control, or the execution of an ETRIGGER command with the event node referenced in its argument.

Event Information Attributes:

CLASS	TYPE
ELEMENT	WINDOW
SEQUENCE	

Notes: The Long List Box gadget in the Implementation section identifies the "go bottom" movement control.

GODOWN

Description: Callback processing can occur when the user selects the gadget's "go down" movement control, or the execution of an ETRIGGER command with the event node referenced in its argument.

Event Information Attributes:

CLASS	TYPE
ELEMENT	WINDOW
SEQUENCE	

Notes: The Long List Box gadget in the Implementation section identifies the "go down" movement control.

GODOWNBIG

Description: Callback processing can occur when the user selects the gadget's "go down big" movement control, or the execution of an ETRIGGER command with the event node referenced in its argument.

Event Information Attributes:

CLASS	TYPE
ELEMENT	WINDOW
SEQUENCE	

Notes: The Long List Box gadget in the Implementation section identifies the "go down big" movement control.

GOTOP

Description: Callback processing can occur when the user selects the gadget's "go top" movement control, or the execution of an ETRIGGER command with the event node referenced in its argument.

Event Information Attributes:

CLASS	TYPE
ELEMENT	WINDOW
SEQUENCE	

Notes: The Long List Box gadget in the Implementation section identifies the "go top" movement control.

GOUP

Description: Callback processing can occur when the user selects the gadget's "go up" movement control, or the execution of an ETRIGGER command with the event node referenced in its argument.

Event Information Attributes:

CLASS	TYPE
ELEMENT	WINDOW
SEQUENCE	

Notes: The Long List Box gadget in the Implementation section identifies the "go up" movement control.

GOUPBIG

Description: Callback processing can occur when the user selects the gadget's "go up big" movement control, or the execution of an ETRIGGER command with the event node referenced in its argument.

Event Information Attributes:

CLASS	TYPE
ELEMENT	WINDOW
SEQUENCE	

Notes: The Long List Box gadget in the Implementation section identifies the go "up big" movement control.

HELP

Description: Callback processing can occur when the user requests help for the gadget or the execution of an ETRIGGER command with the event node referenced in its argument.

Event Information Attributes:

CLASS	TYPE
ELEMENT	WINDOW
SEQUENCE	

Notes: The help key is determined by the underlying windowing platform.

KEYDOWN

Description: Callback processing can occur when the user presses a keycode or sequence or the execution of an ETRIGGER command with the event node referenced in its argument.

Event Information Attributes:

CLASS	SEQUENCE
ELEMENT	TYPE
KEY	WINDOW

Notes: Reference ^$E("KEY") to determine the keycode that caused the event. Keycodes are listed in Appendix A.

KEYUP

Description: Callback processing can occur when the user releases a keycode or sequence or the execution of an ETRIGGER command with the event node referenced in its argument.

Event Information Attributes:

CLASS	SEQUENCE
ELEMENT	TYPE
KEY	WINDOW

Notes: Reference ^$E("KEY") to determine the keycode that caused the event. Keycodes are listed in Appendix A.

PDOWN

Description: Callback processing can occur when the user presses a pointer button or the execution of an ETRIGGER command with the event node referenced in its argument.

Event Information Attributes:

CLASS	PBUTTON	ROW	WINDOW
COL	PPOS	SEQUENCE	
ELEMENT	PSTATE	TYPE	

Notes: Reference ^$E("PBUTTON") to determine the pointer button and any modifier keys depressed when this event type was triggered. The position of the pointer is determined by ^$E("PPOS"), and ^$E("PSTATE") lists of pointer buttons depressed when the event occurred.

Pointer button codes are listed in Appendix A.

Use of this event type for Table gadgets was added by the MDC's version 1.1 specification for the MWAPI.

PDRAG

Description: Callback processing can occur when the user moves the pointer while depressing at least one pointer button, or the execution of an ETRIGGER command with the event node referenced in its argument.

Event Information Attributes:

CLASS	PPOS	TYPE

ELEMENT	PSTATE	WINDOW
PBUTTON	SEQUENCE	

Notes: Reference ^$E("PBUTTON") to determine the pointer button and any modifier keys depressed when this event type was triggered. The position of the pointer is determined by ^$E("PPOS"), and ^$E("PSTATE") lists of pointer buttons depressed when the event occurred.

^$E("PPOS") is undefined when the event is for a Scroll gadget.

Pointer button codes are listed in Appendix A.

Use of this event type for Table gadgets was added by the MDC's version 1.1 specification for the MWAPI.

PMOVE

Description: Callback processing can occur when the user moves the pointer with no buttons depressed or the execution of an ETRIGGER command with the event node referenced in its argument.

Event Information Attributes:

CLASS	PPOS	TYPE
ELEMENT	PSTATE	WINDOW
PBUTTON	SEQUENCE	

Notes: Reference ^$E("PBUTTON") to determine the pointer button and any modifier keys depressed when this event type was triggered. The position of the pointer is determined by ^$E("PPOS"), and ^$E("PSTATE") lists of pointer buttons depressed when the event occurred.

Use of this event type for Table gadgets was added by the MDC's version 1.1 specification for the MWAPI.

PUP

Description: Callback processing can occur when the user releases a pointer button or the execution of an ETRIGGER command with the event node referenced in its argument.

Event Information Attributes:

CLASS	PBUTTON	ROW	WINDOW
COL	PPOS	SEQUENCE	
ELEMENT	PSTATE	TYPE	

Notes: Reference ^$E("PBUTTON") to determine the pointer button and any modifier keys depressed when this event type was triggered. The position of the pointer is determined by ^$E("PPOS"), and ^$E("PSTATE") lists of pointer buttons depressed when the event occurred.

Pointer button codes are listed in Appendix A.

Use of this event type for Table gadgets was added by the MDC's version 1.1 specification for the MWAPI.

SELECT

Description: Callback processing can occur when the user selects or deselects a gadget or choice or the execution of an ETRIGGER command with the event node referenced in its argument.

Event Information Attributes:

CHOICE	ELEMENT	TYPE
CLASS	ROW	WINDOW
COL	SEQUENCE	

Notes: Reference ^$E("CHOICE"), or ^$E("COL") and ^$E("ROW") for Table gadgets, to determine the subscript, or subscripts, associated with the selected choice.

         Use of this event type for Table gadgets was added by the MDC's version 1.1 specification for the MWAPI.

UNFOCUS

Description: Callback processing can occur when the gadget, with this event type defined, loses focus to another gadget defined for the same window or the execution of an ETRIGGER command with the event node referenced in its argument.

Event Information Attributes:

CLASS	OK	WINDOW
ELEMENT	SEQUENCE	
PRIORFOCUS	TYPE	

Notes: If focus moves from the gadget, with this qualifier, to another window, the UNFOCUS event will not occur until focus is returned to a different gadget in the original window.

         If a CHANGE event is defined for the gadget, the triggering of the CHANGE event will occur instead of the UNFOCUS event. For this to occur, the following conditions must be met: (1) the CHANGE attribute's ENABLE Event Specification Attribute must have a true value and (2) the value of the gadget's CHANGED attribute evaluates to true.

Event types can be assigned to ^$W using either the SET or MERGE commands. The syntax shown in Example 5.8 shows an assignment made with the SET command. An assignment made with the MERGE command is made by assigning the subscripts to a global or local array and merging the subscripts into ^$W, as shown in Example 5.9.

```
S ^$W("WIN","G","GAD","EVENT","FOCUS")="FOCUS^WINDOW"
```

EXAMPLE 5.8: *Event Type Assignment Using Set Command*

```
S ARR("WIN","G","GAD","EVENT","FOCUS")="FOCUS^WINDOW"
M ^$W=ARR
```

EXAMPLE 5.9: *Event Type Assignment Using MERGE Command*

Event Specification Attributes

Each EVENT attribute node will have at least one Event Specification Attribute to modify when callback processing can occur for the specified event type. Depending on the event type specified, a second modifier can be used. ENABLE and FILTERIN are the keywords specified by the MWAPI for the restriction of callbacks, and implementers can define their own for their implementations. Implementation-defined keywords will begin with the letter "Z," and are not guaranteed portable. These attributes are maintained as subscripts of the event types they modify. Example 5.10 shows the syntax required for these modifiers. Event Specification Attributes are uppercase keywords that must be enclosed in quotes or assigned as a variable

```
^$W(window name,"G",gadget name,"EVENT",event type,event specification
attribute)=value
```

EXAMPLE 5.10: *Event Specification Node Syntax*

The MWAPI implementation implicitly creates an ENABLE attribute node subscripted from each event type. If the value of the node evaluates to true, and event processing is active for the process, callback processing can occur for the event type specified. If the value is false, a callback will not occur for the event type. The ENABLE attribute is true by default and can be modified at anytime. Example 5.11 shows how this looks.

```
^$W("WIN","G","GAD","EVENT","FOCUS")="FOCUS^WINDOW"
^$W("WIN","G","GAD","EVENT","FOCUS","ENABLE")=1
```

EXAMPLE 5.11: *Enabled Event Node Syntax*

Events in the keyboard and pointer categories (see Table 5.12 and Table 2.2) can have restrictions placed on their ability to process callbacks even if callback processing is enabled for the event type. The event specification attribute FILTERIN restricts callback processing to one or more keys, characters, or pointer codes.

TABLE 5.12: *Event Types That Can Use FILTERIN*

CHAR	KEYUP
CLICK	PDOWN
DBLCLICK	PDRAG
FKEYDOWN	PMOVE
FKEYUP	PUP
KEYDOWN	

Events in the keyboard and pointer categories (see Table 2.2, which categorizes event types) can have restrictions placed on their ability to process callbacks when callback processing is enabled for the event type. The Event Specification Attribute FILTERIN restricts an event to one or more characters, pointers, or key codes. Example 5.12 shows an assignment of the FILTERIN attribute to restrict the gadget's click event to either the user clicking on the window with the left pointer button depressed or the execution of an ETRIGGER with the event node referenced in its *SSVN node reference* and "PB1" assigned to the "PBUTTON" subscript of its *data structure name.* Example 5.13 shows the syntax required for an ETRIGGER trigger of the event.

```
S ^$W("WIN","G","GAD","EVENT","CLICK","FILTERIN")="PB1"
```

EXAMPLE 5.12: *Event Specification Attribute Assignment Using Set Command*

```
S ARRAY("PBUTTON")="PB1"
ETRIGGER ^$W("WIN","G","GAD","EVENT","CLICK"):ARRAY
```

EXAMPLE 5.13: *ETRIGGER with Simulated Left Pointer Button Depressed*

Implementation

This section demonstrates how to create and use fourteen of the fifteen gadgets described as standard by the MDC's version 1.1 specification for the MWAPI. (The GENERIC gadget is described in the Implementation section of the next chapter.) The different gadget types are grouped into the categories described in Table 5.2. Graphical figures of each gadget are presented followed by the code that created the object, and description of the code and use. Concepts covered in earlier chapters are used throughout these examples. For example: the Long List Box gadget demonstrates the concept of stacked ESTARTS described in Chapter 2, and the Event SSVN is referenced numerous times to allow the reuse of code.

Even though the parent window of each gadget is created by default (by using default values), when the gadget is created the parent windows used in these examples have explicitly defined attributes. If these attributes are not explicitly defined, the size of the parent window will be large enough to display the gadgets defined for it at the time of its creation.

Certain output statements use the M WRITE command so the reader can relate them to legacy code. Imagine opening an MTERM window and redirecting the output to the device.

The parent window's attributes for each gadget is shown in *tag*+2 – 5, where *tag* is the name of the tag containing the attributes for the gadget being discussed. The syntax used is similar to the syntax that created window PARENT in the previous chapter. Notice in these examples only the POS, SIZE, TITLE, and EVENT window attributes are used. It is highly recommended that every window have the capability to close, or destroy, itself. Unlike the tag CLOSE^APPWIN, used in the previous chapter, the tag CLOSE, used in these examples, references the Event Information Attribute WINDOW to determine the requesting window to be closed. This information is then used to destroy only that window. This is necessary when there are multiple windows in the current process. Example 5.14 shows the CLOSE tag to destroy the requesting window.

The purpose of tag CLOSE is to process callback requests to close or destroy a window. CLOSE+1 references the Event SSVN in order to determine the window that received the close request, CLOSE+2 kills the window.

```
CLOSE ; close the parent window
+1  S WINDOW=^$E("WINDOW")
+2  K ^$W(WINDOW)
+3  ESTO
+4  Q
```

EXAMPLE 5.14: *Close Tag*

Prior to the initial ESTART for each gadget, focus is set to the gadget or its parent window. Chapter 3 pointed out the syntax of the FOCUS Display attribute allows for an optional second parameter to identify a gadget within the window. If the gadget is capable of receiving focus, it is directed to the gadget.

All the events generated for these examples come from user interaction with the gadget. The routine calls are different for some of the gadgets, so some of their unique qualities can be demonstrated and described. In addition to having unique characteristics, some gadgets share common properties. Each callback routine begins by referencing the Event SSVN to determine the window, element, and element type where the event was directed. In some circumstances the same callback routine can be called to process different event types for the gadget. In such cases, ^$E("TYPE") is referenced to determine the event type to be processed. Since all the callbacks made in this chapter are by gadgets, the element value will always be "G," but each callback routine will check for this value. If additional element types such as menus and timers made the calls, the value of $P(^$E(ELEMENT),",",1) would be different. The approach to callback processing described in this paragraph, and used extensively in this section, was covered by item two in the Implementation section of Chapter 2.

Choice Category

This category of gadgets provides applications with a means to display a list of choices to the user. The MWAPI standard specifies six gadgets for listing choices:

- List Box
- List Button
- List Entry Box
- Long List Box
- Radio Button Set
- Table

The abundance of gadgets for displaying choices gives the programmer much flexibility with the design of the interface. Choices used by each gadget in this category are the values subscripted from the gadget's CHOICE attribute. The maximum stringlength for a choice is 255 characters, and the aggregate of characters in all choices assigned to a gadget must not exceed 16,383. These requirements can be overcome by killing off nodes of choices already viewed. Special code is required in case the user wishes to scroll back to the deleted choices. Several of the gadgets in this example call tag NAMES, with the name of the gadget as the parameter passed, to set up their list of choices.

```
NAMES(N) ; create a list of names
+1  S J=0
+2  F I=
    "DOE,JOHN","DOG,JACK","DOE,JANE","STOOGE,CURLY","CUPIT,RHODA","MOUSE,
MICKEY","TOES,JOE","HABIBI,PHILLIP","STAR,TWINKLE","HAIR,ANGLE","CART,CARL","KITE,CIN
DY","DON,GLUE" D
+3  .S J=J+1
+4  .S W("WINDOW","G",N,"CHOICE",J)=I
+5  Q
```

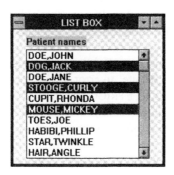

FIGURE.5.2: *List Box*

```
LIST ; list box
+1  K W,^$W
+2  S W("WINDOW","POS")="100,50"
+3  S W("WINDOW","SIZE")="230,200"
+4  S W("WINDOW","TITLE")="LIST BOX"
+5  S W("WINDOW","EVENT","CLOSE")="CLOSE^GADGETS"
+6  S W("WINDOW","G","LIST","TYPE")="LIST"
+7  S W("WINDOW","G","LIST","POS")="20,30"
+8  S W("WINDOW","G","LIST","SIZE")="190,170"
+9  S W("WINDOW","G","LIST","TITLE")="Patient names"
+10 D NAMES("LIST")
+11 S W("WINDOW","G","LIST","SELECTMAX")=3
+12 S W("WINDOW","G","LIST","EVENT","SELECT")="SEL^GADGETS"
+13 S W("WINDOW","G","LIST","EVENT","DESELECT")="SEL^GADGETS"
+14 M ^$W=W
+15 S ^$DI($PD,"FOCUS")="WINDOW,LIST"
+16 ESTA
+17 Q
```

The List Box gadget is an excellent choice for displaying a list of choices due to its ease of use and the functionality it provides to manipulate the list. If the list of choices is too large to display in its entirety, the list is automatically scrolled by selection of one of the movement controls, movement of that the position indicator and clicking within the scroll bar. A call to tag NAMES (see LIST+10) assigns the list of choices. The scrolling region, for this gadget type, is its entire viewing area. The display of scroll bars when all the choices fit in the scrolling region is not required by the MWAPI standard, and is left up to the underlying windowing interface. If the list is too long to display in its entirety, scroll bars will be provided.

Several useful attributes are provided to work with this gadget. LIST+11 uses the SELECTMAX attribute to limit the total number of choices a user can select. This number excludes choices that have been deselected. This example allows the user to select up to three choices. If the value assigned to this attribute is zero, then no explicit limit exists to the number of selections.

One or more choices can appear selected when the gadget is displayed to the user. This is done by setting one or more subscripts descended from the gadget's VALUE attribute to the subscript value associated with the choice in the CHOICE attribute (*item*). Care must be taken when using this approach not to exceed the value of the SELECTMAX attribute. If this value is exceeded or *item* does not exist as a subscript of the CHOICE attribute, an error will occur. If you want an event to be generated for the selected choices, an ETRIGGER command will have to be executed. As noted in the discussion on event processing, automatic event generation does not occur when an SSVN reference value is modified through application code.

The choice at the top of the current viewable list can be determined by referencing the gadget's TOPSHOW attribute. Application code can also assign the value of one of the CHOICE attribute's subscripts to this attribute to cause the associated choice to appear at the top of the list. Regardless the subscript chosen, the collating sequence of the list is maintained.

LIST+12 & 13 call the routines to process select and deselect events respectively. Both routines call the tag SEL, and reference ^$E("TYPE") to determine the event triggered.

```
SEL ; select and deselect events for List Box, Long List Box
+1  W !
+2  S WINDOW=^$E("WINDOW")
+3  S ELEMENT=^$E("ELEMENT")
+4  S ELTYPE=$P($E(ELEMENT),",")
+5  S ELEMENT=$E(ELEMENT,3,$L(ELEMENT))
+6  S TYPE=^$E("TYPE")
+7  S VALUE=^$W(WINDOWINDOW,ELTYPE,ELEMENT,"VALUE")
+8  S CHOICE=^$W(WINDOWINDOW,ELTYPE,ELEMENT,"CHOICE",^$E("CHOICE"))
+9  W !,"A ",TYPE," event has occurred for gadget "_ELEMENT
+10 W !,VALUE," choices have been selected for gadget ",ELEMENT,"."
+11 W !,"The choice just ",TYPE_"ED"," is: "_CHOICE
+12 W !!,"The following choices have been selected:"
+13 S ITEM=""
+14 F  S ITEM=$O(^$W("WINDOW","G",ELEMENT,"VALUE",ITEM)) Q:ITEM=""  D
+15 .W !?5,^$W(WINDOW,ELTYPE,ELEMENT,"CHOICE",ITEM)
+16 W !
+17 Q
```

SEL+7 determines the number of selections made to this gadget, and is written out at SEL+10. The number can increase or decrease as selections and deselections are made, but this value will not be greater than the value of the SELECTMAX attribute. The only exception to this rule is if the value assigned to the SELECTMAX attribute equals zero. If the value is zero indicates no limit imposed. SEL+8 determines the choice selected or deselected by referencing the CHOICE attribute. Since the choices are subscripted from this attribute, ^$E("CHOICE") is referenced to determine the subscript (*item*) associated with the event, and SEL+11 writes out this value. SEL+14 & 15 loop through the VALUE attribute to display all the selected choices. Subscripts descended from this attribute correlate to the subscripts of selected choices descended from the CHOICE attribute.

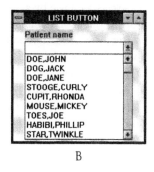

A   B   C

FIGURE 5.3: *List Button*

```
LBUTTON ; list button
+1  K W,^$W
+2  S W("WINDOW","POS")="100,50"
+3  S W("WINDOW","SIZE")="230,200"
+4  S W("WINDOW","TITLE")="LIST BUTTON"
+5  S W("WINDOW","EVENT","CLOSE")="CLOSE^GADGETS"
+6  S W("WINDOW","G","LBUTTON","TYPE")="LISTBUTTON"
+7  S W("WINDOW","G","LBUTTON","POS")="20,30"
+8  S W("WINDOW","G","LBUTTON","SIZE")="190,170"
+9  S W("WINDOW","G","LBUTTON","TITLE")="Patient name"
+10 D NAMES("LBUTTON")
+11 S W("WINDOW","G","LBUTTON","EVENT","SELECT")="SEL1^GADGETS"
+12 S W("WINDOW","G","LBUTTON","EVENT","DESELECT")="SEL1^GADGETS"
+13 M ^$W=W
+14 S ^$DI($PD,"FOCUS")="WINDOW,LBUTTON"
+15 ESTA
+16 Q
```

The List Button gadget allows the application to display a list of choices to the user only if the user selects the gadget. The first box of Figure 5.3 shows how this gadget initially appears to the user. Once the gadget is selected (i.e., by clicking on the gadget), the list will automatically expand to reveal its list of choices, as shown by the next box. The size of the gadget includes the expansion area, and selection will expand the gadget and cover another gadget or out of the parent's application area. The scrolling area is the portion of the gadget below the separator line in the gadget. The scroll bars and the scroll functionality of the list are automatically provided.

Only one item can be selected, at any one time, from the list of choices. Unlike the List Box gadget, this gadget is not specified to use the SELECTMAX attribute to indicate a section limit other than one. When a choice is selected, the gadget closes its list portion, and the choice is displayed, as shown in the last box of Figure 5.3.

In a manner similar to the List Box, the application can cause one of the choices to appear selected when the gadget is displayed to the user. The appearance will look like the third box of Figure 5.3, since the user will not have caused the gadget to expand its list. An application selects a choice by assigning its respective *item* subscript to the gadget's VALUE attribute. If the list is expanded, the selected choice will appear selected in the list. Remember from the discussion on event processing, automatic event generation does not occur when an SSVN reference value is modified through application code. If you want an event to be generated, an ETRIGGER command will have to be executed.

This example uses SEL1^GADGETS as the callback routine to process events for both selection and deselection. Tag SEL could have been used as well but since this gadget type can only have one selected choice at any one time, tag SEL1 identifies this better. Another approach would have been to determine the calling gadget type and add the different code to handle the element.

```
SEL1 ; select and deselect events for List Button and Radio Button Set
+1  S WINDOW=^$E("WINDOW")
+2  S ELEMENT=^$E("ELEMENT")
+3  S ELTYPE=$P($E(ELEMENT),",")
+4  S ELEMENT=$E(ELEMENT,3,$L(ELEMENT))
+5  S TYPE=^$E("TYPE")
+6  .S VALUE=^$W(WINDOW,ELTYPE,ELEMENT,"VALUE")
+7  .S CHOICE=^$W(WINDOWINDOW,ELTYPE,ELEMENT,"CHOICE",VALUE)
+8  W !,"A ",TYPE," event has occurred for gadget "_ELEMENT
+9  W !,"Subscript ",VALUE," has been ",TYPE_"ED","."
+10 W !,"The choice just selected is: "_CHOICE
+11 W !
+12 Q
```

This tag is similar to the callback tag for the List Box gadget, but it has some notable differences. The gadget's VALUE attribute identifies the subscript associated with the choice (see SEL1+6 and 7). The List Button gadget can only have one selected choice at a time. SEL1+10 reflects this by only displaying one choice vs. a list as done for the List Box gadget.

```
LENTRY ; list entry box
+1  K W,^$W
+2  S W("WINDOW","POS")="100,50"
```

```
+3  S W("WINDOW","SIZE")="230,200"
+4  S W("WINDOW","TITLE")="LIST ENTRY BOX"
+5  S W("WINDOW","EVENT","CLOSE")="CLOSE^GADGETS"
+6  S W("WINDOW","G","LENTRY","TYPE")="LISTENTRY"
+7  S W("WINDOW","G","LENTRY","POS")="20,30"
+8  S W("WINDOW","G","LENTRY","SIZE")="190,170"
+9  S W("WINDOW","G","LENTRY","TITLE")="Patient name"
+10 D NAMES("LENTRY")
+11 S W("WINDOW","G","LENTRY","EVENT","SELECT")=
    "SEL2^GADGETS"
+12 S W("WINDOW","G","LENTRY","EVENT","DESELECT")=
    "SEL2^GADGETS"
+13 M ^$W=W
+14 S ^$DI($PD,"FOCUS")="WINDOW,LENTRY"
+15 ESTA
+16 Q
```

The List Entry Box gadget combines the functionality of the Text gadget with a List Box. This gadget is well suited for displaying a selectable list and, with the assistance of application code, allowing the user the opportunity to edit the list of choices. The application can be designed to reference the gadget's VALUE attribute for the text entered, search the list for a match, and display the match or add it to the list of choices. The Text gadget is covered in the Text Category section.

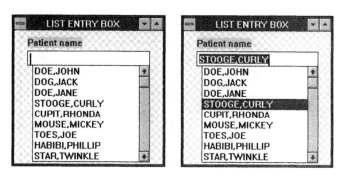

FIGURE 5.4: *List Entry Box*

Scroll bars, and their automatic functionality, can be provided when the list of choices cannot be viewed in its entirety. Unlike the List Box, only one choice can be selected at any one time. The left box in Figure 5.4 shows the gadget as it is initially displayed to the user. The gadget's scrolling area is fixed and does not expand as it does for the List Button gadget. Once a selection is made it redisplays in the text portion of the gadget. The right box in Figure 5.4 shows the choice selected redisplayed in the text portion of the gadget, but, unlike the List Button gadget, this gadget's scrolling region does not contract. SEL2 is called to process both SELECT and DESELECT events for this gadget.

```
SEL2 ; select and deselect events for List Entry Box
+1  S WINDOW=^$E("WINDOW")
+2  S ELEMENT=^$E("ELEMENT")
+3  S ELTYPE=$P($E(ELEMENT),",")
+4  S ELEMENT=$E(ELEMENT,3,$L(ELEMENT))
+5  S TYPE=^$E("TYPE")
+6  S VALUE=^$W(WINDOWINDOW,ELTYPE,ELEMENT,"VALUE")
+7  S SUBSCRIPT=^$E("CHOICE")
+8  S CHOICE=^$W(WINDOWINDOW,ELTYPE,ELEMENT,"CHOICE",SUBSCRIPT)
+9  W !,"A ",TYPE," event has occurred for gadget "_ELEMENT
+10 W !,"Choice subscript ",SUBSCRIPT," has been ",TYPE_"ED","."
+11 W !,"The choice just associated with the event is: "_CHOICE
+12 W !,"The text entered into this gadget is: ",VALUE
+13 W !
+14 Q
```

The VALUE attribute of a List Entry Box gadget contains the text value entered in the text area of the gadget. The user can make an entry into the gadget's text area that is not in the list of choices. Selection is not automatic when the user makes an entry in the text area that matches a choice in the list. The application must make the appropriate assignment to put the text value in the list. If a selection or deselection is made from the list of choices, the value of ^$E("CHOICE") can be referenced to determine the choice subscript associated with the choice selected or deselected (see SEL2+7).

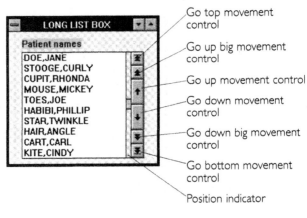

FIGURE 5.5: *Long List Box*

```
LLBOX ; long list box
+1  K W,^$W
+2  S W("WINDOW","POS")="100,50"
+3  S W("WINDOW","SIZE")="230,200"
+4  S W("WINDOW","TITLE")="LONG LIST BOX"
+5  S W("WINDOW","MODAL")="APPLICATION"
+6  S W("WINDOW","EVENT","CLOSE")="CLOSE^GADGETS"
+7  S W("WINDOW","G","LLBOX","TYPE")="LONGLIST"
+8  S W("WINDOW","G","LLBOX","POS")="20,30"
+9  S W("WINDOW","G","LLBOX","SIZE")="190,150"
+10 S W("WINDOW","G","LLBOX","TITLE")="Patient names"
```

```
+11 S  W("WINDOW","G","LLBOX","SELECTMAX")=5
+12 S  W("WINDOW","G","LLBOX","SCROLLRANGE")="0,100"
+13 S  W("WINDOW","G","LLBOX","SCROLLPOS")=50
+14 D  NAMES("LLBOX")
+15 S  W("WINDOW","G","LLBOX","TOPSHOW")=3
+16 S  W("WINDOW","G","LLBOX","EVENT","SELECT")="SEL4^GADGETS"
+17 S  W("WINDOW","G","LLBOX","EVENT","DESELECT")="SEL4^GADGETS"
+18 S  W("WINDOW","G","LLBOX","EVENT","GOUP")="SCROLL1^GADGETS"
+19 S  W("WINDOW","G","LLBOX","EVENT","GODOWN")="SCROLL2^GADGETS"
+20 S  W("WINDOW","G","LLBOX","EVENT","GOUPBIG")="SCROLL3^GADGETS"
+21 S  W("WINDOW","G","LLBOX","EVENT","GODOWNBIG")="SCROLL4^GADGETS"
+22 S  W("WINDOW","G","LLBOX","EVENT","GOTOP")="SCROLL5^GADGETS"
+23 S  W("WINDOW","G","LLBOX","EVENT","GOBOTTOM")="SCROLL6^GADGETS"
+24 M  ^$W=W
+25 S  ^$DI($PD,"FOCUS")="WINDOW,LLBOX"
+26 ESTA
+27 W  !!,"End of nested ESTARTs"
+28 S  ITEM=""
+29 F  S ITEM=$O(^$W("WINDOW","G",ELEMENT,"VALUE",ITEM)) Q:ITEM="" D
+30 .W  !?5,^$W(WINDOW,ELTYPE,ELEMENT,"CHOICE",ITEM)
+31 Q
```

The Long List Box gadget looks and acts like a List Box gadget, but with a few notable differences. The primary difference is in the support for scrolling through the list of choices. This gadget does not automatically provide scrolling functionality for moving through the list of choices. Scroll movements are left to the application allowing the application more versatility.

Six additional event types are specified for the movement controls of this gadget and are defined at tags LLBOX+18–23. The GOUP and GODOWN event types are selected by the depression of the scroll bar buttons with the single arrow up and down respectively. The GOUPBIG and GODOWNBIG event types are associated with depressions of the double arrow up and down selectors respectively. The double arrow up and down keys with the line at the tip of the arrow signify to go to the top (GOTOP) and bottom (GOBOTTOM) respectively. Two additional attributes are specified for the long list box gadget. The SCROLLRANGE attribute (used at LLBOX+12) defines the range of scrolling, and the SCROLLPOS attribute (see LLBOX+13) defines the location in the range of that the position indicator. The code below corresponds to the Long List Box event types listed in tag LLBOX and Table 2.2.

```
SCROLL1    W !,"A request has been received to scroll the list up.",! Q
SCROLL2    W !,"A request has been received to scroll the list down.",! Q
SCROLL3    W !,"A request has been received to scroll the list up a large
           amount.",! Q
SCROLL4    W !,"A request has been received to scroll the list down a large
           amount."
           W ! Q
SCROLL5    W !,"A request has been received to scroll the list to the top.",! Q
SCROLL6    W !,"A request has been received to scroll the list to the bottom.",! Q
```

This gadget's implementation demonstrates the use of nested ESTARTS. Nested ESTARTS are covered in the ESTART section, and item three in the Implementation section of Chapter 2. The code in lines 28 to 30 lists out all the choices selected after all of the nested ESTARTs are terminated. Since only modal windows can stack events, line 5 disables all application windows in the process. When the gadget receives a SELECT or DESELECT event, the code listed below is called to put the current context of the Event SSVN on the stack and return to the event queue.

```
SEL4 ; select events for Long List Box
+1  D SEL
+2  W !,"The current stack level is: ",$ZL
+3  ESTA ; stack ESTART and return to the event queue
+4  W !,"Stack level ",$ZL," popped."
+5  Q
```

Tag SEL is called to print out the choice selected or deselected and all selected choices. The code for tag SEL is shown with the coverage of the List Box gadget. $ZL is an implementation-specific variable that identifies the current stack level. The stacking of the ESTART commands occur when callback processing from a modal window encounters an ESTART command. When the ESTART is encountered at SEL4+3, callback processing is suspended, Event Information Attributes are stacked and become undefined and control is transferred back to the event loop to await the callback for another event. If during callback processing an ESTOP command is executed, the stack is popped, Event Information Attributes are restored to their previous values, and control will resume at the statement after the most recently executed ESTART (SEL4+4). If the most recently executed ESTART is at LLBOX+26, program control will resume at LLBOX+27.

Each time the tag CLOSE is called, the current ESTART level is terminated and control returns to the event queue until final termination of event processing. If three choices are selected, it will take four close events to deactivate event processing: once for each stacked ESTART and once for the initiation of event processing.

```
CLOSE ; close the parent window
+1  W !,"Level "_$ZL_" popped."
+2  ESTO
```

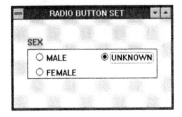

FIGURE 5.6: Radio Button Set

```
RADIO ; create a radio button set gadget
+1  K W,^$W
+2  S W("WINDOW","SIZE")="280,150"
+3  S W("WINDOW","TITLE")="RADIO BUTTON SET"
+4  S W("WINDOW","EVENT","CLOSE")="CLOSE^GADGETS"
+5  S W("WINDOW","G","RADIO","TYPE")="RADIO"
+6  S W("WINDOW","G","RADIO","TITLE")="SEX"
+7  S W("WINDOW","G","RADIO","POS")="25,50"
+8  S W("WINDOW","G","RADIO","SIZE")="230,50"
+9  S W("WINDOW","G","RADIO","CHOICE",1)="MALE"
+10 S W("WINDOW","G","RADIO","CHOICE",2)="FEMALE"
+11 S W("WINDOW","G","RADIO","CHOICE",3)="UNKNOWN"
+12 S W("WINDOW","G","RADIO","VALUE")=3
+13 S W("WINDOW","G","RADIO","ROWCOL")="COL,2,V"
+14 S W("WINDOW","G","RADIO","EVENT","SELECT")="SEL1^GADGETS"
+15 S W("WINDOW","G","RADIO","EVENT","DESELECT")="SEL1^GADGETS"
+16 M ^$W=W
+17 S ^$DI($PD,"FOCUS")="WINDOW,RADIO"
+18 ESTA
+19 Q
```

The Radio Button Set gadget is another element well suited to elicit the selection from a list of choices. The list of choices is displayed in a matrix format, and only one selection can be made at a time. If a selection is made while another choice is selected, the previous choice is automatically deselected. Applications can cause a choice to appear selected by assigning its subscript value (*item*) to the gadget's VALUE attribute. A selected condition is signified by a filled circle next to the choice. RADIO+12 assigns the third choice as the default selection, and displays it as selected when the gadget is created.

RADIO+13 defines the layout of the gadget. The first piece specifies that the choices are to be laid out in columnar fashion. The second parameter specifies the number of columns to be used by the gadget. If the first piece were ROW, the value of the second piece would specify the number of rows for the gadget. The third parameter determines whether the choices are to be filled in row (H) or column (V) order. SEL1 is listed with the List Button gadget and is used to process select and deselect events.

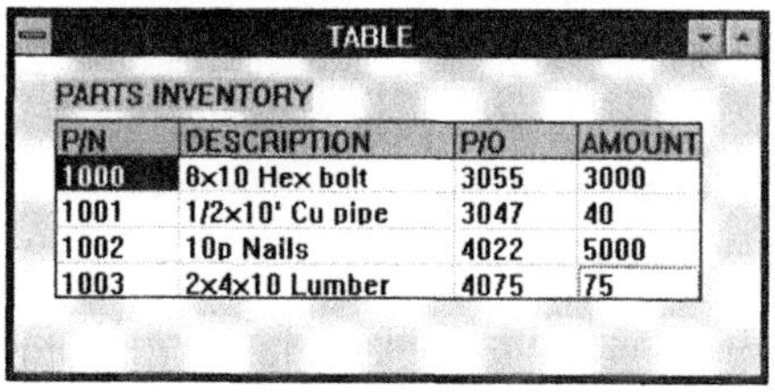

FIGURE 5.7: *Table*

```
TABLE ; create a table gadget
+1  K W,^$W
+2  S W("WINDOW","TITLE")="TABLE"
+3  S W("WINDOW","SIZE")="550,150"
+4  S W("WINDOW","EVENT","CLOSE")="CLOSE^GADGETS"
+5  S W("WINDOW","G","TABLE","TYPE")="T"
+6  S W("WINDOW","G","TABLE","SIZE")="505,85"
+7  S W("WINDOW","G","TABLE","POS")="20,30"
+8  S W("WINDOW","G","TABLE","TITLE")="PARTS INVENTORY"
+9  S W("WINDOW","G","TABLE","TYPE")="TABLE"
+10 S W("WINDOW","G","TABLE","EVENT","SELECT")="SEL7^GADGETS"
+11 S W("WINDOW","G","TABLE","EVENT","DESELECT")="SEL7^GADGETS"
+12 D ROWCOL
+13 M ^$W=W
+14 S ^$DI($PD,"FOCUS")="WINDOW,TABLE"
+15 ESTA
+16 Q
```

The Table gadget was introduced to the MWAPI standard list of gadgets by the MDC's version 1.1 MWAPI specification. Table gadgets are used to display choices in a tabular format different from that of the Radio Button Set gadget. If all of the cells cannot be viewed in their entirety, scrollbars (and their functionality) are automatically provided. Each cell can either contain choices or images, but not both. The code used to create the gadget in this example is very much like the code to create other gadgets in the choice category. The major exception is the call to tag ROWCOL at Table+12. Tag ROWCOL is used to set up the display of choices.

```
ROWCOL ; set up choices for the table gadget
+1  S U="^"
+2  S PART(0)="P/N"_U_"DESCRIPTION"_U_"P/O"_U_"AMOUNT"
+3  S PART(1)=1000_U_"8x10 Hex bolt"_U_3055_U_3000
+4  S PART(2)=1001_U_"1/2x10' Cu pipe"_U_3047_U_40
+5  S PART(3)=1002_U_"10p Nails"_U_4022_U_5000
+6  S PART(4)=1003_U_"2x4x10 Lumber"_U_4075_U_75
+7  F I=0:1:4 F J=1:1:4 D
+8  .S W("WINDOW","G","TABLE","CHOICE",I,J)=$P(PART(I),U,J)
+9  S W("WINDOW","G","TABLE","HROWID")=0
+10 S W("WINDOW","G","TABLE","COL",1,"COLWIDTH")=60
+11 S W("WINDOW","G","TABLE","COL",2,"COLWIDTH")=135
+12 S W("WINDOW","G","TABLE","COL",3,"COLWIDTH")=70
+13 S W("WINDOW","G","TABLE","COL",4,"COLWIDTH")=60
+14 S W("WINDOW","G","TABLE","LEFTSHOW")=1
+15 S W("WINDOW","G","TABLE","TOPSHOW")=1
+16 Q
```

Choices are assigned to Table gadgets in a unique manner from other choice gadgets. Choices are still assigned as values subscripted from the gadgets CHOICE attribute, but an additional subscript is added to identify the column reference. The List Box, Long List Box, List Entry Box, and List Button display one column and many rows of choices. The Table gadget can display many rows and many columns of choices. The assignment of choices to each column and row (cell) requires the row and column to be identified. ROWCOL+7 does just that by using two loops to signify rows and columns, and line 8 makes the assignment to the CHOICE attribute. If the rows and/or columns cannot be viewed in their entirety, scroll bars and their functionality are provided automatically.

Both rows and columns can have headers that do not scroll and that are displayed visually unique from nonheaders. The rows and columns defined by ROW and COL attributes are used for defining headers, so assignment is not required. Headers for columns are defined by assigning the subscript value (*citem*) associated with the column to the HCOLID attribute. Headers for rows are defined by setting the row subscript (*ritem*) to the HROWID attribute. Rows and columns that do not follow the values of HROWID and HCOLID in collating sequence are designated headers. ROWCOL+9 assigns the first row the header for each row.

The height and width of cells in the table gadget can be explicitly defined using the COLWIDTH and ROWHEIGHT Gadget Attributes. If these attributes are not explicitly defined, their values are determined by the underlying windowing interface. The argument to the COLWIDTH attribute node defines the default width of all columns in the gadget, and the argument to ROWHEIGHT specifies a default height for all cells. The default height for all rows is fine for this example, but the default column width is not. Lines 10 through 13 use the COLWIDTH Row and Column Attribute to set the width for each row.

The TOPSHOW attribute value identifies the row of choices to display at the top of the list, and is the same for the List Box, List Entry Box, and the Long List Box. Since a table gadget can display several columns a method is needed to show the choice in the first cell. The value of the LEFTSHOW attribute (see line 14) identifies the column to display to the far left of the gadget. If headers are defined, the top- and left-most cells are below any row headers and to the right of any column headers.

Both SELECT and DESELECT events that occur for the gadget in this example call tag SEL7 for processing. This tag begins in much the same way as the other callback routines listed in this section, the difference is in how the choice(s) for the event is determined. The Event SSVN nodes ROW and COLUMN are referenced to determine the row and column associated with the event (lines 5 and 6).

```
SEL7 ; select and deselect events for TABLE
+1  S ELEMENT=^$E("ELEMENT")
+2  S ELTYPE=$P($E(ELEMENT),",")
+3  S ELEMENT=$E(ELEMENT,3,$L(ELEMENT))
+4  S TYPE=^$E("TYPE")
+5  S ROWSUB=^$E("ROW")
+6  S COLSUB=^$E("COL")
+7  S CHOICE=^$W(WINDOW,ELTYPE,ELEMENT,"CHOICE",ROWSUB,COLSUB)
+8  W !,"A ",TYPE," event has occurred for gadget "_ELEMENT
+9  W !,"The choice just ",TYPE_"ED"," is: "_CHOICE
+10 W !,"The subscripts associated with the selected choice are :"
+11 W ROWSUB,",",COLSUB
+12 Q
```

Text Category

This category of gadgets provides applications methods for displaying and/or eliciting text. The List Entry Box has a text portion that can display and receive text, and an area to display a selectable list of choices. It was covered in the choice category. The MWAPI standard defines the following text category of gadgets:

- Document
- Label
- Text

Each gadget is discussed in the next few sections.

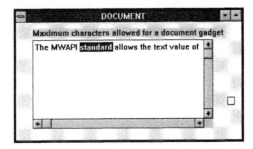

FIGURE 5.8: *Document*

```
DOC ; document
+1  K W,^$W
+2  S W("WINDOW","POS")="100,50"
+3  S W("WINDOW","SIZE")="400,200"
+4  S W("WINDOW","TITLE")="DOCUMENT"
+5  S W("WINDOW","EVENT","CLOSE")="CLOSE^GADGETS"
+6  S X="Maximum characters allowed for a document gadget"
+7  S W("WINDOW","G","DOC","TITLE")=X
+8  S W("WINDOW","G","DOC","TYPE")="DOCUMENT"
+9  S W("WINDOW","G","DOC","POS")="30,30"
+10 S W("WINDOW","G","DOC","SIZE")="320,150"
+11 S X="The MWAPI standard allows the text value of a document"
+12 S X=X_" gadget to be up to 32,767 characters."
+13 S W("WINDOW","G","DOC","VALUE")=X
+14 S W("WINDOW","G","DOC","SCROLL")="5,7"
+15 S W("WINDOW","G","DOC","FRAMED")=1
+16 S W("WINDOW","G","DOC","EVENT","UNFOCUS")="UNFOCUS^GADGETS"
+17 ; the purpose of this check box is to provide another gadget
+18 ; for focus to be redirected
+19 S W("WINDOW","G","CHECK","TYPE")="CHECK"
+20 S W("WINDOW","G","CHECK","POS")="375,125"
+21 S W("WINDOW","G","CHECK","SIZE")="20,20"
+22 M ^$W=W
+23 S ^$DI($PD,"FOCUS")="WINDOW,DOC"
+24 ESTA
+25 Q
```

The Document gadget is used to display or solicit the input of multiple lines of text while providing automatic word processing capabilities. The maximum stringlength for an array node has been extended for this gadget type to a limit of 32,767 characters.

The MWAPI standard does not call for scroll bars to be present when the complete text (see the VALUE attribute at DOC+11–13) can be viewed in the gadget's view window, and their display is up to the implementation. If the text scrolls out of the viewable area, horizontal or vertical scroll bars are presented, although their look-and-feel as well as their functional operation are provided for the underlying windowing platform.

The text that displays in the gadget is its value, and is predefined at DOC+11–13. The value of this gadget could have been provided through user input, but for this example the predefinition is necessary. The word "standard" is highlighted in the display area indicating the word has been selected by either the application or the user. In this example, the selection was made by the user highlighting the word "standard."

At DOC+16, an EVENT node is specified to process UNFOCUS events for the gadget, and the Check Box gadget was created to be the object where focus will be redirected. An UNFOCUS event is generated for gadget DOC when the user causes focus to redirect to another gadget in the same window. Program execution is transferred to UNFOCUS^GADGETS to process the callback. Tag UNFOCUS references the gadget's SELECTVAL attribute to determine the characters selected (see UNFOCUS+7). The gadget's INSELECT attribute is referenced to determine the insertion point in its value, and the number of characters selected. The value (10,8 in this case) indicates the text selection begins at the 10th character in the gadget's value, and 8 characters were selected. An application can cause a portion of the gadget's value to be selected by explicitly defining the INSELECT attribute value. The value of the SELECTVAL attribute will reflect the values chosen by the application. The gadget's value reflects any modification to the selected text.

```
UNFOCUS ; unfocus event
+1  S  WINDOW=^$E("WINDOW")
+2  S  ELEMENT=^$E("ELEMENT")
+3  S  ELTYPE=$P($E(ELEMENT),",")
+4  S  ELEMENT=$E(ELEMENT,3,$L(ELEMENT))
+5  S  VALUE=^$W(WINDOW,ELTYPE,ELEMENT,"VALUE")
+6  S  INSELECT=$G(^$W(WINDOW,ELTYPE,ELEMENT,"INSELECT"))
+7  S  SELECTVAL=$G(^$W(WINDOWINDOW,ELTYPE,ELEMENT,"SELECTVAL"))
+8  W  !,"A change event has occurred for gadget "_ELEMENT
+9  W  !,"The following text was selected"
+10 W  !!?5,SELECTVAL,!!
+11 W  "The insertion point in the original text "
+12 W  "is at position: ",+INSELECT
+13 W  !,"The number of characters chosen is: ",$P(INSELECT,",",2)
+14 Q
```

FIGURE 5.9: *Label*

```
LABEL ; label
+1  K W,^$W
+2  S W("WINDOW","POS")="100,50"
+3  S W("WINDOW","SIZE")="200,100"
+4  S W("WINDOW","TITLE")="LABEL"
+5  S W("WINDOW","EVENT","CLOSE")="CLOSE^GADGETS"
+6  S W("WINDOW","G","LABEL","TYPE")="LABEL"
+7  S W("WINDOW","G","LABEL","POS")="25,20"
+8  S W("WINDOW","G","LABEL","SIZE")="155,20"
+9  S W("WINDOW","G","LABEL","TITLE")="Registration data"
+10 M ^$W=W
+11 S ^$DI($PD,"FOCUS")="WINDOW"
+12 Q
```

The Label gadget is used to display a line of text. The text displayed is the value of the gadget's TITLE attribute. Label gadgets do not receive focus and do not contain EVENT attribute nodes.

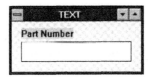

FIGURE 5.10: *Text*

```
TEXT ; create a Text gadget
+1  K ^$W,W
+2  S W("WINDOW","POS")="10,20"
+3  S W("WINDOW","SIZE")="200,75"
+4  S W("WINDOW","TITLE")="TEXT"
+5  S W("WINDOW","EVENT","CLOSE")="CLOSE^GADGETS"
+6  S W("WINDOW","G","TEXT","TYPE")="TEXT"
+7  S W("WINDOW","G","TEXT","POS")="15,30"
+8  S W("WINDOW","G","TEXT","SIZE")="170,30"
+9  S W("WINDOW","G","TEXT","TITLE")="Part Number"
+10 S W("WINDOW","G","TEXT","EVENT","KEYDOWN")="UNFOCUS^GADGETS"
+11 S W("WINDOW","G","TEXT","EVENT","KEYDOWN","FILTERIN")="ENTER"
+12 M ^$W=W
+13 S ^$DI($PD,"FOCUS")="WINDOW,TEXT"
+14 ESTA
+15 Q
```

The Text gadget is useful for displaying, or eliciting, a short (up to 255 characters) modifiable line of text. Text gadgets and document gadget's share more than their word processing capabilities in common. Text gadgets can process the same event types that Document gadgets can, and have nearly the same attribute list. If the gadget's value cannot be viewed in its entirety, scrolling of the text can occur.

If event processing is active, Text+10 specifies a callback processing routine for KEYDOWN events. The processing is restricted by line 11 to the enter key. The routine used to process an unfocus event for the Document gadget is used to process the callback.

Miscellaneous Category

This category consists of the rest of the MWAPI defined gadgets except the Generic Box. The next chapter is devoted to covering the Generic Box, and its unique properties for drawing and displaying objects. The MWAPI standard specifies five gadgets that fit into this category:

- Check Box
- Group Frame
- Push Button
- Scroll
- Symbol

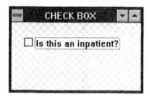

FIGURE 5.11: *Check Box*

```
CHECK ; Check Box
+1  K W,^$W
+2  S W("WINDOW","POS")="100,50"
+3  S W("WINDOW","SIZE")="200,100"
+4  S W("WINDOW","TITLE")="CHECK"
+5  S W("WINDOW","EVENT","CLOSE")="CLOSE^GADGETS"
+6  S W("WINDOW","G","CHECK","TYPE")="CHECK"
+7  S W("WINDOW","G","CHECK","POS")="20,20"
+8  S W("WINDOW","G","CHECK","SIZE")="160,20"
+9  S W("WINDOW","G","CHECK","TITLE")="Is this an inpatient?"
+10 S W("WINDOW","G","CHECK","EVENT","SELECT")="SEL^GADGETS"
+11 S W("WINDOW","G","CHECK","EVENT","DESELECT")="SEL^GADGETS"
+13 M ^$W=W
+14 S ^$DI($PD,"FOCUS")="WINDOW,CHECK"
+15 Q
```

The Check Box gadget is used to solicit a yes-or-no response from the user. The condition of a selection indicates a "yes" response and a deselect condition indicates a "no." A selected condition will fill the square check area with an "X" or other indication of selection. In keeping with a goal of the MWAPI standard, the look and feel of the underlying windowing interface are maintained.

This gadget defines two enabled EVENT nodes for callback processing. The EVENT node at CHECK+10 defines the callback routine for generated select events received for this gadget, and CHECK+11 defines the callback routine for deselect events.

When either a select or deselect event occurs for the gadget, program execution is directed to SEL8^GADGETS for processing of the event. This tag identifies the selection made and references the gadget's VALUE attribute to determine whether a select or

141

deselect event caused the tag to be called. If the event was for a selection, the gadget's value would evaluate to true, otherwise evaluation would result in a false value.

```
SEL8 ; select and deselect events for Check Box
+1  W !
+2  S WINDOW=^$E("WINDOW")
+3  S ELEMENT=^$E("ELEMENT")
+4  S ELTYPE=$P($E(ELEMENT),",")
+5  S ELEMENT=$E(ELEMENT,3,$L(ELEMENT))
+6  S VALUE=^$W(WINDOWINDOW,ELTYPE,ELEMENT,"VALUE")
+7  W !,"A ",$S(VALUE:"select",1:"deselect")," event has occurred for gadget" _ELEMENT
+8  W !,"The value of ",ELEMENT," is ",$S(VALUE:"true",1:"false")
+9  W !
+10 Q
```

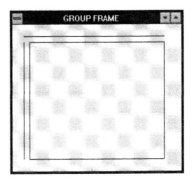

FIGURE 5.12: *Group Frame*

```
FRAME ; group frame
+1  K W,^$W
+2  S W("WINDOW","TITLE")="GROUP FRAME"
+3  S W("WINDOW","POS")="20,20"
+4  S W("WINDOW","SIZE")="300,250"
+5  S W("WINDOW","EVENT","CLOSE")="CLOSE^GADGETS"
+6  ; horizontal line
+7  S W("WINDOW","G","FRAME0","TYPE")="FRAME"
+8  S W("WINDOW","G","FRAME0","POS")="20,20"
+9  S W("WINDOW","G","FRAME0","SIZE")="250,0"
+10 ; rectangle
+11 S W("WINDOW","G","FRAME1","TYPE")="FRAME"
+12 S W("WINDOW","G","FRAME1","POS")="30,30"
+13 S W("WINDOW","G","FRAME1","SIZE")="240,200"
+14 ; vertical line
+15 S W("WINDOW","G","FRAME2","TYPE")="FRAME"
+16 S W("WINDOW","G","FRAME2","POS")="20,30"
+17 S W("WINDOW","G","FRAME2","SIZE")="0,200"
+18 M ^$W=W
+19 S ^$DI($PD,"FOCUS")="WINDOW"
+20 ESTA
+21 Q
```

The Group Frame gadget has several uses, such as acting as a separator in a window, or grouping gadgets. There are three separate gadgets in this example to demonstrate a horizontal and vertical line and a rectangle. The horizontal line is created by the code at FRAME+6–9. Note the value of FRAME0's SIZE attribute defines a positive *hsize* and a zero value for *vsize*. If the vertical coordinate's value is zero, a horizontal line is created (lines 6–9), and a zero-valued horizontal coordinate will produce a vertical line (lines 14–17). Positive values for both coordinates will produce a rectangle (see FRAME+10–13). Group Frame gadget's do not receive focus or contain EVENT attributes.

FIGURE 5.13: *Push Button*

```
PUSH ; push button
+1  K W,^$W
+2  S W("WINDOW","POS")="100,50"
+3  S W("WINDOW","SIZE")="200,150"
+4  S W("WINDOW","TITLE")="PUSH BUTTON"
+5  S W("WINDOW","EVENT","CLOSE")="CLOSE^GADGETS"
+6  S W("WINDOW","G","PUSH","TYPE")="BUTTON"
+7  S W("WINDOW","G","PUSH","POS")="40,50"
+8  S W("WINDOW","G","PUSH","SIZE")="125,40"
+9  S W("WINDOW","G","PUSH","TITLE")="OK"
+10 S W("WINDOW","G","PUSH","EVENT","SELECT")="SEL5^GADGETS"
+11 M ^$W=W
+12 S ^$DI($PD,"FOCUS")="WINDOW,PUSH"
+13 ESTA
+14 Q
```

The Push Button gadget is used to elicit a selection only. Once this gadget type is selected, the user cannot deselect it. This gadget type is useful for asking a question where selection must mean a true response ("ok," "cancel"). Tag SEL5 is called to process SELECT events for this gadget.

```
SEL5 ; select events for PUSH
+1  W !
+2  S WINDOW=^$E("WINDOW")
+3  S ELEMENT=^$E("ELEMENT")
+4  S ELTYPE=$P($E(ELEMENT),",")
+5  S ELEMENT=$E(ELEMENT,3,$L(ELEMENT))
+6  W !,"This gadget has been selected."
+7  Q
```

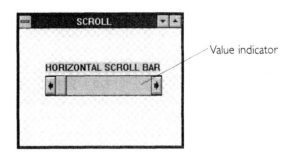

Value indicator

FIGURE 5.14: *Scroll*

```
SCROLL ; scroll gadget
+1  K W,^$W
+2  S W("WINDOW","POS")="100,50"
+3  S W("WINDOW","SIZE")="250,175"
+4  S W("WINDOW","TITLE")="SCROLL"
+5  S W("WINDOW","EVENT","CLOSE")="CLOSE^GADGETS"
+6  S W("WINDOW","G","SCROLL","TYPE")="SCROLL"
+7  S W("WINDOW","G","SCROLL","POS")="40,70"
+8  S W("WINDOW","G","SCROLL","SIZE")="180,30"
+9  S W("WINDOW","G","SCROLL","TITLE")="HORIZONTAL SCROLL BAR"
+10 S W("WINDOW","G","SCROLL","SCROLLRANGE")="1,100"
+11 S W("WINDOW","G","SCROLL","SCROLLBY")="1,20"
+12 S W("WINDOW","G","SCROLL","EVENT","SELECT")="SEL6^GADGETS"
+13 S W("WINDOW","G","SCROLL","EVENT","PDRAG")="SEL6^GADGETS"
+14 M ^$W=W
+15 S ^$DI($PD,"FOCUS")="WINDOW,SCROLL"
+16 ESTA
+17 Q
```

The Scroll gadget provides an application with a means to display scroll bars independent of any other gadget. Scroll bars are automatically provided for many gadgets, but there can be other reasons to display them. Chapter 9 uses two Scroll gadgets in conjunction with two text gadgets to update the values of each. Scroll gadgets can be displayed with a horizontal or vertical format. This example uses the default horizontal orientation. If the gadget is created with a "V" assigned to its SCROLLDIR attribute, the orientation is vertical.

The value range for scrolling is determined by the value of the SCROLLRANGE attribute (see SCROLL+10) and is from 1 to 100 units. The first piece defines the beginning of the scrolling range, and the second parameter defines its end. The SCROLLBY attribute (line 11) identifies the size of small and large scroll movement. A small scroll movement is made by the selection of one of the arrows at either end of the gadget, and will indicate a movement of one unit. A large movement is signified by a selection within the gadget, and indicates a movement of twenty units. Movement made by dragging the value indicator indicates a movement by a variable amount. Tag SEL6 is called to process the events for either movement type.

```
SEL6 ; select and drag events for SCROLL
+1  W !
+2  S WINDOW=^$E("WINDOW")
+3  S ELEMENT=^$E("ELEMENT")
+4  S ELTYPE=$P($E(ELEMENT),",")
+5  S ELEMENT=$E(ELEMENT,3,$L(ELEMENT))
+6  S TYPE=^$E("TYPE")
+7  S RANGE=^$W(WINDOW,ELTYPE,ELEMENT,"SCROLLRANGE")
+8  S ORIGIN=+RANGE
+9  S END=$P(RANGE,",",2)
+10 S VALUE=^$W(WINDOW,ELTYPE,ELEMENT,"VALUE")
+11 W !,"The value indicator "
+12 I TYPE="PDRAG" D
+13 .W:VALUE=ORIGIN "is at the beginning of the scroll gadget."
+14 .I ^$E("PSTATE")="" D
+15 .W "has been moved ",VALUE," units from the origin."
+16 .W:VALUE=END "is at the end of the scroll range."
+17 I TYPE="SELECT" D
+18 .W:VALUE=ORIGIN "is at the beginning of the scroll gadget."
+19 .I VALUE>+ORIGIN,VALUE<END D
+20 .W "has been moved ",VALUE," units from the origin."
+21 .W:VALUE=END "is at the end of the scroll range."
+22 Q
```

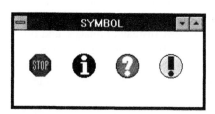

FIGURE 5.15: *Symbol*

```
SYMBOL ; symbol
+1  K W,^$W
+2  S W("WINDOW","POS")="10,50"
+3  S W("WINDOW","SIZE")="260,100"
+4  S W("WINDOW","TITLE")="SYMBOL"
+5  S W("WINDOW","EVENT","CLOSE")="CLOSE^GADGETS"
+6  S W("WINDOW","G","SYM","TYPE")="SYMBOL"
+7  S W("WINDOW","G","SYM","POS")="20,30"
+8  S W("WINDOW","G","SYM","SIZE")="50,50"
+9  S W("WINDOW","G","SYM","RESOURCE")="M,ERROR"
+10 S W("WINDOW","G","SYM1","TYPE")="SYMBOL"
+11 S W("WINDOW","G","SYM1","POS")="80,30"
+12 S W("WINDOW","G","SYM1","SIZE")="50,50"
+13 S W("WINDOW","G","SYM1","RESOURCE")="M,INFO"
+14 S W("WINDOW","G","SYM2","TYPE")="SYMBOL"
+15 S W("WINDOW","G","SYM2","POS")="140,30"
+16 S W("WINDOW","G","SYM2","SIZE")="50,50"
```

```
+17 S W("WINDOW","G","SYM2","RESOURCE")="M,QUEST"
+18 S W("WINDOW","G","SYM3","TYPE")="SYMBOL"
+19 S W("WINDOW","G","SYM3","POS")="200,30"
+20 S W("WINDOW","G","SYM3","SIZE")="50,50"
+21 S W("WINDOW","G","SYM3","RESOURCE")="M,WARN"
+22 M ^$W=W
+23 ESTA
+24 Q
```

One useful application of the Symbol gadget is to display a graphical message to the user. The message can indicate an error (see M,ERROR in line 9), information to the user (see M,INFO in line 13), erroneous input (see M,QUEST in line 17), and a warning (see M,WARN in line 21). These values are specified by the MWAPI standard and are guaranteed portable across platforms. The symbols will take on the look dictated by the underlying windowing platform. The Symbol gadget can also be used to display the contents of a file. This gadget type will not receive focus, and no events will occur for it.

Highlights

The MWAPI specification defines fifteen types of gadgets to be used for specific interaction with the user. User interaction can include text input/output tasks, elicitation of selectable choices, display of images, and other specialized tasks.

Gadgets are the children of windows. Their characteristics are maintained in the Window SSVN and their syntax names their parents. The character "G," which is used in the second subscript of their syntax, identifies the element as a gadget. The MERGE command must be used to create a gadget due to multiple required attributes that must be explicitly defined before the object is created.

Callback processing can occur for most gadgets, and their EVENT node values specify the argument to an M DO command to process the event. The processing of an event can be further modified by two additional subscripts: ENABLE and FILTERIN. The value of the ENABLE subscript activates/deactivates event processing for the event type, and the FILTERIN attribute restricts processing, if enabled, of keyboard and pointer events to certain character, keyboard, and button codes respectively.

The next chapter finished the focus on gadgets with a detailed look at the Generic Box gadget and draw commands.

Exercises

1. Name and categorize the gadgets specified for the MWAPI.
2. Name the minimum required attributes that must be specified before a gadget can be created.
3. Can a gadget be created when the parent is nonexistent?

4. What determines the attributes available to a gadget?

5. Describe the syntax for specifying a gadget's attribute.

6. If the parent window of a gadget is not defined with an explicit size, what default size value is used?

7. If the attributes inherited by a gadget are not modified from their original values, how are their values derived?

8. If the user, via the keyboard, causes focus to be redirected to another gadget in the window that cannot receive focus, how is the redirection be resolved?

9. Does the same attribute have the same value domain regardless the gadget type?

10. How does the syntax for assigning choices to the Table gadget differ from other gadgets in the choice category?

11. If a gadget has both CHANGE and UNFOCUS events enabled while event processing is active, which will occur when the value of the CHANGED attribute is true and focus is redirected to another gadget?

12. When is the FILTERIN Event Specification Attribute appropriate to use to restrict a gadget's event processing?

13. How is the context for an event deferred, stacked and popped?

14. See Exercise 7 in Chapter 4. Add the following gadgets to the window created for that exercise:

    a. Position a 200X130 pixel Document gadget 30 units from the window's origin and centered vertically. Title the gadget "Comments."

    b. Position a List Button gadget at position 30,50 with the title "Company." Assign a list of at least seven company name choices sorted in alphabetical order. Only five choices will display at any one time in the expansion area of the gadget. Assume each choice is 15 units in height.

    c. Create three Label gadgets with the following characteristics:
        The horizontal position of each gadget centers them horizontally in the window, and the horizontal position is for you to decide. The titles are from assignments for each choice: the first piece is the address, second piece is the state, and zip code is the last piece. The gadgets are valued when a selection is made from the List Button gadget.

Endnotes

[1] Version 1.1 of the MWAPI specification changed the error code from "M?1."

[2] Version 1.1 of the MWAPI specification changed the error code from "M?2."

[3] Version 1.1 of the MWAPI specification changed the error code from "M?7."

[4] The MDC's version 1.1 specification for the MWAPI extended the use of this attribute to Check Box, Radio Button Set, and Scroll gadgets.

[5] The MDC's version 1.1 specification for the MWAPI changed this error code from "M?4."

[6] The MDC's version 1.1 specification for the MWAPI changed the error code from "M?7."

[7] The MDC's version 1.1 specification for the MWAPI changed the error code from "M?7."

[8] The MDC's version 1.1 specification for the MWAPI changed the error code from "M?7."

[9] Version 1.1 of the MWAPI specification changed the default from the value of gadget's BCOLOR attribute.

[10] Version 1.1 of the MWAPI specification changed the default from the value of gadget's FCOLOR attribute.

[11] The MDC's version 1.1 specification for the MWAPI changed the error code from "M?3."

[12] The MDC's version 1.1 specification for the MWAPI changed the code from "M?2."

[13] The MDC's version 1.1 extension to the MWAPI changed the error code from "M?1."

[14] The MDC's version 1.1 specification for the MWAPI changed the error code from "M?2."

[15] The MDC's version 1.1 extension to the MWAPI changed the error code from "M?1."

Drawing 6

The last chapter focused on the other fourteen gadget types, and introduced the DRAW and DRAWTYPE attributes used for draw commands. This chapter focuses on the last type with a detailed look at the Generic Box gadget and draw commands. Draw commands give the Generic Box gadget the unique ability to draw geometric shapes, edit pixels, display images, and do the things you would expect from a drawing application.

The Creation and Modification section presents an overview of how draw commands are assigned and the drawing is created in the gadget. Detail coverage of each command is found in the Draw Commands section. A Generic Box gadget is produced with graphical objects in the Implementation section, and includes source code and discussion. After reading this chapter, the reader will have the tools needed to add imagery and drawing capabilities to an application.

Creation and Modification

This section explains how to use draw commands to create and modify objects in the drawing area of the gadget they are assigned. Drawing capabilities are only available to gadgets specified to use the DRAW and DRAWTYPE attributes. Currently only the Generic Box gadget is so specified by the MWAPI specification, and the drawing area is the entire area of the gadget. Drawing objects involves the assignment of draw commands to nodes descended from the gadget's DRAW attribute, and the subscript values must be nonnegative numeric values. If an application attempts to assign a negative valued subscript, an error will occur with a code of "M47."[1] The value of the DRAW attribute is automatically updated to indicate the number of descended draw commands. The only modification an application can make to this attribute node is to kill it and its descendants. This will set the node's value to zero and destroy all drawing in the gadget. The DRAWTYPE attribute specifies the type of draw commands assigned to descendant nodes of the DRAW attribute. "MDRAW" is the standard type and is guaranteed portability. Types beginning with the letter "Z" are reserved for implementation values, and may not be portable.

Draw commands are assigned as arguments to subscript nodes descended from the gadget's DRAW attribute. The Draw Commands section lists and details all the MWAPI (MDRAW type) specified draw commands. Each draw command is executed in the collating order of their subscripts to produce objects, pictures, and attributes to describe characteristics for following node values. Example 6.1 demonstrates the syntax of draw commands as they appear in the Window SSVN.

```
^$W("WINDOW","G","GENERIC","DRAW")=2
^$W("WINDOW","G","GENERIC","DRAW",0)="FCOLOR,65535,0,65535"
^$W("WINDOW","G","GENERIC","DRAW",1)="LINE,20,20,100,20"
^$W("WINDOW","G","GENERIC","DRAWTYPE")="MDRAW"
```

EXAMPLE 6.1: *Draw Commands and Attributes Example*

Assignments can be made using either the M SET or M MERGE commands. The value of the DRAW attribute not assigned, and is included to show that it automatically updates to indicate the number of descended draw commands. The value of the DRAWTYPE attribute node will default to "MDRAW," and is shown in this example to define the type of draw commands. The Generic Box "GENERIC" in the application window "WINDOW" is used in this example as the object to display the results of the commands. The object drawn in this example is an MDRAW type magenta line extending from coordinates 20,20 to 100,20 relative to the origin of the gadget's viewport. The argument to subscript zero assigns the foreground color characteristic for the line to magenta. The value of the following node is executed to produce the line.

Each drawing shares a common set of characteristics. Pen size, draw mode, fill pattern, unit of measurement, background color, and foreground color are common to all draw commands, and inherit default values from the parent window and host windowing system. Default characteristics can be changed anytime to affect the commands that follow the node in collating order, and will remain in effect until changed in the argument of a descended subscript.

Drawing objects include geometric shapes, bitmapped images, line size, text, foreground and background colors, and fill patterns. The Draw Commands that create these objects are detailed in the Draw Commands section along with all other MWAPI-specified draw commands. The next section covers "MDRAW" draw commands in detail.

Draw Commands

The MWAPI standard defines eighteen commands for drawing objects, displaying images, and editing pixels. The MWAPI specification also permits the use of implementation-defined Draw Commands. Draw commands starting with "Z" are reserved for use in defining implementation-specific commands, and are not guaranteed to be portable. Draw commands are assigned to DRAW attribute subscript nodes in uppercase. An attempt to assign a draw command that is not specified for use by the MWAPI specification will cause an error to occur with a code of "M46."[2] The MWAPI standard defines "MDRAW" draw commands, and they are listed in Table 6.1.

MWAPI defined draw commands can be divided into the following functional categories:

Color:	Color characteristics of draw commands are defined by this category.
Image:	Draw commands in this category permit the display of images produced with another applications.
Line Drawing:	These commands are used to draw geometric shapes.
Properties:	This category consists of common characteristics used by draw commands.
Text:	This category defines the font and text drawn in the gadget.

TABLE 6.1: *Draw Commands Categorized*

Category	Draw Command	Category	Draw Command
COLOR	BCOLOR	PROPERTIES	DMODE
	FCOLOR		FILLPAT
IMAGE	BITMAP		PEN
	PICTURE		UNITS[1]
LINE DRAWING	ARC	TEXT	DRAWTEXT
	BOX		FFACE
	LINE		FSIZE
	OVAL		FSTYLE
	PIE		
	POINT		

[1] This command was added to the MWAPI specification by version 1.1.

Draw commands are listed below using the format presented in Table 6.2. If any of the section(s) are not necessary to the description of the command, the section(s) will not be shown.

TABLE 6.2: *Draw Command Description Format*

COMMAND NAME	
Description:	This section describes the command's function.
Syntax:	This section lists the syntax required for this draw command.
Domain:	This section lists the domain of allowable values for this command. If the assigned values are not within the domain, an error will occur with a code of "M47."[3]
Default:	This section lists default values.
Notes:	This section contains notes on this command.

ARC

Description: This command draws an arc from a start point to the end point using the specified radius.

Syntax: `ARC,hpos,vpos,radius,startangle,endangle`

Domain: The domain of values for the *hpos*, *vpos*, and *radius* parameters are numeric literals. The domain for the *startangle* and *endangle* parameters are degree measurements.

Notes: The *hpos* and *vpos* parameters are measured relative to the origin (0,0) of the gadget, the center of the circle that includes the arc.

The distance from the center of the circle to its circumference is defined by the *radius* parameter.

The start and end positions (stated in degrees) of the arc are defined by the *startangle* or *endangle* parameters respectively, and the resulting arc is drawn in a counterclockwise direction. Zero values for both *startangle* and *endangle* produce a circle.

Zero degrees is the rightmost point on the horizontal axis.

BCOLOR

Description: This command specifies the current background color for draw commands that follow in collating order.

Syntax: `BCOLOR,color,fillmode`

Domain: The domain of values for the *color* parameter are color definitions specified by the amount of red, green, and blue (RGB), and the syntax is: *rcolor,gcolor,bcolor*. Appropriate color values lie between 0 and 65535. The domain for the *fillmode* parameter is either OPAQUE, TRANSPARENT, or an Implementation-defined value. See the FILLMODE draw command for the details for fillmode parameters.

Default: The default value for the *color* parameter is the current value of the gadget's BCOLOR attribute, and the default for the *fillmode* parameter is TRANSPARENT.

Notes: A *fillmode* value of OPAQUE will cover over any previously displayed draw commands until the value is changed to TRANSPARENT.

Color values are listed in Appendix A.

BITMAP

Description: This draw command displays a bitmap image at the *hpos* and *vpos* coordinates in the gadget.

Syntax: `BITMAP,hpos,vpos,extresource`

Domain: The domain of values for the *hpos* and *vpos* parameters are numeric literals. The domain of values for the *extresource* parameter are:

Value	Description
F,*fileid*	This is for a file specifier. The path to the file containing the bitmap image is specified by *fileid*.
R,*resourceid*	This is for a resource identifier. The resource is specified by *resourceid*.

Implementation Value   This value is determined by the vendor's implementation of the MWAPI and is not standard.

Notes: The *hpos* and *vpos* parameters are measured relative to the origin (0,0) of the gadget, and defines the origin of the image.

BOX

Description: This command draws a rectangular object.

Syntax: BOX,*hpos1*,*vpos1*,*hpos2*,*vpos2*

Domain: The domain of values for the parameters are numeric literals.

Notes: The upper left corners of the rectangle is defined by *hpos1* and *vpos1*, and the lower right corner is defined by *hpos2* and *vpos2*. Each corner is measured relative to the gadget's origin.

The box is filled using the current fill pattern and draw background color.

DMODE

Description: This command determines how draw commands affect the pixels in their drawing.

Syntax: DMODE,*dmode*

Domain: The values for *dmode* are:

Value	Description
SOLID	This value causes pixels to display in the current foreground or background color as appropriate.
XOR	When this value is used, the color of each new pixel is determined by performing an XOR operation between the pixel in the drawing area and the current foreground or background color as appropriate. This operation normally produces the opposite color.
Implementation Value	This value is determined by the vendor's implementation of the MWAPI and is not standard.

Default: The default value for the *dmode* parameter is SOLID.

DRAWTEXT

Description: This command specifies the text to appear at the coordinates specified by the *hpos* and *vpos* parameters.

Syntax: DRAWTEXT,*hpos*,*vpos*,*chars*

Domain: The domain of values for the *hpos* and *vpos* parameters are numeric literals.
The domain for the *chars* parameter include any control or graphic character.

Notes: The text displayed by this command uses the current font face, font size, and font style defined for drawing objects in the current gadget.

The *hpos* and *vpos* parameters specify the location of the upper left corner of the character cell of the first character. A character cell is a conceptual rectangular area that encompasses a character.

The character cell is filled using the current fill pattern and draw background color.

FCOLOR

Description: This command specifies the current foreground color for draw commands that follow in collating order.

Syntax: FCOLOR,*color*

Domain: The domain of values for the *color* parameter is a color definition specified by the amount of red, green, and blue (RGB), and the syntax is *rcolor,gcolor,bcolor*. Appropriate color values lie between 0 and 65535.

Default: The default for the color parameter is the current value of the gadget's FCOLOR attribute.

Color values are listed in Appendix A.

FFACE

Description: This command specifies the current typeface to use for drawing text in the current gadget.

Syntax: FFACE,*fontface*

Domain: The domain for the *fontface* parameter is one of the fontface values defined by the TYPEFACE attribute of the current Display SSVN. One of the values listed below can also be used:

Font Name	Description
M,DEFAULT	This is the default typeface defined for the underlying windowing system. If there is no underlying windowing platform, the MWAPI defines this fontface.
M,FIXED	This is a nonproportional typeface.
M,SANS	This is a proportional typeface from the sans-serif family.
M,SERIF	This is a proportional typeface from the serif family.
Implementation Value	This value begins with a "Z," and can be defined by the M implementation.

Default: The default for *fontface* is the current value assigned to the gadget's FFACE attribute.

If the specified value cannot be supported by the underlying windowing platform, a substitute is used.

FILLPAT

Description: This command specifies the current pattern to fill the background of specified objects.

Syntax: FILLPAT,*fillpatern*

Domain: The values for *fillpattern* are:

Value	Description
BDIAGONAL	This value displays a pattern of diagonal lines running from lower left to upper right.
CROSSHATCH	This value displays a pattern of vertical and horizontal lines crisscrossing each other.

DCROSSHATCH	This value displays lines running diagonally from lower right to upper left and from lower left to upper right.
FDIAGONAL	This value displays lines running from lower left to upper right.
HORIZONTAL	This value displays horizontal lines.
NONE	This value displays no filling.
SOLID	This value displays the area filled with the current draw foreground color.
VERTICAL	This value displays vertical lines.
Implementation Value	This value is determined by the vendor's implementation of the MWAPI and is not standard.

Default: The default value for the *fillpattern* parameter is determined by the underlying windowing interface.

Notes: Fill patterns use the current draw foreground color and draw mode.

FSIZE

Description: This command specifies the current size of text to be used by draw commands.

Syntax: `FSIZE,fontsize`

Domain: The domain of values for the *fontsize* parameter is a positive numeric value that specifies point size (1/72 inch) in the fontface in use.

Default: The default value for *fontsize* is the current value of the gadget's FSIZE attribute.

Notes: If *fontface* is a subscript of the logical display's TYPEFACE attribute, use one of its descendant subscripts for the value of this attribute.

        If the value of this attribute cannot be supported, a substitute is used.

FSTYLE

Description: This command specifies the current type style to be used by draw commands.

Syntax: `FSTYLE,fontstyle`

Domain: The domain of values for the *fontstyle* parameter are:

Value	Description
NORMAL	The text is displayed in a normal style.
BOLD	The text is displayed in bold.
ITALIC	The text is displayed in italics.
ULINE	The text is displayed underlined
Implementation Value	The text is displayed in an implementation-defined manner. Values beginning with "Z" are reserved for implementation values.

Default: The default value for the *fontstyle* parameter is the current value of the gadget's FSTYLE attribute.

Notes:	The values listed for *fontstyle* are combined using the comma as a delineator: BOLD,ULINE. The value NORMAL cannot be combined with other values.
	If the value requested for *fontstyle* cannot be provided, an alternative value is assigned by the underlying windowing interface. In any case, any reference to this attribute will reflect the actual value.

LINE

Description:	This command draws a line from one position to another.
Syntax:	LINE,hpos1,vpos1,hpos2,vpos2
Domain:	The domain of values for the *hpos* or *vpos* parameters are numeric literals.
Notes:	The *hpos* and *vpos* parameters are measured relative to the origin (0,0) of the gadget that the draw command is assigned in the unit of measurement specified by the UNITS draw command.
	The *hpos1* and *vpos1* identify the beginning of the line, and *hpos2* and *vpos2* define the end coordinates.

OVAL

Description:	This command draws an ellipse.
Syntax:	OVAL,hpos1,vpos1,hpos2,vpos2
Domain:	The domain of values for the *hpos* or *vpos* parameters are numeric literals.
Notes:	The *hpos* and *vpos* parameters are measured relative to the origin (0,0) of the gadget that the draw command is assigned in the unit of measurement specified by the UNITS draw command.
	The parameters *hpos1*, *vpos1*, *hpos2* and *vpos2* defines an invisible rectangular area that encompasses the ellipse.
	The ellipse is filled using the current fill pattern and draw background color.

PENSIZE

Description:	This command defines the thickness of the lines, measured in pixels, for drawing the outline (foreground) of objects.
Syntax:	PENSIZE,pensize
Domain:	The domain of values for the *pensize* parameter are integers.
Default:	The default value for the *pensize* parameter is determined by the underlying windowing platform.
Notes:	A *pensize* value of zero indicates no apparent drawing by pen.

PICTURE

Description:	This command draws a picture at coordinates defined by *hpos* and *vpos*.
Syntax:	PICTURE,hpos,vpos,extresource
Domain:	The domain of values for the *hpos* and *vpos* parameters are numeric literals. The domain of values for the *extresource* parameter are:

Value	Description
F,*fileid*	This is for a file specifier. The path to the file containing the bitmap image is specified by *fileid*.
R,*resourceid*	This is for a resource identifier. The resource is specified by *resourceid*.
Implementation Value	This value is determined by the vendor's implementation of the MWAPI and is not standard.

Notes: The *hpos* and *vpos* parameters are measured relative to the origin (0,0) of the gadget, and defines the origin of the picture.

PIE

Description: This command draws a pie object.

Syntax: `PIE,hpos,vpos,radius,startangle,endangle`

Domain: The domain of values for the *hpos*, *vpos*, and radius parameters are numeric literals. The domain for the *startangle* and *endangle* parameters are degree measurements.

Notes: The *hpos* and *vpos* parameters are measured relative to the origin (0,0) of the gadget and define the center of a circle that contains the arc section of the object.

The distance from the center of the circle to the arc is defined by the *radius* parameter.

The start and end positions (stated in degrees) of the arc are defined by the *startangle* or *endangle* parameters respectively, and the resulting arc is drawn in a counterclockwise direction. Zero values for both *startangle* and *endangle* produce a circle.

Zero degrees is the rightmost point on the horizontal axis.

Lines are drawn to connect both ends of the arc to the center of the circle to produce the pie.

The pie is filled using the current fill pattern and draw background color.

POINT

Description: This command draws a point at the position specified.

Syntax: `POINT,hpos,vpos`

Domain: The domain of values for *hpos* and *vpos* are numeric literals.

Notes: The *hpos* and *vpos* parameters are measured relative to the origin (0,0) of the gadget to define the position of the point.

UNITS

Description: This command specifies the unit of measurement for draw commands in the current gadget.

Syntax: UNITS,*unitspec*

Domain: The domain of values for the *unitspec* parameter is shown below.

Value	Description
CHAR[,*chars*]	This value specifies that the position is measured relative to the size of a character in the basis font. The value domain for the *chars* parameter is one or more characters.
PIXEL	This value specifies that the position measurement is measured in pixels.
POINT	This value specifies that the position is measured in points. The size of a point is 1/72 of an inch.
REL[,*hscale,vscale*]	This value specifies a relative measurement with respect to a basis size. The parameters *hscale* and *vscale* have the domain of numeric literal values.
Implementation Value	This value is determined by the vendor's implementation of the MWAPI and is not standard.

Default: The default value is the current value of the gadget's UNITS attribute.

Notes: The basis font for a unit of measurement of CHAR is specified by the FFACE, FSIZE, and FSTYLE Draw Commands or their default values, as appropriate. If the *chars* parameter is specified, and not equal to the emptystring, the average width of all characters specified is used to determine the unit of measurement.

    If the unit of measurement is REL, the basis size is the size of the gadget's area. If *hscale* and *vscale* are not specified they will default to 100.

Implementation

This section demonstrates an implementation of the Generic Box gadget to demonstrate a few draw commands. This demonstration will give the reader an idea of how to use Draw Commands to create images and elicit user-defined parameter values.

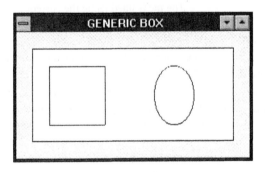

FIGURE 6.1: *Generic Box*

```
GENERIC ; Generic Box
+1  K ^$W,W
+2  S W("WINDOW","POS")="10,20"
+3  S W("WINDOW","SIZE")="290,150"
+4  S W("WINDOW","TITLE")="GENERIC BOX"
```

```
+5  S W("WINDOW","EVENT","CLOSE")="CLOSE^GADGETS"
+6  S W("WINDOW","G","GEN","TYPE")="GENERIC"
+7  S W("WINDOW","G","GEN","POS")="20,20"
+8  S W("WINDOW","G","GEN","SIZE")="250,110"
+9  S W("WINDOW","G","GEN","EVENT","PDRAG")="PDRAG^GADGETS"
+10 S W("WINDOW","G","GEN","EVENT","PDOWN")="PDOWN^GADGETS"
+11 S W("WINDOW","G","GEN","EVENT","PUP")="PUP^GADGETS"
+12 S W("WINDOW","G","GEN","DRAWTYPE")="MDRAW"
+13 S W("WINDOW","G","GEN","DRAW",1)="FILLPAT,NONE"
+14 S W("WINDOW","G","GEN","DRAW",2)="OVAL,150,20,200,90"
+15 S W("WINDOW","G","GEN","DRAW",3)="BOX,20,20,90,90"
+16 S W("WINDOW","G","GEN","DRAW",4)="PENSIZE,2"
+17 M ^$W=W
+18 ESTA
+19 Q
```

The code at lines GENERIC+1 through 11 define characteristics for the parent window and the Generic Box gadget for the display of the objects created by the draw commands used in this implementation. The Draw Commands used in this implementation are of the type MDRAW (see line 12). Lines 13 through 16 are nodes subscripted from the gadget's DRAW attribute that contain, as their arguments, the commands that created the drawing shown. The value of the DRAW attribute node automatically updates itself to reflect the number of Draw Commands used in the gadget. Draw Commands are executed in the collating order of the subscripts descended from the gadget's DRAW attribute.

The first command (see line 13) specifies that no fillpattern is used for the commands shown. This explicit definition for this command overrides the default fill pattern defined for the underlying windowing platform. Lines 14 and 15 draw an oval and box using the current pen size, foreground and background color, and draw mode. The default pen size is changed for draw commands that follow the new definition (see line 16) in collating sequence.

Additional drawings can be added to this gadget either specified by application code or user input. Pointer and keyboard events that can be processed to determine the type and characteristics for new draw commands. Lines 9 through 11 define events that can be used to process PDRAG, PDOWN, and PUP events to determine the type and coordinates for additional objects. The example below determines the user specified coordinates for, and causes, a line to be drawn.

```
PDOWN ; If the correct pointer button is depressed, get the pointer position.
+1  S PBUTTON=^$E("PBUTTON")
+2  I PBUTTON="PB1" D
+3  .S PPOS=^$E("PPOS")
+4  .S SHPOS=$P(PPOS,",",1)
+5  .S SVPOS=$P(PPOS,",",2)

PDRAG ; process mouse movement while a mouse button is depressed
+1  S PBUTTON=^$E("PBUTTON")
+2  S PPOS=^$E("PPOS")
+3  Q
```

```
PUP ; get the pointer position when the pointer button is released.
+1  S  PPOS=^$E("PPOS")
+2  S  EHPOS=$P(PPOS,",",1)
+3  S  EVPOS=$P(PPOS,",",2)
+4  S  SUB=$O(^$W("WINDOW","G","GEN","DRAW",""),-1)+1.1
+5  S  X="LINE,SHPOS,SVPOS,EHPOS,EVPOS"
+6  S  ^$W("WINDOW","G","GEN","DRAW",SUB)=X
+7  Q
```

Tag PDOWN references the Event SSVN to determine the pointer button depressed. If the button is the primary (or left) one, the Event SSVN is again referenced to determine the starting horizontal and vertical position for the line. These coordinates are measured relative to the origin of the gadget. Tag PUP determines the ending position and causes the line to be drawn. The pen size used to draw the line is two pixels wide. Line 16 of tag Generic overrides the default pen size for draw commands that follow in collating order. PUP+1 through 6 get ending coordinates and assign the "LINE" draw command to the subscript following the last. The assignment of the command creates the object. Tag PDRAG can be used to determine the pointer position as it moves.

The value of the gadget's DRAW attribute automatically updates to a value of five to indicate the number of Draw Commands descended. Note this value may or may not be the same number as the last descended subscript used. PUP+6 uses the subscript value of 5.1 to demonstrate this difference.

Highlights

The MWAPI specification provides the capability for including drawings of objects into a GUI application. The types of objects that can be drawn include geometric shapes, bitmapped images, and text. These objects are explicitly created by draw commands, and the Generic Box gadget serves as the canvass.

The Generic Box gadget uses the DRAWTYPE and DRAW element attributes to specify drawings. The arguments to nodes descended from the DRAW attribute consist of Draw Commands. The resulting drawing is created by executing each command in collating order of the DRAW attribute subscripts. The value of the gadget's DRAW attribute automatically updates to reflect the current number of descended Draw Commands.

As draw commands are assigned, the current background and foreground color, pensize, fillpattern, and unit of measurement are used. Default values are used for these characteristics unless modified. Once modified the new value is the current value used by all draw commands that follow the redefinition in collating order.

Exercises

1. How does the MWAPI create drawing objects?

2. Can any gadget draw with draw commands?

3. What is the purpose of the DRAW attribute?

4. What is the purpose of the DRAWTYPE attribute?

5. How can the common characteristics be changed from one draw command to the next?

6. Add a Generic Box gadget to the window built in Exercise 7 of Chapter 4. Create a pie chart alternating each 90 degrees blue, red, green, and yellow.

Endnotes

[1] The version 1.1 specification changed the error code from "M?2."

[2] The MDC's version 1.1 type A extension for the MWAPI changed the error code from "M?1."

[3] The version 1.1 specification changed the error code from "M?2."

Menus and Timers

7

Menus and timers are both children of windows used to perform specialized tasks. A menu consists of a list of choices and may appear much like a gadget in the choice category, but distinct differences exist in how their items are characterized. Menu choices can be characterized individually whereas gadget choices have a distinct dependency on the parent element. The list of attributes available to describe the characteristics of menu choices, and their appearance in menus, is more extensive than those available to gadget choices.

One of the major differences between menus and gadgets is in the area of event processing. Each menu choice can have its own event node so callbacks may be directed to the individual choice. In contrast, a callback for a gadget's selection would be directed to the element's event node where processing follows the same path regardless of choice. Another major difference is the ability to link menu choices into a hierarchy of options. The selection of one menu choice can cause another menu to display with another selection that causes yet another menu to appear—building a hierarchical structure of choices. You have more flexibility in the way choices appear in menus than you do with gadgets in the choice category.

The Creation and Modification section explains how menus and timers are created and how their characteristics are modified. The attributes specified for both menus and timers are discussed in the Menu and Timer Attributes section. The attributes available for describing characteristics of menu choices are covered in the Choice Attributes section. The Implementation section uses source code and figures to demonstrate the use of menus and timers. Highlights and Exercise sections complete the chapter. After reading this chapter, you will be able to make your windows applications more robust and user friendly with menus and timers.

Creation and Modification

The syntax for the assignment of menu and timer attributes is similar to the syntax for assigning attributes to gadgets (see Example 7.1).

```
^$W(window name,element type,element name,element attribute)=value
```

EXAMPLE 7.1: *Menu and Timer Attribute Syntax*

The *window name* subscript uniquely identifies the parent window of the menu or timer, and is limited to a maximum stringlength of thirty-one alphanumeric characters. The *element type* subscript is "M" when referring to a menu, and "T" when referring to a timer. The *element name* subscript uniquely identifies the menu or timer from any other menu or timer assigned to the window, and is also limited to thirty-one alphanumeric characters. The attribute keywords used for describing the element's characteristics are defined as the fourth or *element attribute* subscript. The value of the node assigns quality, or quantity, to the attribute.

Menu

A menu consists of one or more choices descended from the elements CHOICE attribute (see Example 7.2).

```
^$W(window name,"M",element name,"CHOICE",item)=value
```

EXAMPLE 7.2: *Menu Choice Assignment Syntax*

Menu choices are maintained as subscript values to a menu's CHOICE attribute. The *item* subscript identifies the node of a choice, and its value is a selectable entity. The value may not exceed 255 characters in length, and a single window can contain a maximum of 255 menu choices. Menus can be used in a variety of ways:

1. A menu can be used as the menubar of its parent.
2. It can be designed to display, or pop-up, anywhere in the application area of its parent independent of the menubar or menu item.
3. A menu can be specified to pop-up and display adjacent to a selectable item.

A menubar displays its list of choices in a horizontal orientation typically under its parent window's title area. The positioning of a menubar is a question of look and feel, and determined by the underlying windowing platform. The window's MENUBAR attribute specifies the name of the menu to use as the menubar for the window. Example 7.3 defines menu "SUB" with two choices, and designates it the menubar of window "WIN."

```
S W("WIN","MENUBAR")="SUB"
S W("WIN","M","SUB","CHOICE",1)="FILE"
S W("WIN","M","SUB","CHOICE",2)="EDIT"
M ^$W=W
```

EXAMPLE 7.3: *Submenu Specification*

A pop-up menu displays choices in a vertical format descended from a menubar choice or elsewhere in its parent window. Example 7.4 shows the syntax for designating menu "SUB1" the pop-up menu for choice "FILE" in menu "SUB." When "FILE" is selected, "SUB1" pops-up and displays adjacent and descended from the choice. The value of the SUBMENU Choice Attribute node specifies the submenu for the choice it is descended. Submenus can continue their descent to a maximum of seven levels. The width of a submenu display is determined by the longest choice assigned to it.

```
S W("WIN","M","SUB","CHOICE",1)="FILE"
S W("WIN","M","SUB","CHOICE",1,"SUBMENU")="SUB1"
S W("WIN","M","SUB1","CHOICE",1)="NEW"
M ^$W=W
```

EXAMPLE 7.4: *Descendant Pop-Up Menu*

An application can be coded so a menu will pop up anywhere within the application area of its parent window. The element's POS attribute is used to determine its origin, and may be absolute or relative to another object. Both the implementation section of this chapter and Chapter 9 demonstrate pop-up menus with origin relative to the current pointer position. The element's VISIBLE attribute is required to make this type of menu visible. Example 7.5 shows the code required to display menu "SUB3" at position 30,30. The values of the POS and VISIBLE attributes are ignored when the menu is used as a menubar or submenu.

```
S W("WIN","M","SUB3","POS")="30,30"
S W("WIN","M","SUB3","VISIBLE")=1
S W("WIN","M","SUB3","CHOICE",1)="CUT"
M ^$W=W
```

EXAMPLE 7.5: *Independent Pop-Up Menu*

Timer

A timer is an element used to generate an event at the expiration of a specified time interval, and has no visual representation. Timers are identified by their names, and may not exceed thirty-one alphanumeric characters in length. A single window can contain a maximum of seven timer elements. Example 7.6 creates the timer "TIMER" with a time interval of three hundred seconds. If the timer's interval is allowed to elapse, an interval event will occur.

```
S ^$W("WIN","T","TIMER","INTERVAL")=300
```

EXAMPLE 7.6: *Timer Created*

If all of the following statements are true, a timer's time interval will begin to elapse and trigger an event when it expires:

1. The timer has an enabled EVENT attribute node.
2. Event Processing is active for the M process.
3. The current window and all ancestor windows are active.
4. The element is active.
5. The timer is assigned a valid argument to its INTERVAL attribute.

If the specified time interval elapses, a callback is directed to the element's enabled event node's value for processing. Modification of any of an active timer's attribute values or completion of its callback processing restarts the element with the current interval value. A timer is canceled by making any of the above conditions false or using the timer's node reference as the argument to the KILL command. An application can use the ETRIGGER command to cause a timer event to occur, but this will not restart the element.

Menu and Timer Attributes

This section describes the attributes available to define the characteristics of menus and timers. The attributes for menu choices are presented in the next section.

Nine MWAPI attributes are listed in this section: seven are available to menus and five to timers. The element types that can use each attribute is explained during the detailed examination of each keyword. Implementation- and application-defined attributes are also permitted. Keywords starting with "Y" are reserved for application attributes, and are limited to a maximum stringlength of thirty-one characters. Application attributes permit application-specified values to be stored within the structure of an objects definition and should logically pertain to the element, although this is not a requirement. Keywords starting with "Z" are reserved for implementation-specified attributes. Attributes defined by the MWAPI are standard and portable across vendor implementations of the MWAPI. Implementation attributes defined by the vendor's implementation are not standard and may not be portable. Table 7.1 lists the attributes available for use by menus and timers by their functional categories:

1. *Action:* The category defines actions performed by timers.

2. *Appearance:* This attribute specified the look of the pointer over the element.

3. *Property:* This category specifies qualities of the element.

4. *State:* This category specify the state of the element.

TABLE 7.1: *MWAPI-Defined Menu and Timer Attributes*

CATEGORY	ATTRIBUTE	CATEGORY	ATTRIBUTE
ACTION	EVENT	STATE	ACTIVE
APPEARANCE	PTYPE[1]		VISIBLE
PROPERTY	CHOICE		
	ID		
	INTERVAL		
	POS		
	UNITS		

[1] The MDC's version 1.1 specification added the PTYPE attribute to the list.

Table 7.2 identifies the attributes for menus and timers.

TABLE 7.2 *Menu and Timer Attributes*

ATTRIBUTE	MENU	TIMER
ACTIVE	X	X
CHOICE	X	
EVENT		X
ID	X	X
INTERVAL		X
POS	X	
PTYPE	X	X
UNITS	X	
VISIBLE	X	

Menu and timer attributes are described in Table 7.3. The attributes are listed in alphabetical order and do not necessarily pertain to both element types. If an attempt is made to assign an attribute to either a menu or timer that is not specified for the attribute, an error with a code of "M46" will occur.[1] When a particular attribute is described, the element type specified for its use is identified. The values assigned to an attribute must fall within a certain domain defined for the attribute. If an attempt is made to assign a value to an attribute that is not within its domain, an error will occur with a code of "M47."[2]

TABLE **7.3:** *Attribute Description Format*

ATTRIBUTE NAME	
Description:	This section describes the attribute's function.
Syntax:	If the subscript syntax differs from that shown in Example 7.1, or if the argument can have more than one parameter, this section shows the syntax.
Domain:	This section lists the domain of values for the attribute.
Default:	This section specifies the default value for the attribute.
Notes:	This section lists any pertinent notes about this attribute. This section will cover any modifications made to this attribute definition by the MDC's version 1.1 specification for the MWAPI. If there are no further notes to list, this section will not exist.

ACTIVE

Description:	If this attribute describes a menu, the value determines whether a user may interact with the menu. If this attribute describes a timer, the value determines whether the element may be started or is active.
Domain:	The domain of values is an expression that evaluates to true or false.
Access:	The value of this attribute may be assigned when the window is being created, modified after creation, and referenced.
Default:	The default value is true.
Notes:	If the value of this attribute evaluates to true, the element is active. If the evaluation is false, the element is inactive.
	Users may only interact with active menus.
	A timer must be active in order for its interval value to expire.

CHOICE

Description:	This attribute specifies via descendant nodes choices that is displayed in the menu.
Syntax:	^$W(*window name*,"M",*element name*,"CHOICE",*item*)=*choice*
Domain:	There is no value at the subscript level of this attribute, only for descendant nodes. The first three subscripts are the same as mentioned in Example 7.1. The fourth subscript identifies this attribute. The fifth-level subscript maintains a unique node for each choice, and the *choice* argument is the text of an entity to display in the menu.
Access:	The value of this attribute may be assigned when the window is being created, modified after creation, and referenced.
Default:	There is no default value for this attribute.
Notes:	If callback processing occurs for a menu choice, the value of ^$E("CHOICE") will indicate the *item* subscript associated with the *choice* selected.
	If the *choice* argument contains an ampersand character (&) followed by a character other than an ampersand, the choice may be selected by the depressing the character on the keyboard. For instance: MS Windows displays an

underscore under the character following the ampersand to indicate selection of the choice by depressing the character on the keyboard. If the choice is inactive, selection cannot occur.

If an ampersand character is to be displayed in the choice, precede it with one ampersand. Keyboard selection will not occur by selecting the ampersand character on the keyboard.

Use of this attribute and its descendant subscripts are found in the Choice Attributes section of this chapter.

EVENT

Description: This attribute specifies via descendant node(s) callback routine(s) for specified event types.

Syntax: `^$W(window name,"T",element name,"EVENT",event type)=value`

The element type "T" is used because this attribute is only available to timers.

Domain: There is no value at the subscript level of this attribute, only for descendant nodes. Timer is the only *event type* specified for use by timer elements. *Value* is the name of a routine that will process the event.

Access: Descendant nodes of this attribute may be assigned when the window is being created, modified after creation, and referenced for their value.

Default: There is no default value for this attribute.

Notes: Events that occur for menus are associated with their choices, and are covered in the Choice Attributes section

The value of ^$E("TYPE") will contain the event type keyword that triggered the callback.

ID

Description: This attribute specifies an internal identifier that assists the underlying windowing interface in accessing the element.

Domain: The standard does not specify a domain of values for this attribute.

Access: This attribute may only be referenced for its value.

Default: There is no default value for this attribute.

Notes: The value of this attribute may differ from the name of the element. If an event occurs for an element, its name is used in ^$E("ELEMENT") to identify it.

INTERVAL

Description: This attribute specifies the elapsed time, in seconds, of a timer.

Domain: The value of this attribute must be a numeric literal greater than zero.

Access: The value of this attribute may be assigned when the window is being created, modified after creation, and referenced.

Default: There is no default value for this attribute.

Notes: If a timer's interval expires, it will normally restart from its current value, and an interval event will occur. If the timer's event is triggered by ETRIGGER execution, the interval will not automatically reset.

POS

Description: This attribute specifies the origin (0,0) of a menu that pops up independent of the menubar, or menu choice.

Syntax: hpos[,[vpos][,unitspec]] or ,vpos[,unitspec]

Domain: The domain of values for the *hpos* and *vpos* parameters are numeric literals. (Version 1.1 of the MWAPI specification modified these parameters to include negative values.) The domain of values for the *unitspec* component is:

Value	Description
CHAR[,*chars*]	This value specifies that the position is measured relative to the size of a character in the basis font of the menu. The *chars* parameter has the domain of one or more characters.
PIXEL	This value specifies that the position measurement is measured in pixels.
POINT	This value specifies that the position is measured in points. The size of a point is 1/72 of an inch.
REL[,*hscale*,*vscale*]	This value specifies a relative measurement with respect to a basis size. The parameters *hscale* and *vscale* have the domain of numeric literal values.
Implementation Value	This value is determined by the vendor's implementation of the MWAPI, is not standard, and the first character is "Z."

Access: The value of this attribute may be assigned when the window is being created, modified after creation, and referenced.

Default: There is no default value for this attribute.

Notes: If the assignment of *hpos* or *vpos*, but not both, is not specified, after the menu is created, the default is the current value for that parameter.

If an *hpos* or *vpos* value is assigned that cannot be provided by the windowing platform, a suitable value is determined by the windowing platform.

If the *unitspec* parameter is not explicitly specified when value is assigned to this attribute, it will default to the current value of the window's UNITS attribute.

The basis font for a unit of measurement of CHAR is specified by the FFACE, FSIZE, and FSTYLE attribute of the parent window, or their default values, as appropriate. If the *chars* parameter is specified and not equal to the emptystring, the average width of all characters specified is used to determine horizontally the unit of measurement for the font.

If the unit of measurement is REL, the basis size is the size of the parent window. If *hscale* or *vscale* are not specified they will default to 100.

If the menu is used as the menubar, or a submenu, the value of this attribute is ignored.

PTYPE

Description: This attribute specifies the pointer appearance when the pointer is over the object.

Domain: The domain of values is one of the following values:

Value	Description
M,CROSS	This value specifies a pointer appearance of cross-hairs.
M,IBEAM	This value specifies a pointer appearance of I-beam.
M,WAIT	This value specifies a pointer appearance of a waiting state.
F,fileid	This is for a file specifier. The path to the file is specified by fileid.
R,resourceid	This is for a resource identifier. The resource is specified by resourceid.
Implementation Value	This value is determined by the vendor's implementation of the MWAPI, is not standard and the first character is "Z."

Access: The value of this attribute may be assigned when the window is being created, modified after creation, and referenced.

Default: This attribute has no default value.

Notes: If the PTYPE attribute of the current logical display is defined, its value will have precedence over the pointer appearance. The value of an element's PTYPE attribute has precedence over the value of the parent window's PTYPE attribute.

   If the window's logical display does not have a pointer device connected (^$DI($PD,"PTR") is undefined), the value of this attribute is ignored.

   The values for F,fileid and R,resourceid are platform and hardware dependent and may not be portable.

   This attribute was added to the MWAPI specification by The MDC's version 1.1 specification.

UNITS

Description: This attribute defines the unit of measurement for the menu.

Domain: The domain of values is shown below.

Value	Description
CHAR[,chars]	This value specifies that the position is measured relative to the size of a character in the basis font of the menu. The value domain for the chars parameter is one or more characters.
PIXEL	This value specifies that the position measurement is measured in pixels.
POINT	This value specifies that the position is measured in points. The size of a point is 1/72 of an inch.
REL[,hscale,vscale]	This value specifies a relative measurement with respect to a basis size. The parameters hscale and vscale have the domain of numeric literal values.

Implementation Value   This value is determined by the vendor's implementation of the MWAPI, is not standard and the first character is "Z."

Access: The value of this attribute may be assigned when the element is being created, modified after creation, and referenced.

Default: The default value is the value of the parent's UNITS attribute.

Notes: The value of this attribute serves as the default *unitspec* value of the element's POS attribute.

The basis font for a unit of measurement of CHAR is specified by the FFACE, FSIZE, and FSTYLE attribute of the parent window, or their default values, as appropriate. If the *chars* parameter is specified, and not equal to the emptystring, the average width of all characters specified is used to determine horizontal the unit of measurement for the font.

If the unit of measurement is REL, the basis size is the size of the parent window. If *hscale* or *vscale* are not specified they will each default to 100.

VISIBLE

Description: This attribute specifies whether the pop-up menu (independent of a menu choice) is visible or not.

Domain: The domain of values is an expression that evaluates to true or false.

Access: The value of this attribute may be assigned when the window is being created, modified after creation, and referenced.

Default: The default value is true.

Notes: This attribute is not relevant for menus displayed as menubars or submenus. If this attribute is assigned to a menubar or submenu, its value is ignored.

If the value of this attribute evaluates to true, the menu is visible. If the value of this attribute evaluates to false, the menu is invisible.

If an application assigns a value to this attribute that evaluates to true and the element is invisible, it will become visible. If the assigned value evaluates to false, and the element is visible, it will become invisible. The effect may not be seen if the element is obscured.

Choice Attributes

This section focuses on the attributes available to menu choices. Choice Attributes are case-sensitive keywords used to define the characteristics of choices descended from a menu's CHOICE attribute. Example 7.7 shows the syntax for a menu's Choice Attribute.

```
^$W(window name,"M",menu name,"CHOICE",item,choice attribute)=value
```

EXAMPLE 7.7: *Menu Choice Attribute Syntax*

The first three subscripts are as mentioned above in the Creation and Modification section. The fourth subscript is the menu's "CHOICE" attribute, and the *item* subscript indicates the node containing the choice. The *choice attribute* subscript is a Choice attribute keyword from Table 7.4, and defines a characteristic of the choice. The *value* argument specifies a value from the domain specified for the attribute, and assigns quality. If an application attempts to assign a value for a Choice attribute that is not specified by its domain of values, an error will occur with a code of "M47."[3]

The MWAPI standard specifies seven attribute keywords available to characterize menu choices. Implementation- and application-defined attributes are also permitted. Keywords starting with "Y" are reserved for application attributes, and are limited to a maximum stringlength of thirty-one characters. Application attributes permit application specified values to be stored within the structure of an objects definition, and should logically pertain to the element though this is not a requirement. Keywords starting with "Z" are reserved for implementation-specified attributes. Attributes defined by the MWAPI are standard and portable across vendor implementations of the MWAPI. Implementation attributes are defined by the vendor's implementation are not standard and may not portable. Table 7.4 lists MWAPI-defined Choice attributes by functional category:

1. *Appearance:* Attributes in this category specify the appearance of the choice within a menu.
2. *Property:* This category defined the items that belong to a menu choice.
3. *Selection:* This attribute allows an alternate method for quick choice selection.
4. *State:* This category list quality of a choice.

TABLE 7.4: *MWAPI-Defined Menu Choice Attributes*

CATEGORY	ATTRIBUTE	CATEGORY	ATTRIBUTE
APPEARANCE	MARKER	SELECTION	ACCELERATOR
	SEPARATOR	STATE	ACTIVE
PROPERTY	SUBMENU		EVENT
	AID		

The format introduced in Table 7.3 is used to cover the detail explanations of each standard Choice Attribute listed above. If an attempt is made to assign an attribute that is not specified for choices, an error code of "M46" will result.[4] The values that may be assigned to an attribute must fall within a certain domain defined for the attribute. If an attempt is made to assign a value to an attribute that is not within its domain, an error will occur with a code of "M47."[5]

ACCELERATOR
Description: This attribute specifies a key sequence that will cause the choice to be selected.
Domain: The domain of allowable values is a keycode.
Access: The value of this attribute may be assigned when the window is being created and referenced.

Default:	There is no default value for this attribute.
Notes:	The key sequence used by this attribute is in addition to including an ampersand in the name of the choice.
	Keycodes are listed in Appendix A.

ACTIVE

Description:	This attribute specifies whether the choice is enabled or disabled for selection.
Domain:	The domain of allowable values is an expression that evaluates to true or false.
Access:	The value of this attribute may be assigned when the window is being created, modified after creation, and referenced.
Default:	The default value is true.
Notes:	If the value of this attribute evaluates to true, both user and application selections of the choice may occur.

If the value of this attribute evaluates to false:

The choice is displayed in reverse video or some manner to indicate that it is disabled for selection.
The user will not be able to cause the choice to be selected.
Any previous selection of the choice is deselected.

If an application attempts to select an inactive choice, an error will occur with an error code of "M47."

AID

Description:	This attribute is provided so an application dependent value can be associated with the choice.
Domain:	The domain of allowable values is one or more characters.
Access:	The value of this attribute may be assigned when the window is being created, modified after creation, and referenced.
Default:	There is no default value for this attribute.
Notes:	This attribute is similar to an application attribute, and with the benefit of portability among conforming MWAPI implementations.

EVENT

Description:	This attribute specifies the event node for the choice identified by *item* in its syntax. The value of the descended subscript identifies the callback routine to process events for the choice.
Syntax:	`^$W(window name,element type,element name,"CHOICE",item,"EVENT",event type)=value`
Domain:	There is no value at the subscript level of this attribute. The only event type specified for a menu choice is "SELECT." The *item* subscript identifies a choice, and the node's argument designates one, or more, callback routines.
Access:	Descendant nodes of this attribute may be assigned when the window is being created, modified after creation, and referenced for their value.

Default: There is no default value for this attribute.

Notes: When a choice is selected, ^$E("CHOICE") will contain the *item* subscript of the choice. Reference ^$W(window name,"M",element name,"CHOICE",^$E("CHOICE")) to get the choice selected.

MARKER

Description: This attribute specifies an image to be displayed to the left of the choice.

Domain: The domain of allowable values is listed below:

Value	Description
M,BULLET	This is an image of a bullet item.
M,CHECK	This is an image of a check mark.
M,DIAMOND	This is an image of a diamond.
Resource ID	A resource id specifies a valid resource to be included.
File ID	A file ID indicates the path to a valid file identifier to be included.
Implementation Value	This identifier specifies a valid implementation value.

Access: The value of this attribute may be assigned when the window is being created, modified after creation, and referenced.

Default: There is no default value for this attribute.

SEPARATOR

Description: This attribute causes a visual separator to be displayed, in a pop-up or sub-menu, after the choice. The separator is usually a horizontal line. The use of this attribute in a menubar may cause subsequent choices to appear right justified.

Domain: The only value that may be assigned to this attribute is the emptystring.

Access: The value of this attribute may be assigned when the window is being created and referenced.

Default: There is no default value for this attribute.

Notes: The display characteristics created by this attribute are dictated by the look and feel of the underlying windowing interface.

SUBMENU

Description: This attribute designates the menu to be used as the submenu for the choice.

Domain: The domain of values are child menus of the window.

Access: The value of this attribute may be assigned when the window is being created, modified after it has been created and referenced.

Default: There is no default value for this attribute.

Notes: The Creation and Modification section above discusses the use of this attribute.

If the menu named in the argument is not a child of the current window or is the name of the current menu, an "M48"[6] error will occur.

Event Processing

This section expands on the topic of event processing that was introduced in Chapter 2, with a look at processing menu choice and timer events. If a callback is directed to a menu ($P(^$E("ELEMENT"),",",1)="M"), it is received by one of the choices and not the element itself. Example 7.8 shows the event syntax used for menu choices, and Example 7.9 shows the syntax used by timers.

`^$W(window name,"M",menu name,"CHOICE",item,"EVENT",event type)=value`

EXAMPLE 7.8: *Menu Choice Event Syntax*

`^$W(window name,"T",timer name,"EVENT",event type)=value`

EXAMPLE 7.9: *Timer Event Syntax*

Event Types

If an event occurs for a menu choice with an enabled *event type* node defined to process the event, reference ^$E("WINDOW") to determine the window for which the event occurred, and ^$E("ELEMENT") to find menus name and element type. The value of ^$E("CHOICE") is the *item* subscript of the selected choice. The WINDOW and ELEMENT nodes of the Event SSVN contain the same information for a timer's callback. The event types specified for menus and timers are "select" and "timer," respectfully. Table 7.4 presents the format to used to describe the event types.

TABLE 7.5: *Event Type Description Format*

EVENT TYPE	
Description:	This section indicates when callback processing may occur for the event type. The descriptions for user-triggered events assume the window alone has focus. ^$DI($PD,"FOCUS") contains only the name of the window.
Event Information Attributes:	This section lists the Event Information attributes available to describe the event object.
Notes:	Where appropriate, this section will provide notes on the attribute.

SELECT

Description:	Callback processing can occur for this event type when a user selects a menu choice or the event node is referenced in the argument of an executed ETRIGGER command.

Event Information Attributes:

CHOICE	ELEMENT	TYPE
CLASS	ROW	WINDOW
COL	SEQUENCE	

Notes: Reference ^$E("CHOICE") to determine item subscript of the choice selected.

TIMER

Description: Callback processing can occur for this event type when a timer's interval expires or the event node is referenced in the argument of an executed ETRIGGER command.

Event Information Attributes:

CLASS	TYPE
ELEMENT	WINDOW
SEQUENCE	

Event Specification Attributes

Event Specification Attributes modify the characteristics of callback processing for the event types they are assigned. Since neither menu choices nor timers are specified to use event types in the pointer, keyboard, or character categories (defined in Chapter 2), the FILTERIN keyword is inappropriate. The ENABLE Event Specification Attribute is also appropriate, and toggles the ability of a node to receive a callback. Implementation-defined keywords are permitted and will begin with the letter "Z." Attributes defined by the MWAPI are standard and portable across vendor implementations of the MWAPI. Implementation attributes that are defined by the vendor's implementation are not standard and may not be portable. If an application attempts to specify a keyword other than ENABLE, FILTERIN, or an implementation-defined attribute, an error will occur with a code of "M46."[7] Examples 7.10 and 7.11 show the syntax used for the assignment to a menu choice and timer respectively.

```
^$W(window name,"M",menu name,"CHOICE",item,"EVENT",event type,event specification
attribute)=value
```

EXAMPLE 7.10: *Menu Choice Event Specification Attribute Syntax*

```
^$W(window name,"T",timer name,"EVENT",event type, event specification
attribute)=value
```

EXAMPLE 7.11: *Timer Event Specification Attribute Syntax*

The assignment of an Event Type node automatically causes an implicit assignment of an ENABLE Event Specification Attribute for the node. Table 7.6 presents the format to be used for the detailed coverage of this attribute.

TABLE **7.6**: *Event Specification Attribute Format*

ATTRIBUTE NAME	
Description:	This section describes the attribute's function.
Domain:	This section lists the domain of allowable values for the attribute.
Access:	This section lists the method(s) of usage for the attribute.
Default:	This section specifies the default value for the attribute.
Notes:	This section lists any pertinent notes about this attribute. This section will cover any modifications made to this attribute definition by the MDC's version 1.1 specification for the MWAPI. If there are no further notes to list, this section will not exist.

ENABLE

Description:	This modifier specifies whether callback processing is enabled for the *event type* specified in the node.
Domain:	The domain of values for this modifier is an expression that evaluate to true or false.
Access:	The value of this attribute may be assigned when the window is being created, modified after creation, and referenced.
Default:	The default value is true.
Notes:	If the value of this specifier is true, callback processing is enabled for the event type. If the value of this attribute is false, callback processing is disabled for the event type.

Implementation

This section demonstrates the use of all menu types and a timer. Each example is shown with source code and descriptions of use. You will learn how to add menus and timers to windows applications to make them more robust and user friendly.

Menu

This subsection begins by demonstrating menu definitions and designating their use as a menubar or submenu. The demonstration begins by creating a window with a menubar and a submenu with simple characteristics defined. After displaying the result in Figure 7.1 and explaining the source code, complication is added with additional menu characteristics. Choice Attributes are added to the previous menu definitions and additional submenus are added to the menubar. Figure 7.2 shows how the resulting window now appears. This subsection is concluded with demonstrations of independent pop-up menu. Source code is included and explained for all demonstrations.

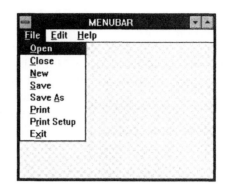

FIGURE 7.1: *Menu A*

```
MENU1 K W,^$W
+1    S W("W","POS")="20,20"
+2    S W("W","SIZE")="300,200"
+3    S W("W","EVENT","CLOSE")="CLOSE^MENU"
+4    S W("W","TITLE")="MENUBAR"
+5    ; begin simple menu definitions
+6    S W("W","M","MAIN","CHOICE",1)="&FILE"
+7    S W("W","M","MAIN","CHOICE",2)="&EDIT"
+8    S W("W","M","MAIN","CHOICE",3)="&HELP"
+9    ; FILE menu
+10   S W("W","M","SUB1","CHOICE",1)="&Open"
+11   S W("W","M","SUB1","CHOICE",2)="&Close"
+12   S W("W","M","SUB1","CHOICE",3)="&New"
+13   S W("W","M","SUB1","CHOICE",4)="&Save"
+14   S W("W","M","SUB1","CHOICE",5)="&Print"
+15   S W("W","M","SUB1","CHOICE",6)="P&rint Setup"
+16   S W("W","M","SUB1","CHOICE",7)="E&xit"
+17   ; specify window's menubar
+18   S W("W","MENUBAR")="MAIN"
+19   ; associate a submenu with choice "FILE" of menu "MAIN"
+20   S W("W","M","MAIN","CHOICE",1,"SUBMENU")="SUB1"
+21   ; create the objects
+22   M ^$W=W
+23   ESTA
+24   Q

CLOSE ; close window
+1    K ^$W("W")
+2    ESTOP
+3    Q
```

Menu "MAIN" is created with three choices in lines 6 through 8, and lines 10 through 16 create menu "SUB1" with seven choices. The ampersand (&) in the values designate keyboard selection by depressing the character following the ampersand. If the choice is disabled, selection cannot occur. As Figure 7.1 shows, the ampersand is not displayed, and the character following is displayed in a manner to indicate it may be used to select the choice.

The argument to the window's MENUBAR attribute node is used to designate the menubar for the window. The menu "MAIN" is designated in line 18 to be used as the menubar of window "W." If the argument of the MENUBAR attribute names a child menu of the current window before the window is created, the menu is the menubar. If the designation is made after the window has been created, the menu may not serve as the menubar. The underlying windowing platform may not allow adding a menubar after the window has been created.

The Choice Attribute SUBMENU is used in line 20 to designate menu "SUB1" as the menu to display adjacent to the first choice in menu "MAIN" when displayed. Menu "SUB1" will remain invisible, regardless the value of its VISIBLE attribute, until choice "FILE" is selected. The value of the VISIBLE attribute is ignored when the menu is either a menubar or submenu.

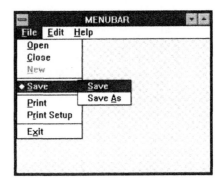

FIGURE 7.2: *Menu B*

```
MENU2; Choice Attributes and more submenus
+1   ; EDIT submenu
+2   S W("W","M","SUB2","CHOICE",1)="&Undo"
+3   S W("W","M","SUB2","CHOICE",2)="&Redo"
+4   S W("W","M","SUB2","CHOICE",3)="&Find"
+5   S W("W","M","MAIN","CHOICE",2,"SUBMENU")="SUB2"
+6   ; SAVE submenu
+7   S W("W","M","SUB3","CHOICE",1)="&Save"
+8   S W("W","M","SUB3","CHOICE",2)="Save &As"
+9   S W("W","M","SUB1","CHOICE",4,"SUBMENU")="SUB3"
+10  ; Choice Attributes that modify menu and choice display
+11  S W("W","M","SUB1","CHOICE",3,"ACTIVE")=0
+12  S W("W","M","SUB1","CHOICE",3,"SEPARATOR")=""
+13  S W("W","M","SUB1","CHOICE",4,"SEPARATOR")=""
+14  S W("W","M","SUB1","CHOICE",6,"SEPARATOR")=""
+15  S W("W","M","SUB1","CHOICE",4,"MARKER")="M,DIAMOND"
+16  ; events
+17  S W("W","M","SUB1","CHOICE",1,"EVENT","SELECT")="SEL^MENU"
+18  S W("W","M","SUB1","CHOICE",2,"EVENT","SELECT")="SEL^MENU"
```

```
+19  S  W("W","M","SUB1","CHOICE",3,"EVENT","SELECT")="SEL^MENU"
+20  S  W("W","M","SUB1","CHOICE",5,"EVENT","SELECT")="SEL^MENU"
+21  S  W("W","M","SUB1","CHOICE",6,"EVENT","SELECT")="SEL^MENU"
+22  S  W("W","M","SUB1","CHOICE",7,"EVENT","SELECT")="CLOSE^MENU"
+23  S  W("W","M","SUB2","CHOICE",1,"EVENT","SELECT")="SEL^MENU"
+24  S  W("W","M","SUB2","CHOICE",2,"EVENT","SELECT")="SEL^MENU"
+25  S  W("W","M","SUB3","CHOICE",3,"EVENT","SELECT")="SEL^MENU"
+26  S  W("W","M","SUB3","CHOICE",1,"EVENT","SELECT")="SEL^MENU"
+27  S  W("W","M","SUB3","CHOICE",2,"EVENT","SELECT")="SEL^MENU"
+28  M  ^$W=W
+29  Q
```

The code above adds an additional submenu to the menubar created in Figure 7.1 (a submenu to choice "SAVE" of menu "SUB1") and introduces additional Choice attributes. Figure 7.2 shows the result. The Choice Attribute introduced at line 9 specifies menu "SUB3," the submenu to be displayed when the fourth choice of menu "SUB1" (SAVE) is selected. This hierarchy is shown in Figure 7.2 when the sequence FILE then SAVE is chosen. The hierarchy of submenus can continue to a maximum of seven levels.

Choice Attributes can also be used to modify the display of menus and choices. Figure 7.2 shows how the appearance of menu "SUB1" has been altered by lines 11 through 15. The choice NEW is made inactive at line 11 and is displayed in a fashion to indicate such. The method for displaying an inactive menu choice is dependent on the look and feel of the underlying windowing platform, and a typical fashion is gray. Separator, or horizontal lines, are specified at lines 12 through 14, and can be used to logically group choices. A separator line is displayed following the choice specified. The definition at line 12 refers to choice NEW, and the separator is displayed before the next choice in the menu. A diamond is specified as the marker for the fourth choice in menu "SUB1." Optionally, line 15 could have specified some other object to display next to the choice.

```
SEL ; process SELECT events
+1  S  T=^$E("CHOICE")
+2  S  T1=$P(^$E("ELEMENT"),",",2)
+3  W  !,"The choice subscript ",T
+4  W  !,"has been chosen from menu: ",T1
+5  S  X=$TR(^$W("W","M",T1,"CHOICE",T),"&","")
+6  W  !,"The action requested is to: ",X
+7  Q
```

The EVENT Choice Attribute in lines 17 through 27 define the callback routines to be called when a menu choice is selected. The same tag and routine serve as the processing routine for most of the choices. Tag SEL+1 references the Event SSVN to determine the subscript of the selection. The menu where the choice exist is determined at line 2. The subscript is used at line 5 to determine the corresponding choice selected, and $TRANSLATE removes any occurrence of an ampersand. The callback routine for the EXIT choice differs from the other choices by calling the same routine specified for closing the window. This is appropriate and gives the user another way over the System Control Menu Box (described in Chapter 4) to close the window.

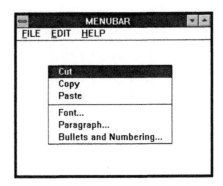

FIGURE 7.3: *Independent Pop-up Menu*

```
POP   ; define pop-up menu
+1    S W("W","M","POPUP","CHOICE",1)="Cut"
+2    S W("W","M","POPUP","CHOICE",2)="Copy"
+3    S W("W","M","POPUP","CHOICE",3)="Paste"
+4    S W("W","M","POPUP","CHOICE",3,"SEPARATOR")=""
+5    S W("W","M","POPUP","CHOICE",4)="Font..."
+6    S W("W","M","POPUP","CHOICE",5)="Paragraph..."
+7    S W("W","M","POPUP","CHOICE",6)="Bullet and Numbering"
+8    ; hook to the window
+9    S W("W","EVENT","CLICK")="POPUP^MENU"
+10   S W("W","EVENT","CLICK","FILTERIN")="PB3"
+11   M ^$W=W
+12   Q

POPUP ; display the pop-up menu
+1    S ^$W("W","M","POPUP","VISIBLE")=1
+2    S ^$W("W","M","POPUP","POS")=^$("PPOS")
+3    Q
```

Figure 7.3 shows the pop-up menu that was created by merging the code in tag POP into the Window SSVN and clicking the rightmost mouse button in the application area of the window. When the window receives a valid click event, tag POPUP is called to display the origin (0,0) of menu "POPUP" at the position of the pointer device (see POPUP+2). Since the menu is independent of the menubar, and not a submenu, POS and VISIBLE attributes must be defined. The value of the VISIBLE and POS attributes are ignored when implemented as the menubar or a submenu. Since the pop-up menu displays at the pointer position, the menu's POS attribute is set, in line 2, to the position of the pointer when the event occurred.

Timer

This subsection demonstrates the use of a timer. The source code used is included along with some descriptive text.

```
TIMER ; create a timer for the window
+1    S W("W","T","TIME","INTERVAL")=60
+2    S W("W","T","TIME","EVENT","TIMER")="TIME^MENU"
+3    M ^$W=W
+4    Q

TIME  ; ring the bell
+1    W *7
+2    Q
```

A timer element is added to window "W" in tag TIMER. Line 1 sets the interval to sixty seconds, and line 2 specifies the callback routine to process its events. Tag TIME rings the bell every minute until the timer is stopped.

Highlights

Menus and timers are specialized children of a window. Menus are displayable objects that present a number of selectable choices to a user. The choices that make up menus differ from those of Gadgets in the choice category by their typical usage and by additional characteristics. Menu choices are, by convention, used to cause an immediate action to occur: file, edit, or exit. Timers are used to time certain events, such as inactivity. If the specified period of time expires, a timer event will occur. The processing routine can reference ^$E("SEQUENCE") to determine if an event has taken place during the element's interval. If the timer is not stopped, it will restart with its current INTERVAL value.

A child menu may serve as the menubar of a window. The display of the menubar is determined by the look-and-feel characteristics of the windowing platform. The orientation is normally horizontal and at the top of the window or display. Choices are displayed distributed along the menubar.

Menus may also be of the pop-up variety displayed descended from the menubar, or elsewhere independent of the menubar. Additional menus can be tied to each choice and display adjacent to each other when the choice is selected. Submenus may continue to a depth of seven levels. The positioning of a pop-up menu, independent of the menubar, is determined by the POS attribute, and its visibility depends on the VISIBLE attribute's value. The values of the POS and VISIBLE attributes are ignored in a menu when used as the menubar or a submenu.

Each menu choice can be characterized individually by their own Choice Attributes. This contrasts with the way Gadgets of the choice category handle choices. The Choice attributes available to menu choices are more comprehensive than those for Gadget choices. Choice Attributes can be used to:

1. Alter the display of a Menu's list or a single choice.
2. Specify whether event processing may occur, and the callback routine for individual choices.
3. Specify a submenu to display adjacent to a choice when selected.

183

4. Specify a method for selection via the keyboard.

5. Specify a portable application-defined attribute.

This chapter concludes the focus on elements that began with Chapter 5. Elements make up the basic tools for interacting with the user and are a vital part of any GUI application. The next chapter covers the special variables and error processing available to an M process running the MWAPI.

Exercises

1. How do menus differ from gadgets in the choice category?

2. Describe the methods for using menus.

3. Can menus receive events?

4. What is the maximum menu depth for a window?

5. How does a menu become the menubar of a window?

6. What is a timer used for and identify a common use?

7. How does the expiration of a timed ESTART command differ from the expiration of a timer?

8. Why is the use of the FILTERIN Event Specification Attribute inappropriate for menus and timers?

9. How many timers may a window have?

10. Create a submenu for the window created in Exercise 7 of Chapter 4 with the following choices: File, Edit, and Help. Permit selection by choosing the first character of each choice. Create a submenu for "File" with three choices, including "Exit." An ETRIGGER is executed to destroy the window when "Exit" is chosen. Change the window's processing routine for a click event to display the submenu at the pointer coordinates.

Endnotes

[1] The MDC's version 1.1 specification changed the error code from "M?1."
[2] The MDC's version 1.1 specification changed the error code from "M?2."
[3] The MDC's version 1.1 specification changed the error code from "M?2."
[4] The MDC's version 1.1 specification changed the error code from "M?1."
[5] The MDC's version 1.1 specification changed the error code from "M?2."
[6] The MDC's version 1.1 specification changed the error code from "M?3."
[7] The MDC's version 1.1 extension to the MWAPI changed the error code from "M?1."

Special Variables and Functions

8

The MWAPI introduces special variables and functions to the M language for working with the unique properties of GUI applications. These new capabilities are explained in this chapter, along with a sample program to demonstrate their use. MWAPI special variables are covered in the Special Variables section. The new functions return information regarding the current font, and are covered in the Functions section. A sample program using a modified version of the Table gadget presented in Chapter 5 is used in the Implementation section to demonstrate the functions and special variables introduced in this chapter.

Special Variables

This section covers the special variables available to an M process running a conforming implementation of the MWAPI. $ECODE and $ETRAP are part of the 1995 ANSI M standard, and are included here to help clarify MWAPI error processing.

$ER[EF]   When an error occurs because of an MWAPI SSVN node, $ER will contain the reference. This is true no matter whether the error is due to a display, an entity or an element. This variable is demonstrated in the Implementation section.

$EC[ODE] $EC is a special variable name (SVN) that contains a comma delineated string of error codes. The comma character is the first character in the string of error codes and the last character in the string. When a process is activated, the value of $EC equals the emptystring. Program execution continues normally until a value (or values) is assigned to this variable. Application code can modify the value of this variable.

$ET[RAP] $ET is a special variable name (SVN) that can be set to code to execute if an error occurs. If an error occurs and the value of this variable is not the empty string, an implicit M EXECUTE command executes the value of $ET as its argument.

$PD[ISPLAY] $PD is a special variable that returns the name of the current logical display.

Functions

The MWAPI introduces $WFONT, $WTFIT, and $WTWIDTH to work with fonts. Each of these functions returns information about the font indicated by their parameters. If the information is not available for the specified font, the function returns an emptystring. The parameters required for these intrinsic functions are described in Table 8.1.

TABLE 8.1: *Function Parameters*

Parameter	Value
fontface:	The value of this parameter is the name of one of the fontfaces indicated by the third subscript of ^$DI($PD,"TYPEFACE"), or one of the following MWAPI fontfaces: M,DEFAULT M,FIXED M,SANS M,SERIF
fontsize:	The value of this parameter is the size of the font specified by the fontface parameter. If fontface is included in ^$DI($PD,"TYPEFACE"), fontsize should be one of descended subscript values.
fontstyle:	The value of this attribute indicates a style for fontface from one, or a comma delineated string, of the following styles: NORMAL BOLD ITALIC ULINE Implementation Value NORMAL cannot be combined with any other value.
unitspec:	The value of this parameter indicates the unit of measurement for the fontface parameter, and must be one of the following values: PIXEL POINT If the value of this parameter is not PIXEL or POINT, an error occurs with an error code equal to "M53."[1]
expr:	Test string expression.
numexpr:	Area (width) measured in unitspec unit of measurement.

[1] The MDC's version 1.1 specification for the MWAPI changed the error code from "M?8."

$WFONT

Description:	This function returns a comma delineated string about the font described by its parameters. The information is returned in the following format:

"*height,maxchar,avgchar*"

Where *height* indicates the height of the character cell plus external leading. The *maxchar* parameter indicates the maximum width of a character. The average width of a character is indicated by *avgchar*. The domain for these parameters are nonnegative numeric values.

Syntax:	`$WFONT(fontface,fontsize,fontstyle,unitspec)`

$WTFIT

Description:	This function returns the number of characters in the specified font and unit of measurement (*expr*) that can be displayed fully in the specified area (*numexpr*).
Syntax:	`$WTFIT(expr,numexpr,fontface,fontsize,fontstyle,unitspec)`

$WTWIDTH

Description:	This function returns the width of *expr* in the specified font and unit of measurement.
Syntax:	`$WTWIDTH(expr,fontface,fontsize,fontstyle,unitspec)`

Implementation

The sample program in this section uses a modified version of the Table gadget described in the Implementation section of Chapter 5 to demonstrate how MWAPI functions and special variables can be used to aid in GUI development. The functions described in the Functions section permit the allocation of a dynamic display area when the text to be displayed is unknown. This is an excellent example of *late binding,* or *dynamic allocation,* and will make the interface easier to develop. The use of $PD has been used and described throughout this book, and is used in this program. An intentional error condition has been created in tag ERROR to demonstrate $ER and $EC. The code used in Chapter 5 for the Table gadget is listed here for clarity, but the main differences are in tags SPVARS and ERROR.

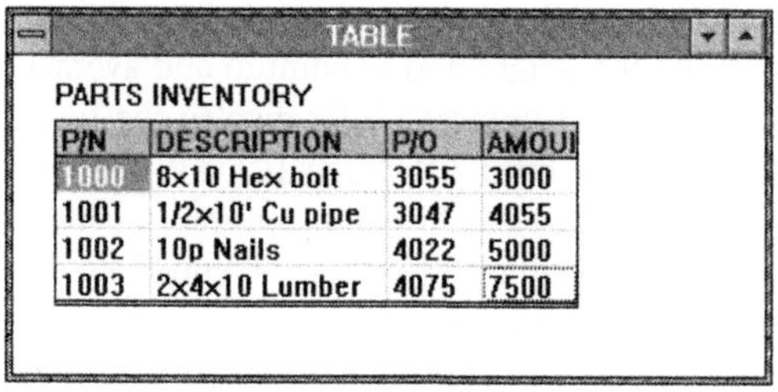

FIGURE 8.1: *Table*

```
TABLE ; table gadget
+1    K W,^$W
+2    S $ET="G ERROR^GADGETS"
+3    S W("WINDOW","TITLE")="TABLE"
+4    S W("WINDOW","SIZE")="370,150"
+5    S W("WINDOW","EVENT","CLOSE")="CLOSE^GADGETS"
+6    S W("WINDOW","G","TABLE","TYPE")="TABLE"
+7    S W("WINDOW","G","TABLE","POS")="20,30"
+8    S W("WINDOW","G","TABLE","TITLE")="PARTS INVENTORY"
+9    S W("WINDOW","G","TABLE","TYPE")="TABLE"
+10   S W("WINDOW","G","TABLE","EVENT","SELECT")="SEL7^GADGETS"
+11   S W("WINDOW","G","TABLE","EVENT","DESELECT")="SEL7^GADGETS"
+12   D ROWCOL
+13   M ^$W=W
+14   S ^$DI($PD,"FOCUS")="WINDOW,TABLE"
+15   ESTA
+16   Q

ROWCOL; set up choices for the table
+1    S U="^"
+2    S PART(0)="P/N"_U_"DESCRIPTION"_U_"P/O"_U_"AMOUNT"
+3    S PART(1)=1000_U_"8x10 Hex bolt"_U_3055_U_3000
+4    S PART(2)=1001_U_"1/2x10' Cu pipe"_U_3047_U_4055
+5    S PART(3)=1002_U_"10p Nails"_U_4022_U_5000
+6    S PART(4)=1003_U_"2x4x10 Lumber"_U_4075_U_7500
+7    F I=0:1:4 F J=1:1:4 D
+8    .S W("WINDOW","G","TABLE","CHOICE",I,J)=$P(PART(I),U,J)
+9    S W("WINDOW","G","TABLE","HROWID")=0
+10   D SPVARS
+11   S W("WINDOW","G","TABLE","COL",1,"COLWIDTH")=X1
+12   S W("WINDOW","G","TABLE","COL",2,"COLWIDTH")=X2
+13   S W("WINDOW","G","TABLE","COL",3,"COLWIDTH")=X3
+14   S W("WINDOW","G","TABLE","COL",4,"COLWIDTH")=X4
+15   S W("WINDOW","G","TABLE","LEFTSHOW")=1
+16   S W("WINDOW","G","TABLE","TOPSHOW")=1
+17   Q
```

SPVARS; determine column widths and show special variables

Functions are used to determine the column width needed to fully display the text in array "PART," and the gadget's size (see lines 5 through 18). $WFONT is used in line 5 to determine the height and maximum and average width of a character in the current font. The width required to fully display the text for each column is found by using $WTWIDTH (see lines 7 through 10). $WTFIT returns the number of characters that may be displayed by a cell in each column (see lines 11 through 14 and 30 through 33). The width of the table gadget is determined by the assignment in line 16. The size of the maximum character for the font is added to each column to make space for the display of grid lines in the gadget. The height required by the gadget is determined by multiplying the number of row by the height and external leading of the character cell (see lines 15 and 17). Two pixels times the number of rows is added to the height for the grid lines. The values for the X and Y coordinates are assigned to the gadget's SIZE attribute in line 18. This procedure dynamically allocates the gadget's area when the size of the display text is not fully understood, or only the area required to display the value is used. The output of this tag shows the values used and is shown below line 34.

```
+1 ;
+2 S FSIZE=^$DI($PD,"FSIZE")
+3 S FSTYLE=^$DI($PD,"FSTYLE")
+4 S UNITS=^$DI($PD,"UNITS")
```

Since there has been no change in the font defined for the current logical display, the values from the display may be used. $PD is used as a shorthand method of indicating the name of the current logical display.

```
+5  S FSPEC=$WFONT(FFACE,FSIZE,FSTYLE,UNITS)
+6  S T=$P(FSPEC,",",2) ; 1 blank in the maximum character width
+7  S X1=$WTWIDTH($P(PART(2),U,1),FFACE,FSIZE,FSTYLE,UNITS)+T
+8  S X2=$WTWIDTH($P(PART(2),U,2),FFACE,FSIZE,FSTYLE,UNITS)+T
+9  S X3=$WTWIDTH($P(PART(2),U,3),FFACE,FSIZE,FSTYLE,UNITS)+T
+10 S X4=$WTWIDTH($P(PART(0),U,4),FFACE,FSIZE,FSTYLE,UNITS)+T
+11 S T1=$WTFIT($P(PART(2),U,1),X1+T,FFACE,FSIZE,FSTYLE,UNITS)
+12 S T2=$WTFIT($P(PART(2),U,2),X2+T,FFACE,FSIZE,FSTYLE,UNITS)
+13 S T3=$WTFIT($P(PART(2),U,3),X3+T,FFACE,FSIZE,FSTYLE,UNITS)
+14 S T4=$WTFIT($P(PART(0),U,4),X4+T,FFACE,FSIZE,FSTYLE,UNITS)
+15 S X=+FSPEC
+16 S GX=X1+X2+X3+X4+5
+17 S GY=X*5+(2*4) ; include space for the grid lines
+18 S W("WINDOW","G","TABLE","SIZE")=GX_","_GY
+19 W !,"The principal display for this M process is: ",$PD
+20 W !,"The height of the character cell plus external leading "
+21 W "is ",+FSPEC," ",UNITS,"S."
+22 W !,"The maximum width for a character in this font is "
+23 W $P(FSPEC,",",2)," ",UNITS,"S."
+24 W !,"The average width for a character in this font is "
+25 W $P(FSPEC,",",3)," ",UNITS,"S."
+26 W !,"The width of the 1st column is ",X1," ",UNITS_"S."
+27 W !,"The width of the 2nd column is ",X2," ",UNITS_"S."
+28 W !,"The width of the 3rd column is ",X3," ",UNITS_"S."
+29 W !,"The width of the 4th column is ",X4," ",UNITS_"S."
+30 W !,T1," characters will fit in the 1st column."
+31 W !,T2," characters will fit in the 2nd column."
+32 W !,T3," characters will fit in the 3rd column."
+33 W !,T4," characters will fit in the 4th column."
+34 Q
```

```
The principal display for this M process is: 300
The height of the character cell plus external leading is 16 PIXELS.
The maximum width for a character in this font is 14 PIXELS.
The average width for a character in this font is 7 PIXELS.
```

```
The width of the 1st column is 46 PIXELS.
The width of the 2nd column is 115 PIXELS.
The width of the 3rd column is 46 PIXELS
The width of the 4th column is 72 PIXELS.
4 characters will fit in the 1st column.
15 characters will fit in the 2nd column.
4 characters will fit in the 3rd column.
6 characters will fit in the 4th column.

CLOSE ; close the parent window
+1  S WINDOW=^$E("WINDOW")
+2  K ^$W(WINDOW)
+3  ESTO
+4  Q


SEL7 ; select and deselect events for TABLE
+1  ;
+2  S ELEMENT=^$E("ELEMENT")
+3  S ELTYPE=$P($E(ELEMENT),",")
+4  S ELEMENT=$E(ELEMENT,3,$L(ELEMENT))
+5  S TYPE=^$E("TYPE")
+6  S ROWSUB=^$E("ROW")
+7  S COLSUB=^$E("COL")
+8  S VALUE=^$W(WINDOW,ELTYPE,ELEMENT,"VALUE",ROWSUB,COLSUB)
+9  S CHOICE=^$W(WINDOW,ELTYPE,ELEMENT,"CHOICE",ROWSUB+10,COLSUB)
```

Line 9 produces an error because it references a nonexistent cell in the Table gadget. When the flow of execution is directed (see line 1) to tag ERROR, the SSVN reference that caused the error is written to the screen. The value of $EREF is ^$W("WINDOW","G","TABLE","CHOICE",12,1).

```
+10 W !,"A ",TYPE," event has occurred for gadget "_ELEMENT
+11 W !,"The choice just ",TYPE_"ED"," is: "_CHOICE
+12 W !,"The subscripts associated with the selected choice are :"
+13 W ROWSUB,",",COLSUB
+14 W !
+15 Q
ERROR ;display $EREF
+1  W !,"$EREF = ",$ER
+2  W !,"$ECODE = ",$EC
+3  S $EC="" ; reset error handling
+4  Q
```

Highlights

The MWAPI specification introduces several useful special variables and functions to work with the unique properties of a GUI environment. These variables and functions are available to any process running a conforming implementation of the MWAPI.

An application can determine the current logical display by referencing the variable $PD. The examples in this book use $PD to reference the current logical display, and make the reference more flexible than hard coding the value. The listing of M error codes has been modified to include entries specific to the workings of the MWAPI. If an error occurs because of a MWAPI SSVN node, the value of $ECODE will contain the MWAPI error code, and $EREF returns a reference to the node. The combination of error code and $EREF reference serves as useful debugging tools.

Three text-related functions are introduced: $WFONT, $WTFIT, and $WTWIDTH. These functions are useful in development and helpful in dynamically determining the area needed to display a string of characters.

The next chapter brings the combined information in this book together in a functional application. The program provides an opportunity to introduce some additional aspects of the MWAPI specification.

Exercises

1. List and briefly describe the special variables and functions introduced by the MWAPI specification.

2. What function is used to find the width necessary to display a string of text?

3. If an error occurs, what variable will contain the error code? SSVN node reference?

4. How can font functions aid in the development process?

Summary

9

The previous chapters discussed the tools needed to develop standard windowing applications using the MWAPI. This chapter brings these methods and concepts together into a functional application. The checking account database application was designed to reinforce what has been taught and demonstrated, show how objects can be designed to work with each other, and introduce the capability for dynamic binding. Figures of the interfaces and source code are included so you can follow along and see how the application was created.

The figures in the previous chapters were created with MS Windows 3.1 as the underlying windowing platform. They maintain the environment's look-and-feel characteristics. The figures in this chapter use MS Windows NT as the platform, and inherit its respective look-and-feel characteristics. The syntax of the source code is exactly the same for both, demonstrating how the look and feel of the underlying platform is maintained regardless of the platform. Figure 9.1 shows the main interface into the application.

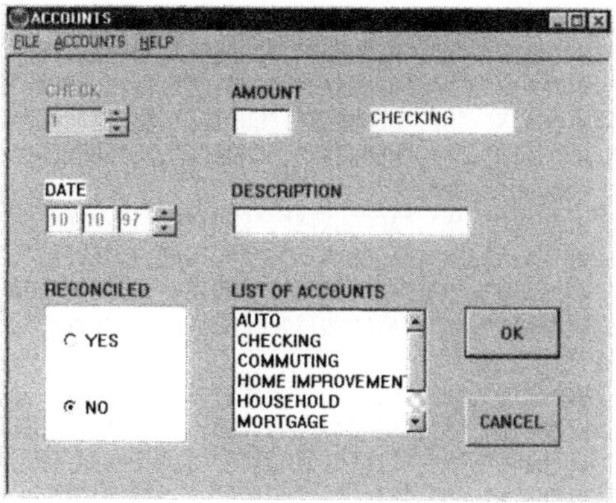

FIGURE 9.1: *Check Book Interface*

The positioning of the elements of the window shown in Figure 9.1 demonstrates a coherence of order: the checking label follows the amount that follows the check number, and "date" and "reconciled" are positioned below each other. Note that the source code specifies the elements and the values of their POS attributes in random order. If all the definitions to be used when an interface is created are defined, the order used for organizing the arguments is not significant. When the statements are merged into the Window SSVN, they are assigned in collating order. The effects of merging the source code into the Window SSVN are displayed only after all the assignments have taken place, both intrinsic and explicit.

```
EN   S $ET="G ERR" ; define error handler
; Other windows may be in use, so kill only those used by this application.
N W K^$W("MAIN"),^$W("HELP"),^$W("ERR")
MAIN ; main window
+1   S W("MAIN","TITLE")="ACCOUNTS"
+2   S W("MAIN","POS")="40,40"
+3   S W("MAIN","SIZE")="500,350"
+4   S W("MAIN","MENUBAR")="MENUBAR"
+5   S W("MAIN","NEXTG")="NUMBER"
+6   S W("MAIN","DEFBUTTON")="OK"
+7   S W("MAIN","EVENT","CLOSE")="CLOSE^CHECKING"
+8   S W("MAIN","G","NUMBER","ACTIVE")=0
+9   S W("MAIN","G","NUMBER","NEXTG")="SCROLL1"
```

The first time window MAIN alone receives focus (^$DI($PD,"FOCUS") is equal to "MAIN"), the statement made by line 5 will direct input to Gadget NUMBER. The statement at line 8 defines NUMBER to be an inactive gadget, and cannot receive focus. Since the gadget's NEXTG attribute defines a gadget that cannot receive focus, focus is directed to its value (see line 9). If the user presses the return key when the window has focus (window or window and child), line 6 indicates a select event may occur for Gadget OK. If the EVENT attribute node does not exist or is disabled in OK, callback processing will not occur.

```
+10  ; menus
+11  S W("MAIN","M","MENUBAR","CHOICE",1)="&FILE"
+12  S W("MAIN","M","MENUBAR","CHOICE",1,"SUBMENU")="FILE"
+13  S W("MAIN","M","MENUBAR","CHOICE",2)="&ACCOUNTS"
+14  S W("MAIN","M","MENUBAR","CHOICE",2,"SUBMENU")="ACCOUNTS"
+15  ; accounts menu
+16  S W("MAIN","M","ACCOUNTS","CHOICE",1)="&CHECKING"
+17  S W("MAIN","M","ACCOUNTS","CHOICE",1,"EVENT","SELECT")="SEL^CHECKING"
+18  S W("MAIN","M","ACCOUNTS","CHOICE",2)="&SAVINGS"
+19  S W("MAIN","M","ACCOUNTS","CHOICE",2,"EVENT","SELECT")="SEL^CHECKING"
+20  ; file menu
+21  S W("MAIN","M","FILE","CHOICE",1)="&NEW"
+22  S W("MAIN","M","FILE","CHOICE",1,"EVENT","SELECT")="NEW^CHECKING"
+23  S W("MAIN","M","FILE","CHOICE",1,"SEPARATOR")=""
+24  S W("MAIN","M","FILE","CHOICE",2)="&PRINT"
+25  S W("MAIN","M","FILE","CHOICE",2,"EVENT","SELECT")="PRINT^CHECKING"
```

```
+26  S W("MAIN","M","FILE","CHOICE",2,"ACTIVE")=0
+27  S W("MAIN","M","FILE","CHOICE",2,"SEPARATOR")=""
+28  S W("MAIN","M","FILE","CHOICE",3)="&SAVE"
+29  S W("MAIN","M","FILE","CHOICE",3,"EVENT","SELECT")="FILE^CHECKING"
+30  S W("MAIN","M","FILE","CHOICE",4)="SAVE &AS"
+31  S W("MAIN","M","FILE","CHOICE",4,"ACTIVE")=0
+32  S W("MAIN","M","FILE","CHOICE",4,"SEPARATOR")=""
+33  S W("MAIN","M","FILE","CHOICE",5)="E&XIT"
+34  S W("MAIN","M","FILE","CHOICE",5,"EVENT","SELECT")="CLOSE^CHECKING"
+35  ;gadgets
+36  ; check number
+37  S W("MAIN","G","NUMBER","TYPE")="TEXT"
+38  S W("MAIN","G","NUMBER","POS")="30,40"
+39  S W("MAIN","G","NUMBER","SIZE")="50,25"
+40  S W("MAIN","G","NUMBER","BCOLOR")="65535,65535,0"
+41  S W("MAIN","G","NUMBER","TITLE")="CHECK"
+42  ; set the initial value with the last check number used + 1
+43  S MWNUM=$P($G(^CHECK(0)),"^",2)+1
+44  S W("MAIN","G","NUMBER","VALUE")=MWNUM
+45  ; scroll for check number
+46  S W("MAIN","G","SCROLL1","TYPE")="SCROLL"
+47  S W("MAIN","G","SCROLL1","POS")="80,40"
+48  S W("MAIN","G","SCROLL1","SIZE")="20,25"
+49  S W("MAIN","G","SCROLL1","SCROLLDIR")="V"
+50  S W("MAIN","G","SCROLL1","SCROLLRANGE")="1,10000"
+51  S W("MAIN","G","SCROLL1","NEXTG")="AMOUNT"
+52  S W("MAIN","G","SCROLL1","VALUE")=MWNUM
+53  S W("MAIN","G","SCROLL1","EVENT","SELECT")="SCROLL^CHECKING"
```

Gadgets NUMBER and SCROLL1 demonstrate the use of two elements working in conjunction with each other to get and display a value. Since NUMBER is inactive, the user cannot directly assign its value. The design for this application has the user use SCROLL1 to change the value of NUMBER. The value of NUMBER is initially set equal to the value of SCROLL1, and equality is maintained by tag SCROLL. When callback processing is directed to the processing routine for SCROLL1, the value is assigned to NUMBER. The application can also cause a select event for SCROLL1. Tag ETR is called in several places to generate such an event. Since the gadget's SCROLLBY attribute is not explicitly defined, the default of one increment or decrement of the gadget's value is used for each click on the scroll arrows.

```
+54  ; check amount
+55  S W("MAIN","G","AMOUNT","POS")="185,40"
+56  S W("MAIN","G","AMOUNT","SIZE")="50,25"
+57  S W("MAIN","G","AMOUNT","TYPE")="TEXT"
+58  S W("MAIN","G","AMOUNT","TITLE")="AMOUNT"
+59  S W("MAIN","G","AMOUNT","NEXTG")="SCROLL2"
+60  ; description of the transaction
+61  S W("MAIN","G","DESCRIPTION","POS")="185,120"
+62  S W("MAIN","G","DESCRIPTION","SIZE")="200,25"
+63  S W("MAIN","G","DESCRIPTION","TYPE")="TEXT"
```

```
+64  S W("MAIN","G","DESCRIPTION","TITLE")="DESCRIPTION"
+65  S W("MAIN","G","DESCRIPTION","NEXTG")="ACCOUNTS"
+66  ; date - month
+67  S W("MAIN","G","MONTH","TYPE")="TEXT"
+68  S W("MAIN","G","MONTH","POS")="30,120"
+69  S W("MAIN","G","MONTH","SIZE")="30,25"
+70  S W("MAIN","G","MONTH","ACTIVE")=0
+71  ; date - day
+72  S W("MAIN","G","DAY","TYPE")="TEXT"
+73  S W("MAIN","G","DAY","POS")="60,120"
+74  S W("MAIN","G","DAY","SIZE")="30,25"
+75  S W("MAIN","G","DAY","ACTIVE")=0
+76  ; date - year
+77  S W("MAIN","G","YEAR","TYPE")="TEXT"
+78  S W("MAIN","G","YEAR","POS")="90,120"
+79  S W("MAIN","G","YEAR","SIZE")="30,25"
+80  S W("MAIN","G","YEAR","ACTIVE")=0
+81  ; values for MONTH, DAY and YEAR
+82  S MWDATE=$H
+83  D MMDDYY(MWDATE)
+84  S W("MAIN","G","MONTH","VALUE")=MWMTH
+85  S W("MAIN","G","DAY","VALUE")=MWDAY
+86  S W("MAIN","G","YEAR","VALUE")=MWYR
+87  ; scroll for date
+88  S W("MAIN","G","SCROLL2","TYPE")="SCROLL"
+89  S W("MAIN","G","SCROLL2","POS")="120,120"
+90  S W("MAIN","G","SCROLL2","SIZE")="20,25"
+91  S W("MAIN","G","SCROLL2","SCROLLDIR")="V"
+92  S W("MAIN","G","SCROLL2","SCROLLRANGE")="-30,30"
+93  S W("MAIN","G","SCROLL2","NEXTG")="DESCRIPTION"
+94  S W("MAIN","G","SCROLL2","EVENT","SELECT")="SCROLL^CHECKING"
```

The user cannot directly assign value to gadgets MONTH, DAY, and YEAR, and the method for updating these values is similar to the method used for Gadget NUMBER. When user causes the value of SCROLL2 to change, the new value is added to the internal date to determine the values of MONTH, DAY, and YEAR. Since the gadget's SCROLLBY attribute is not explicitly defined, the default of one increment or decrement of the gadget's value is used for each click on the scroll arrows.

```
+95  ; reconciled group
+96  S W("MAIN","G","RECONCILED","TYPE")="RADIO"
+97  S W("MAIN","G","RECONCILED","POS")="30,200"
+98  S W("MAIN","G","RECONCILED","SIZE")="120,110"
+99  S W("MAIN","G","RECONCILED","TITLE")="RECONCILED"
+100 S W("MAIN","G","RECONCILED","CHOICE",1)="YES"
+101 S W("MAIN","G","RECONCILED","CHOICE",2)="NO"
+102 S W("MAIN","G","RECONCILED","NEXTG")="OK"
+103 ; list of accounts
+104 D ACCOUNTS ; get choices in alphabetical order
+105 S W("MAIN","G","ACCOUNTS","TYPE")="LIST"
+106 S W("MAIN","G","ACCOUNTS","POS")="185,200"
```

196

```
+107  S  W("MAIN","G","ACCOUNTS","SIZE")="165,115"
+108  S  W("MAIN","G","ACCOUNTS","TITLE")="LIST OF ACCOUNTS"
+109  S  W("MAIN","G","ACCOUNTS","NEXTG")="RECONCILED"
+110  ; ok button
+111  S  W("MAIN","G","OK","TYPE")="BUTTON"
+112  S  W("MAIN","G","OK","POS")="380,200"
+113  S  W("MAIN","G","OK","SIZE")="80,40"
+114  S  W("MAIN","G","OK","TITLE")="OK"
+115  S  W("MAIN","G","OK","NEXTG")="CANCEL"
+116  S  W("MAIN","G","OK","EVENT","SELECT")="FILE^CHECKING"
+117  ; cancel button
+118  S  W("MAIN","G","CANCEL","TYPE")="BUTTON"
+119  S  W("MAIN","G","CANCEL","POS")="380,270"
+120  S  W("MAIN","G","CANCEL","SIZE")="80,40"
+121  S  W("MAIN","G","CANCEL","TITLE")="CANCEL"
+122  S  W("MAIN","G","CANCEL","EVENT","SELECT")="RESTORE^CHECKING"
```

FIGURE 9.2: *Pop-up File Menu*

```
+123  S  W("MAIN","EVENT","CLICK")="POPUP^CHECKING"
+124  S  W("MAIN","EVENT","CLICK","FILTERIN")="PB3"
```

If the user causes a click event for the window MAIN when the rightmost pointer button is depressed, tag POPUP is called to process the event. Lines 123 and 124 define these attributes. POPUP displays the menu "FILE" as a pop-up menu at the current position of the pointer. This is achieved by defining the menu's POS and VISIBLE attributes (see tag POPUP). ^$E("PPOS") is referenced to position the menu at the current pointer position, and it is made visible by assigning one to the VISIBLE attribute. Prior to the call to POPUP the menu's POS and VISIBLE attributes are not explicitly defined, but afterwards they are. This menu is also used for the submenu for choice "file" in the menubar. It may appear contradictory for a menu to be displayed adjacent to the menubar while its POS attribute has been explicitly set to some other coordinate value. This works because the POS and VISIBLE attribute values are ignored when the menu is used as the menubar or a submenu.

```
+125  TIMER ; set the inactivity timer - close if no activity
+126  S  MWTIME=300
+127  S  W("MAIN","T","TIMER","INTERVAL")=MWTIME
+128  S  W("MAIN","T","TIMER","EVENT","TIMER")="CHKACT^CHECKING"
```

The syntax in lines 126 through 127 define a timer object that will generate an event and call tag CHKACT every three hundred seconds unless canceled. The purpose of this timer is to check for inactivity. Each time a callback is received, tag CHKACT compares the event sequence to its previous value to determine activity. If no activity occurred during three hundred seconds, an ETRIGGER execution triggers a close event for the parent window. If there has been activity, the timer restarts from its current interval value.

FIGURE 9.3: *Help Window*

```
+129 S W("MAIN","M","MENUBAR","CHOICE",3)="&HELP"
+130 S W("MAIN","M","MENUBAR","CHOICE",3,"EVENT","SELECT")="HELP^CHECKING"
```

The default size for a window is an area that will surround all its visible child gadgets whose POS attribute values do not include negative numbers. If choice HELP is selected, tag HELP will dynamically allocate a window with only gadgets specified. This window demonstrates dynamic allocation. It also demonstrates that any window can be created by defining only its gadgets. The window becomes immediately visible upon the conclusion of the MERGE operation into ^$W. When the Gadget "OK" is selected, only window "HELP," and its children, are destroyed.

```
+131 ; account notification label
+132 S W("MAIN","G","NOTE","TYPE")="LABEL"
+133 S W("MAIN","G","NOTE","POS")="300,40"
+134 S W("MAIN","G","NOTE","SIZE")="120,20"
+135 S W("MAIN","G","NOTE","TITLE")="CHECKING"
+136 S W("MAIN","G","NOTE","FCOLOR")="65535,0,0"
+137 M ^$W("MAIN")=W("MAIN") ; create window main
+138 ; date - label
+139 S W("MAIN","G","DATE","TYPE")="LABEL"
+140 S W("MAIN","G","DATE","POS")="30,100"
+141 S FACE=^$DI($PD,"FFACE")
+142 S STYLE=^$DI($PD,"FSTYLE")
+143 S SIZE=^$DI($PD,"FSIZE")
+144 S UNITS=^$DI($PD,"UNITS")
```

```
+145 S X=$WTWIDTH("DATE",FACE,SIZE,STYLE,UNITS)
+146 S Y=+$WFONT(FACE,SIZE,STYLE,UNITS)
+147 S W("MAIN","G","DATE","SIZE")=X_","_Y
+148 S W("MAIN","G","DATE","TITLE")="DATE"
+149 M ^$W("MAIN","G","DATE")=W("MAIN","G","DATE") ; create gadget DATE
```

Gadget's NOTE and DATE are both label gadgets, and they take different approaches to determine the areas to allocate for the displays of their values. The SIZE attribute defined for the gadgets shown in this chapter allocate an arbitrary area for their display. Given the actual size of the object, or text value, this may be wasteful. DATE demonstrates how to use MWAPI font functions to determine the exact size needed. The current font of the current logical display is used to determine the font values needed by these functions.

Both elements and elements can be added to the parent at anytime as demonstrated with gadget "DATE." The assignment of elements to windows and windows to logical displays cannot be made when their maximum numbers have been reached. The assignment of a menubar for a window, after it has been created, can be ignored by the host windowing system.

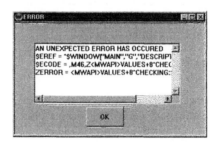

FIGURE 9.4: *Error Window*

```
+150 ; error window
+151 S X=^$DI($PD,"SIZE")
+152 S Y=$P(X,",",2),X=+X
+153 S X=X\2-200,Y=Y\2-113
+154 S W("ERR","POS")=X_","_Y
+155 S W("ERR","VISIBLE")=0
+156 S W("ERR","TITLE")="ERROR"
+157 S W("ERR","SIZE")="400,225"
+158 S W("ERR","G","MESS","POS")="40,40"
+159 S W("ERR","G","MESS","SIZE")="310,125"
+160 S W("ERR","G","MESS","TYPE")="DOCUMENT"
+161 S W("ERR","G","MESS","SCROLL")="1,1"
+162 S W("ERR","G","OK","POS")="150,170"
+163 S W("ERR","G","OK","SIZE")="80,40"
+164 S W("ERR","G","OK","TYPE")="BUTTON"
+165 S W("ERR","G","OK","TITLE")="OK"
+166 S W("ERR","G","OK","EVENT","SELECT")="CLOSE^CHECKING"
+167 M ^$W("ERR")=W("ERR") ; create the error window
```

199

If an error occurs during execution of this program, tag ERR is called to handle it. The code from lines 151 to 167 define the window that is displayed to notify the user of the error and give some indication of the problem. Window ERR is created invisible until execution is directed to tag ERR. When an error occurs, the window's VISIBLE attribute is set to one, and the window is displayed in the center of the current logical display. The code at line 151 gets the size of the current logical display, lines 152 and 153 determine the horizontal and vertical coordinates that will position the error window in its center. After the calculations are done, the window's position is assigned in line 154. The error information is concatenated in tag ERR using the ASCII codes for a carriage return and line feed. When the error window displays the text is formatted, as shown by Figure 9.4.

```
+168 S ^$DI($PD,"FOCUS")="MAIN"
+169 ESTA 9000
+170 Q
```

As line 169 indicates, event processing is active for 9000 seconds. Since the ESTART command includes a time-out, test of $T will indicate how event processing was terminated. If an ESTOP command execution terminates processing, $T will have the value of one. A zero value indicates will indicate termination in another manner, such as expiration of the time-out period.

```
ERR ; Handle any errors
N X
K ^$W("MAIN")
N X S ^$W("ERR","VISIBLE")=1
S X="AN UNEXPECTED ERROR HAS OCCURED"_$C(13,10)
S X=X_"$EREF = "_$ER_$C(13,10)_"$ECODE = "_$EC
S X=X_$C(13,10)_"ZERROR = "_$ZE
; $C(13,10) is the code for a carriage return line feed
S ^$W("ERR","G","MESS","VALUE")=X
Q
;
ACCOUNTS ; creates accounts list in alphabetical order.
N P
S P="CHECKING^SAVINGS^HOUSEHOLD^UTILITIES^AUTO"
S P=P_"^MORTGAGE^HOME IMPROVEMENT^COMMUTING"
F I=1:1:8 D
.S W("MAIN","G","ACCOUNTS","CHOICE",$P(P,"^",I))=$P(P,"^",I)
Q
;
SEL ; Process select events for ACCOUNTS menu
D WINELM
S X=^$E("CHOICE")
S X=^$W(WINDOW,"T",ELEMENT,"CHOICE",X)
; The name of the choice may include an ampersand, so filter any.
S X=$TR(X,"&")
S ^$W("MAIN","G","NOTE","TITLE")=X
Q
```

```
;
CLOSE ; destroy a window
D WINELMT
K ^$E("OK")
K ^$W(WINDOW)
ESTO:WINDOW="MAIN"
Q
;
CHKACT     ; If there is no activity in 300 seconds, quit the program.
S NEWSEQ=^$E("SEQUENCE")
I NEWSEQ-1=SEQUENCE D
.; Since no events occurred during the timer interval, trigger a close event for
the "MAIN"
.; window.
.ETR ^$W("MAIN","EVENT","CLOSE")
.S SEQUENCE=NEWSEQ
Q
;
WINELMT ; Determine the window, element type and name for the event
; Get the sequence of each event so a comparison can be made in tag CHKACT.
S SEQUENCE=^$E("SEQUENCE")
; Get the name of the window where the event was directed. The value may not be the
; window with focus.
S WINDOW=^$E("WINDOW")
S X=$G(^$E("ELEMENT")) ; If the event occurred for an element, X will follow null.
S ELTYPE=$P(X,",",1) ; Get the element's type.
S ELEMENT=$P(X,",",2) ; Get the element's name.
Q
;
ETR ; Trigger a select event for SCROLL1.
ETR ^$W("MAIN","G","SCROLL1","EVENT","SELECT") Q
;
SCROLL ; this tag processes SELECT events for the SCROLL gadgets
D WINELMT
S X=^$W("MAIN","G",ELEMENT,"VALUE")
I ELEMENT="SCROLL1" D
.; Update NUMBER's value to that of SCROLL1.
.S ^$W("MAIN","G","NUMBER","VALUE")=X
.D LOOKUP(X)
I ELEMENT="SCROLL2" D
.; Increment the date.
.S MWSDATE=$G(MWSDATE,MWDATE)
.D DATE(MWSDATE+X)
Q
;
LOOKUP(X) ; Display the detail for a check.
S CHECK0="",U="^"
S IEN=$O(^CHECK("B",X,""))
S:IEN CHECK0=^CHECK(IEN,0)
S MWNUM=X,MWDATE=$P(CHECK0,U,2),MWDESC=$P(CHECK0,U,3)
S MWREC=$P(CHECK0,U,4),MWACC=$P(CHECK0,U,5)
S MWAMT=$P(CHECK0,U,6)
```

```
S:'MWDATE MWDATE=+$H
S MWSDATE=MWDATE
S:MWREC="" MWREC=2
D VALUES ; Assign values to gadgets in window MAIN.
Q
;
RESTORE ; Cancel and restore the old values.
S X=$S(MWNUM=1:1,1:MWNUM-1)
S W("MAIN","G","SCROLL1","VALUE")=X
D ETR
; Trigger a select event for SCROLL1 and get and display the values.
Q
;
UPDATE ; Increment the check number.
S MWNUM=$P($G(^CHECK(0)),"^",2)+1
S ^$W("MAIN","G","SCROLL1","VALUE")=MWNUM
Q
;
NEW ; new record
D UPDATE
D ETR ; Trigger a select event for SCROLL1 and display the new values.
Q
;
VALUES ; Assign values to the gadget in MAIN.
; Clear all selected choices from "ACCOUNTS."
K ^$W("MAIN","G","ACCOUNTS","VALUE")
; The check number and date are assigned by tags SCROLL an MMDDYY
; respectively
; List of gadgets to assign values and display.
S X="DESCRIPTION^RECONCILED^ACCOUNTS^AMOUNT"
S T=MWDESC_U_MWREC_U_MWACC_U_MWAMT
F I=1:1:4 D
.S GADGET=$P(X,U,I)
.I GADGET="ACCOUNTS" D Q
..S:$P(T,U,I)]"" ^$W("MAIN","G",GADGET,"VALUE",$P(T,U,I))=""
.S ^$W("MAIN","G",GADGET,"VALUE")=$P(T,U,I)
D DATE(MWDATE)
Q
;
HELP ; Create and display the help window only when called.
N X
S X("HELP","G","MESS","POS")="40,40"
S X("HELP","G","MESS","SIZE")="200,125"
S X("HELP","G","MESS","TYPE")="DOCUMENT"
S T="THIS APPLICATION WAS DEVELOPED TO DEMONSTRATE AND DESCRIBE A MWAPI APPLICATION"
S X("HELP","G","MESS","VALUE")=T
S X("HELP","G","OK","POS")="80,165"
S X("HELP","G","OK","SIZE")="80,40"
S X("HELP","G","OK","TYPE")="BUTTON"
S X("HELP","G","OK","TITLE")="OK"
S X("HELP","G","OK","EVENT","SELECT")="CLOSE^CHECKING"
M ^$W("HELP")=X("HELP") ; create the help window
```

```
Q
;
FILE ; file the data
S X="",U="^"
; check number
S $P(X,U,1)=$G(^$W("MAIN","G","NUMBER","VALUE"))
; check date
S $P(X,U,2)=MWDATE
; description of the check
S $P(X,U,3)=$G(^$W("MAIN","G","DESCRIPTION","VALUE"))
; reconcile 1-YES/2-NO
S $P(X,U,4)=^$W("MAIN","G","RECONCILED","VALUE")
; account
S $P(X,U,5)=$O(^$W("MAIN","G","ACCOUNTS","VALUE",""))
; amount
S $P(X,U,6)=$G(^$W("MAIN","G","AMOUNT","VALUE"))
;
S IEN=$O(^CHECK("B",+X,""))
I 'IEN D
.S IEN=$P($G(^CHECK(0)),U,3)+1
.S $P(^CHECK(0),U,3)=IEN ; last ien used
.S $P(^CHECK(0),U,2)=+X ; last check number used
.S ^CHECK("B",+X,IEN)=""
S ^CHECK(IEN,0)=X
D NEW
S ^$DI($PD,"FOCUS")="MAIN"
Q
;
SELECT ; process SELECT events
D WINELMT
I ELEMENT="ACCOUNTS",WINDOW="MAIN" D
.S X=^$E("CHOICE")
.S ACCOUNT=^$W(WINDOW,ELTYPE,ELEMENT,"CHOICE",X)
Q
;
DATE(X) ; Set month, day, year values.
D MMDDYY(X)
S ^$W("MAIN","G","MONTH","VALUE")=MWMTH
S ^$W("MAIN","G","DAY","VALUE")=MWDAY
S ^$W("MAIN","G","YEAR","VALUE")=MWYR
Q
;
MMDDYY(X) ; Get month, day and year
S %DN=X D 400^%DO
S MWMTH=$P(%DS,"/",1),MWDAY=$P(%DS,"/",2)
S MWYR=$P(%DS,"/",3)
Q
;
POPUP ; popup menu at cursor position
S ^$W("MAIN","M","FILE","POS")=^$E("PPOS")
S ^$W("MAIN","M","FILE","VISIBLE")=1
Q
```

Future Directions

The MDC is continuing to enhance this unique standard for GUI development. The real beauty of the MWAPI lies in its power, simplicity, and portability. The future developments such as Dynamic Data Exchange (DDE) support promises to make the MWAPI even more of a beauty.

The proliferation of windowing environments shows the direction market demand is putting on software development. The days of "roll and scroll" interfaces is numbered. GUI development is the game of today and will probably go on well into the future. The MWAPI offers a straightforward ANSI-approved method to meet the growing software demand.

There is a new frontier opening up for the M developer and it is with Internet applications and corporate intranets. Although the Internet itself is not new, its growing popularity is a recent phenomenon. Server software exists to access M databases and applications, so the M language is a natural choice for the string-handling needs of servers and clients. Conceivably M applications can be downloaded to client browsers and run using the resources of the host. Let the applications be written using the MWAPI and the client can have a consistent interface while preserving the platform's look-and-feel characteristics. The future indeed looks bright for the MWAPI, so jump on the wagon now.

Codes

This appendix lists MWAPI codes in three sections:

- Section One lists all keyboard, pointer button, and character codes.
- Error codes are listed in Section Two.
- Colors and their associated RGB values are shown in Section Three.

Section One

This section identifies the codes that indicate characters and keys from the keyboard and pointer buttons on the pointer device. Character and keycodes share many codes in common; however the difference is in the way a character can be represented.

The intention for character codes is to enable applications to focus on the characters received, rather than the keyboard action that produced the characters. This insulates applications from substantial complexity since keyboard design and languages are diverse. The following codes are common to indicate characters and keys on the keyboard:

1. The set of function keys indicated by Table A.1.
2. Characters represented by their graphical form: A for an uppercase "A" and 1 for the number "1." These characters are not represented by their ASCII value equivalents.
3. The word "COMMA." This word is used to indicate a comma character when the string of codes contains one or more comma delineators: A,COMMA,B.
4. An implementation defined value.

The domain for keycodes also includes modifier codes listed in Table A.2. These codes are used to describe characters only when used in conjunction with another code in the domain: the user pressing a code from the list above while a modifier key is pressed.

The plus character follows a modifier: ALT+A or CTRL+ALT+DEL. The SHIFT and SHIFTR modifiers are never used in combination with a graphic character.

Multiple key and character codes can be specified in the same string when delineated by comma characters. The string may not contain a mixture of code types. When a FILTERIN Event Specification Attribute nodes value lists multiple codes, all indicated codes must be indicated before the stated event type can receive a call back. Key and character codes can be shown by keyboard input, or stated in the data structure name component of the syntax of an executed ETRIGGER command.

TABLE A.1: *Function Key Codes*

CATEGORY	CODES	CATEGORY	CODES
CURSOR KEYS	UP	NON GRAPHIC	PAGEDOWN
	DOWN	(continued)	PAGEUP
	RIGHT		PAUSE
	LEFT		RET
FUNCTION KEYS	F1 – 24		SCRLLOCK
	PF1 – 4		SEL
NON GRAPHIC	BACKSPC		TAB
	BREAK	NUMERIC KEYPAD KEYS	NUM0 - 9
	CAPSLOCK		NUMDEC
	DEL		NUMDEL
	END		NUMDIV
	ENTER		NUMENTER
	ESC		NUMLOCK
	FIND		NUMMINUS
	HOME		NUMMULT
	INS		NUMPLUS
	NEXT		

TABLE A.2: *Modifier Key Codes*

ALT	CTRL
ALR	CTRLR
COMMAND	OPTION
COMPOSE	SHIFT
COMPOSER	SHIFTR

Buttons on the pointer device are represented by pointer buttons listed and described in Table A.3.

TABLE A.3: *Pointer Button Codes*

CODE	DESCRIPTION
PB1	Leftmost or only button.
PB2	If the pointer has three buttons, this code indicates the middle button.
PB3	Rightmost button.

Section Two

MWAPI error codes are listed in Table A.4. See the body of this book for cross references of these codes with version 1.0. The codes listed here will be used with future MWAPI enhancements.

TABLE A.4: *MWAPI Error Codes*

V 1.1	DESCRIPTION
M46	The attribute name is invalid for the display or entity.
M47	The value assigned is not within the attribute's domain.
M48	Reference made to a nonexistent entity.
M49	The attempt to set focus is invalid.
M50	Open command references a non-MTERM window.
M51	Attempt to destroy an MTERM window prior to closing it.
M52	The entity is missing a required attribute.
M53	The font function is using an invalid parameter.
M54	Non-modal child window specified or a modal parent.
M55	The nesting of the ESTART command is invalid.

Section Three

Table A.5 lists colors along with their RGB definitions. Colors are defined by their amounts of red, green, and blue colors (RGB).

TABLE A.5: *Color Codes*

COLOR	RGB VALUE
Black	0,0,0
Blue	0,0,65535
Cyan	0,65535,65535
Green	0,65535,0
Grey	49150,49150,49150
Red	65535,0,0
White	65535,65525,65535
Yellow	65535,65535,0

Answers to **Appendix** **B**
Chapter Exercises

This appendix contains the answers to the Exercise sections of each chapter. The answers in this appendix are grouped by chapter.

Chapter One

1. An in-depth knowledge of any windowing system's API is not necessary for the development of a complete windowing application using the MWAPI. Development using the standard MWAPI will provide portable applications that will run unmodified on any supported windowing or hardware platform. The MWAPI specification does allow for the customization of applications for a particular windowing or hardware platform.

2. The MWAPI system provides a system of inheritance designed for the passing down from the windowing platform to descendent objects look and feel characteristics in an attempt to maintain these characteristics in the descendent objects.

3. The MWAPI standard specifies an MWAPI implementation may operate separately from an underlying windowing platform. The implementation will provide the support that otherwise would have been provided to the MWAPI by an underlying windowing platform.

4. Logical displays are descended from the windowing platform, or the MWAPI implementation. Windows are descended from logical displays, and may also be descended from other windows. Gadgets, menus, and timers are inherited from windows. An event loop exists within each M process running an implementation of the MWAPI to detect and notify applications of events.

5. The MWAPI specification uses SSVNs to create and maintain the characteristics of objects. The Display SSVN (^$DI) contains the characteristics that make up logical displays. The Window SSVN (^$W) maintains the characteristics for all windowing entities. The Event SSVN (^$E) is used to return the characteristics of events to call back routines for processing.

6. Attributes are keywords used to describe characteristics of MWAPI objects. They are maintained as subscripts descended from the name of the object, or entity, they describe. Attributes assigned to an object, or entity, are maintained in the SSVN designed for the object or entity.

7. The values assigned to an attribute must fall within a specified value domain specified for the attribute. An error will occur if the assigned value is outside the domain for an attribute.

8. Not all attributes may be assigned to, nor are appropriate for, all object types. The type of object determines the attributes that may be used to describe it. An error will occur if an attribute is assigned to an inappropriate object.

9. MWAPI entities are created by the assignment of their attribute nodes to the Window SSVN.

10. Yes, terminal emulation is provided for legacy code by MTERM windows.

Chapter Two

1. The name of the Event SSVN is ^$EVENT and can be abbreviated as ^$E.

2. An application should reference the values of ^$E("WINDOW") and ^$E("ELEMENT") to determine an entity for which the call back occurred. The value of ^$E("WINDOW") will identify the window where the event occurred. A further check of ^$E("ELEMENT") should be made to determine if the event occurred for an element of the window. This approach will tell an application where callback processing is being directed regardless how the event was triggered.

3. Events normally occur as the result of user interaction with entities. An application may also cause an event to occur by executing an ETRIGGER command.

4. The modification to an SSVN reference will not cause a MWAPI event to occur.

5. The important differences between the MWAPI's call back approach to event processing and polling are: Define an event type to process within an entity's definition and when it occurs the MWAPI system throws an object defining characteristics of the event to the entity's event node for processing.

6. The ESTART command activates event processing and the ESTOP command deactivates it.

7. The ENABLE and FILTERIN Event Specification Attributes may be used to control the processing of certain specified event types when event processing is active. The ENABLE attribute determines whether event processing is enabled for the event type. The FILTERIN attribute specifies any keyboard or pointer

button codes that must be associated with the event before callback processing may occur.

8. After the execution of an ESTOP command, program execution continues with the code following the most recently executed ESTART command.

9. The processing for an event can be deferred by the execution of an ESTART command during callback processing. When this occurs, the contents of ^$E is placed on the stack and control is returned to the event loop.

10. Event processing may be deactivated by execution of the ESTOP command, time-out of the activity ESTART command, or temporarily during callback processing. Event processing temporarily deactivated during callback processing is reactivated when the current processing is complete.

11. The ETRIGGER command provides an application with a means to cause a event to occur.

12. The syntax of the ETRIGGER command permits the assignment of certain Event Information Attributes to be included in ^$E. This is necessary because not all the information required to describe an event fully is always available when triggered by an ETRIGGER.

Chapter Three

1. A physical display device may contain multiple logical displays.

2. The Display SSVN is used to describe the environment of logical displays where entities may exist and function.

3. The characteristics of each logical display are subscripted from the name of the logical display they describe. The first level subscript in ^$DI is the name of a logical display. It must be unique and acts to separate one from another.

4. Logical displays may overlap, but may not be shared among, or within, an M process. Logical displays are not visual objects, but they do occupy distinct, non-sharable, areas.

5. $PD is an intrinsic variable that returns the value of the current logical display.

6. The children of a logical display can only be windows, but a window does not have to be the child of a logical display. A window may be created as the child of another window. Since a window is not necessarily the direct descendent of a logical display, its default characteristics are not inherited from the display where it lives.

7. The initial values for these attributes are derived by settings of the underlying windowing platform or the MWAPI implementation.

8. Entities already created are not affected by the modification to an inherited Display Attribute node's value. All subsequently created entities will use the modified value.

9. User action will automatically cause focus to be updated to indicate the entity the user has selected.

Chapter Four

1. The parent of all MTERM windows is a logical display. An application window's PARENT attribute determines its parent. If the attribute node is undefined, its parent is a logical display. A defined PARENT attribute node will name another window the parent.

2. The MWAPI specification defines MTERM and application windows. MTERM windows provide terminal emulation for older code, and can be opened, used, and closed as a device. Application windows are GUI front ends to M code, may have child windows, contain elements, and process call backs. Implementors are permitted to define their own window types for their products.

3. A window consists of an application area, viewport, and window frame. The application area is a virtual space for the placement of the window's elements, and may provide the basis for their position. The viewport is an area of the window that allows the user to view some portion of the application area. A frame may surround a window's viewport, and can contain a menubar, a title bar with the window's title, and window controls.

4. A window is created by merging at least one of its attributes into the Window SSVN. A window created in this manner may default to an application. An MTERM window's TYPE attribute node must equal "MTERM" in such an assignment. An MTERM window is created and made visible by executing an OPEN command for an MTERM device.

5. A window can be created by the assignment of at least one of its attributes into the Window SSVN due to default values for unspecified and required characteristics.

6. All event types subscripted from an objects EVENT attribute node are able to receive call back processing, and the default is disabled by changing the node's ENABLE Event Specification Attribute to a zero value. The FILTERIN Event Specification Attribute is used by certain event types to restrict call back processing to certain character, key, and pointer button codes.

7. Example source code for the solution:

```
S WNAME="WINDOW"
K W,^$W(WNAME)
S WHSIZE=450,WVSIZE=250
S DSIZE=^$DI($PD,"SIZE")
S WHPOS=+DSIZE\2-(WHSIZE\2),WVPOS=$P(DSIZE,",",2)\2-(WVSIZE\2)
S W(WNAME,"POS")=WHPOS_","_WVPOS
S W(WNAME,"SIZE")=WHSIZE_","_WVSIZE_",POINT"
S W(WNAME,"TITLE")="Window Exercise"
S W(WNAME,"EVENT","CLOSE")="CLOSE^MWEXERC"
S W(WNAME,"EVENT","CLICK")="CLICK^MWEXERC"
S W(WNAME,"EVENT","CLICK","FILTERIN")="PB1"
S W(WNAME,"COLOR")="0,0,65525"
M ^$W(WNAME)=W(WNAME)
```

```
S ^$DI($PD,"FOCUS")="WINDOW"
ESTART
Q
;
CLOSE ; destroy a window
W !,"CLOSE"
S WCALLER=^$E("WINDOW")
K ^$W("WINDOW")
ESTOP
Q
;
CLICK ; process a click event
K W S DEV="TERM"
S W(DEV,"TITLE")="Pointer Position"
S W(DEV,"TYPE")="MTERM"
M ^$W(DEV)=W(DEV)
O DEV:::"MTERM"
U DEV W !?15,^$("PPOS")
R X C DEV K ^$W(DEV)
Q
```

Chapter Five

1. The choice category includes gadgets capable of displaying a list of selectable choices:

```
LIST BOX
LIST BUTTON
LIST ENTRY BOX
LONG LIST BOX
RADIO BUTTON SET
TABLE
```

The text category is made up or gadgets capable of displaying and eliciting text:

```
DOCUMENT
TEXT
LABEL
```

The LIST ENTRY BOX is a hybrid combining TEXT and LIST BOX gadgets into a common object. The third, miscellaneous category, includes the rest:

```
CHECK BOX
GENERIC BOX
GROUP FRAME
PUSH BUTTON
SCROLL
SYMBOL
```

2. At a minimum, an objects type, position, and size must be defined before creation.

3. Yes, the percent will be created using default values.

4. The list of attributes that can be assigned to a gadget is determined by the element's type.

5. The first subscript is the name of the parent window. The second subscript is the key letter "G" for gadget, and the third subscript is the name of the element. The attribute described is the keyword for the fourth subscript, and the node's value assigns quantity or quality to the attribute.

6. If the parent window's size is not specified through explicit assignment, it defaults large enough to encompass all visible gadgets with non-negative position coordinates.

7. Default values are passed down to gadgets from their parent windows.

8. The process looks at the NEXTG attributes of each gadget, indicated by the previous gadget's NEXTG attribute, for a gadget that may receive focus. This process is continued until either a gadget is found that can receive focus or the search fails. If the search finds no gadget to receive focus, focus will remain with the original gadget.

9. Value domains are usually the same for each attribute regardless of gadget type. The domain for a few attributes depend on the gadget type.

10. Tables are the only gadget types in the choice category that use cells to contain choices. The syntax for assigning choices to these gadgets must specify the rows and columns that define cells.

11. The gadget will receive a call back for a change event, and no unfocus event will occur.

12. The FILTERIN Event Specification Attribute is used to restrict certain event types to the addition of user keyboard or pointer button actions.

13. If during call back processing an ESTART command is executed, the event is deferred by stacking its characteristics for later processing. During execution the window must have its MODAL attribute node equal to "APPLICATION." Each executed ESTOP command or ESTART timeout will pop event characteristics off the stack.

14. Example source code for the solution:

```
S W(WNAME,"G","DOC","TYPE")="DOCUMENT"
S GVPOS=$P(^$W(WNAME,"SIZE"),",",2)\2
S W(WNAME,"G","DOC","POS")="30,"_GVPOS
S W(WNAME,"G","DOC","SIZE")="200,130"
S W(WNAME,"G","DOC","TITLE")="Comments"
S W(WNAME,"G","LBUTTON","TYPE")="LISTBUTTON"
S W(WNAME,"G","LBUTTON","TITLE")="Company"
S W(WNAME,"G","LBUTTON","POS")="30,50"
S W(WNAME,"G","LBUTTON","SIZE")="200,110"
S W(WNAME,"G","LBUTTON","EVENT","SELECT")="SEL^MWEXERC"
S C="SAIC,GEOMED INC.,WASHER INC.,INTELLECT CORP.,BOWER BROTHERS"
S C=C_",FORK CORP.,WEATHERBY INC.,BOBS SON"
F I=1:1 S X=$P(C,",",I) Q:X="" D
.S W(WNAME,"G","LBUTTON","CHOICE",X)=X
```

```
S GHPOS=+^$W(WNAME,"SIZE")\2
S W(WNAME,"G","LABEL1","TYPE")="LABEL"
S W(WNAME,"G","LABEL1","POS")=GHPOS_",50"
S W(WNAME,"G","LABEL1","SIZE")="100,15"
S W(WNAME,"G","LABEL2","TYPE")="LABEL"
S W(WNAME,"G","LABEL2","POS")=GHPOS_",70"
S W(WNAME,"G","LABEL2","SIZE")="100,15"
S W(WNAME,"G","LABEL3","TYPE")="LABEL"
S W(WNAME,"G","LABEL3","POS")=GHPOS_",90"
S W(WNAME,"G","LABEL3","SIZE")="100,15"
M ^$W(WNAME,"G")=W(WNAME,"G")
ESTART
Q
SEL S CHOICE=^$E("CHOICE")
; example ^COMPANY node
S ^COMPANY("SAIC")="10260 CAMPUS POINT COURT^SAN DIEGO,CA^92121"
S X=$G(^COMPANY(CHOICE),^COMPANY("SAIC"))
S ^$W(WNAME,"G","LABEL1","TITLE")=$P(X,"^",1)
S ^$W(WNAME,"G","LABEL2","TITLE")=$P(X,"^",2)
S ^$W(WNAME,"G","LABEL3","TITLE")=$P(X,"^",3)
Q
```

Chapter Six

1. Each draw command assigned to descendant nodes of the gadget's DRAW attribute is executed in collating sequence of its subscript to draw objects.

2. The Generic Box is the only gadget defined by the MWAPI to use draw commands. Implementor's of the MWAPI are permitted to define gadget types specified to use draw commands, but these are not guaranteed the portability of standard definitions.

3. Draw commands are assigned to descendent nodes, and the DRAW attribute node's value specifies the number of descended commands.

4. The value of the DRAWTYPE attribute's node identifies the type of draw commands assigned to descendant nodes of the gadget's DRAW attribute.

5. The values for the pen size, draw mode, fill pattern, unit of measurement, and background and foreground color can be changed to affect draw commands that follow in collating order of their DRAW attribute subscripts through the assignment of their respective draw commands.

6. Example source code for the solution:

```
S W(WNAME,"G","GEN","TYPE")="GENERIC"
S W(WNAME,"G","GEN","POS")=GHPOS_","_GVPOS
S W(WNAME,"G","GEN","SIZE")="200,130"
S W(WNAME,"G","GEN","DRAW",1)="BCOLOR,0,0,65535,TRANSPARENT"
S W(WNAME,"G","GEN","DRAW",2)="PIE,100,65,50,0,90"
S W(WNAME,"G","GEN","DRAW",3)="BCOLOR,65535,0,0,TRANSPARENT"
S W(WNAME,"G","GEN","DRAW",4)="PIE,100,65,50,90,180"
```

```
S W(WNAME,"G","GEN","DRAW",5)="BCOLOR,0,65535,0,TRANSPARENT"
S W(WNAME,"G","GEN","DRAW",6)="PIE,100,65,50,180,270"
S W(WNAME,"G","GEN","DRAW",7)="BCOLOR,0,0,65535,TRANSPARENT"
S W(WNAME,"G","GEN","DRAW",9)="PIE,100,65,50,270,360"
M ^$W(WNAME,"G","GEN")=W(WNAME,"G","GEN")
ESTART
Q
```

Chapter Seven

1. Menu choices can be characterized individually, whereas gadget choices have a distinct dependency on the parent element. The selection of a menu choice is by convention associated with some immediate action such as opening a file, printing, and closing the window.

2. The methods for using menus are:

    A. A menu can be used as the menubar of its parent. A menu used in this manner is typically permanently displayed horizontally in the application area of its parent application window beneath the title bar. The display and placement of a window's menubar is maintained as defined by the current host windowing environment. The value of the window's MENUBAR attribute node specifies the menu in its menubar.

    B. A menu can be specified to pop-up and display adjacent to a selectable choice. The selection of a designated choice will cause a submenu of choices to display adjacent to it. The value of a choice's SUBMENU Choice Attribute defines the menu to use as its submenu.

    C. A menu can display, or pop-up independent of a menubar or menu choice. The values of the POS and VISIBLE attribute nodes define the position and visibility of a menu used in this fashion. If the menu is used as either the menubar or a submenu, the values of these attributes are ignored.

3. Events occur for the choices contained in menus and not the element.

4. Menu hierarchy of submenus descended from any given choice can continue to a maximum depth of seven levels.

5. The value of the MENUBAR window attribute defines the menu in its menubar. If a window is created with this attribute defined, its value may be modified to change the menu in the menubar.

6. A timer is used to time something by triggering an event upon the expiration of a defined time interval. A common use is to determine activity.

7. The normal expiration of a timer triggers a timer event and resets from its current interval value. When the timeout specified for an ESTART command expires event processing is terminated for the stack level, no event is automatically triggered, the value of $T is zero and code execution continues following the initiating ESTART command for the terminated stack level.

8. Since neither menu choices or timers are specified to use event types in the pointer, keyboard or character categories (defined in Chapter Two), the FILTERIN keyword is inappropriate.

9. A window may have a maximum of seven timer elements.

10. Example source code for the solution:

```
S W(WNAME,"MENUBAR")="MAIN"
S W(WNAME,"EVENT","CLICK")="POP^MWEXERC"
S W(WNAME,"M","MAIN","CHOICE",1)="&File"
S W(WNAME,"M","MAIN","CHOICE",1,"SUBMENU")="SUB"
S W(WNAME,"M","MAIN","CHOICE",2)="&Edit"
S W(WNAME,"M","MAIN","CHOICE",3)="&Help"
S W(WNAME,"M","SUB","CHOICE",1)="&New"
S W(WNAME,"M","SUB","CHOICE",2)="&Open"
S W(WNAME,"M","SUB","CHOICE",2,"SEPARATOR")=""
S W(WNAME,"M","SUB","CHOICE",3)="E&xit"
S W(WNAME,"M","SUB","CHOICE",3,"ACCELERATOR")="CTRL+K"
S W(WNAME,"M","SUB","CHOICE",3,"EVENT","SELECT")="ETR^MWEXERC"
M ^$W(WNAME)=W(WNAME) ; recreate window for the menubar
ESTART
W !,"EXIT" Q
POP S PPOS=^$E("PPOS")
S ^$W(WNAME,"M","SUB","POS")=PPOS
S ^$W(WNAME,"M","SUB","VISIBLE")=1
Q
ETR ETR ^$W(WNAME,"EVENT","CLOSE")
Q
```

Chapter Eight

1. The special variable $PD returns the name of the current logical display. The function $WFONT returns a comma delineated string defining the height of a character cell and the maximum and minimum widths of the specified font and unit of measurement.

   The $WTFIT function returns the number of characters in the specified font and unit of measurement that can be displayed fully in the specified area.

   The $WTWIDTH function returns the width of a specified string in the specified font and unit of measurement.

2. The width needed to fully display a text string is found using the $WTWIDTH function.

3. If an error occurs $ECODE ($EC) contains a comma delineated string with the error code. If the error is committed to a node of one of the three MWAPI SSVN's, the value of $EREF ($ER) is the node where it occurred.

4. Font functions aid in such things as the determination of size and the number of characters that will display in a given area.

Objects at a Glance

Appendix **C**

OBJECTS

This appendix was designed to be used as an aid during application development. Each object, or object type, is listed with its attributes, applicable event types, and syntax. Illustrations of the visual elements are included within Chapters 1 through 9, so you can envision how the window and element will look in your application. The goal is to provide a quick reference; the details will be found in Chapters 1 through 9.

LOGICAL DISPLAY

Attributes

BCOLOR
CLIPBOARD
COLOR
COLORTYPE
FCOLOR
FFACE
FOCUS
FSIZE
FSTYLE
KEYBOARD
PEN
PLATFORM
PTR

PTYPE
SIZE
SPECTRUM
TBCOLOR
TFCOLOR
TYPEFACE
UNITS

Notes

1. Use $PD when referring to the current logical display.

2. Attribute syntax:

```
S ^$DI(display name,display attribute)=value
```

WINDOW

The MWAPI defines two types of windows: application and MTERM. Application windows provide the basis for a GUI front end complete with the ability to have child windows and elements. MTERM windows provide terminal emulation to M applications using legacy code.

Notes

1. A window name is limited to 31 characters.

2. An M process can not have more than 31 windows.

APPLICATION

Attributes

ACTIVE
BCOLOR
COLOR
DEFBUTTON
DISPLAY
EVENT
FCOLOR
FFACE
FSIZE
FSTYLE
ICON

ICONIFY
ID
ITITLE
MENUBAR
MIN
MODAL
NEXTG
PARENT
POS
PTYPE
RESIZE
SCROLL
SIZE
SIZEMIN
SIZEWIN
TBCOLOR
TFCOLOR
TIED
TITLE
TYPE
UNITS
TYPE
VISIBLE

Event Types

CHAR
CLICK
CLOSE
DBLCLICK
FOCUS
HELP
KEYDOWN
KEYUP
MAX
MIN
MOVE
PDOWN
PDRAG
PMOVE
PUP
RESIZE
RESTORE
UNFOCUS

Note

1. TYPE attribute value equals APPLICATION.

MTERM

Attributes

DISPLAY
MODAL
POS
RESIZE
SIZE
TITLE
TYPE
UNITS

Event Types

NONE

Notes

1. TYPE attribute value equals MTERM.
2. The following syntax will create a MTERM window and make it visible: O device:::"MTERM"
3. Attribute syntax:

```
S ^$W(window name,window attribute)=value
```

4. Event syntax:

```
S ^$W(window name,"EVENT",event type)=processing routine(s)
```

ELEMENT

This section presents quick reference information on the elements. To aid in the selection of a particular gadget to use for a particular task, gadgets are listed on this page by their respective categories. These categories correspond to those in Chapter Five. The following pages provide reference on each element type, and are listed in alphabetical order.

Notes

1. The name of an element can not exceed 31 characters.

2. An M process can not contain more than 2,047 elements.

3. The title of an element can not exceed 255 characters in length.

GADGETS

Choice Category

This category of gadgets provides the applications with a means to display a list of choices to the user. The MWAPI standard specifies six gadgets for listing choices:

LIST BOX
LIST BUTTON
LIST ENTRY BOX
LONG LIST BOX
RADIO BUTTON SET
TABLE

Text Category

Use a gadget from this category when the task is for the input or display of text. The LIST ENTRY BOX is a TEXT gadget combined with a list of choices. The following gadgets are for text only:

DOCUMENT
LABEL
TEXT

Miscellaneous Category

This category merely lists the gadgets that do not fit into one of the categories listed above.

CHECK BOX
GENERIC BOX
PUSH BUTTON
SCROLL
SYMBOL

Notes

1. A window can not have more than 255 gadgets.

2. A choice is limited to 255 characters in length.

CHECK BOX

Attributes

ACTIVE
BCOLOR
CANCEL
CANCHANGE
CHANGED
EVENT
FCOLOR
ID
NEXTG
POS
PTYPE
SIZE
TFFACE
TFSIZE
TFSTYLE
TITLE
TYPE
UNITS
VALUE
VISIBLE

Event Types

CHANGE
DESELECT
FOCUS
HELP
SELECT
UNFOCUS

Notes

1. TYPE attribute value equals CHECK.

2. Attribute syntax:

```
^$W(window name,"G",gadget name,gadget attribute)=value
```

3. Event syntax:

```
^$W(window name,"G",gadget name,"EVENT",
event type)=processing routine(s)
^$W(window name,"G",gadget name,"EVENT",event type,
event specification attribute)=value
```

4. The value of the SIZE attribute includes the gadget's title.

DOCUMENT

Attributes

ACTIVE
BCOLOR
CANCEL
CANCHANGE
CHANGED
CHARMAX
EVENT
FCOLOR
FFACE
FRAMED
FSIZE
FSTYLE
ID
INSELECT
NEXTG
POS
PTYPE
SCROLL
SELECTVAL
SIZE
TBCOLOR
TFCOLOR
TFFACE
TFSIZE
TFSTYLE
TITLE
TPOS
TYPE
UNITS
VALUE
VISIBLE

Event Types

CHANGE
CHAR
FOCUS
HELP
KEYDOWN
KEYUP
UNFOCUS

Notes

1. TYPE attribute value equals DOCUMENT.

2. Attribute syntax:

   ```
   ^$W(window name,"G",gadget name,gadget attribute)=value
   ```

3. Event syntax:

   ```
   ^$W(window name,"G",gadget name,"EVENT",
   event type)=processing routine(s)
   ^$W(window name,"G",gadget name,"EVENT",event type,event
   specification attribute)=value
   ```

4. The value of the SIZE attribute does not include the gadget's title.

5. The VALUE attribute reflects the text entered.

6. Up to 32,767 characters can be assigned to the VALUE attribute.

GENERIC BOX

Attributes

ACTIVE
BCOLOR
CANCEL
DRAW
DRAWTYPE
EVENT
FCOLOR
FFACE
FRAMED
FSIZE
FSTYLE
ID
NEXTG
POS
PTYPE
SIZE
TYPE
UNITS
VALUE
VISIBLE

Event Types

CHAR
CLICK

DBLCLICK
FOCUS
HELP
KEYDOWN
KEYUP
PDOWN
PDRAG
PMOVE
PUP
UNFOCUS

Draw Commands

ARC
BCOLOR
BITMAP
BOX
FCOLOR
FFACE
FILLPAT
FSIZE
FSTYLE
LINE
MODE
OVAL
PENSIZE
PICTURE
PIE
POINT
TEXT
UNITS

Notes

1. TYPE attribute value equals GENERIC.

2. Attribute syntax:

   ```
   ^$W(window name,"G",gadget name,gadget attribute)=value
   ```

3. Event syntax:

   ```
   ^$W(window name,"G",gadget name,"EVENT",
   event type)=processing routine(s)
   ^$W(window name,"G",gadget name,"EVENT",event type,event
   specification attribute)=value
   ```

4. The value of the SIZE attribute does not include the gadget's title.

5. An M process cannot contain more than 2,047 draw commands.

GROUP FRAME

Attributes

BCOLOR
FCOLOR
ID
NEXTG
POS
PTYPE
SIZE
TFFACE
TFSIZE
TFSTYLE
TITLE
TYPE
UNITS
VISIBLE

Event Types

NONE

Notes

1. TYPE attribute value equals FRAME.
2. Attribute syntax:

```
^$W(window name,"G",gadget name,gadget attribute)=value
```

3. The value of the SIZE attribute does may not include the gadget's title.

LABEL

Attributes

BCOLOR
FCOLOR
FRAMED
ID
NEXTG
POS
PTYPE
SIZE
TFFACE

TFSIZE
TFSTYLE
TITLE
TYPE
UNITS
VISIBLE

Event Types

NONE

Notes

1. TYPE attribute value equals LABEL.
2. Attribute syntax:

   `^$W(window name,"G",gadget name,gadget attribute)=value`

3. The value of the SIZE attribute includes the gadget's title.

LIST BOX

Attributes

ACTIVE
BCOLOR
CANCEL
CANCHANGE
CHANGED
CHOICE
EVENT
FCOLOR
FFACE
FSIZE
FSTYLE
ID
NEXTG
POS
PTYPE
SELECTMAX
SIZE
TBCOLOR
TFCOLOR
TFFACE
TFSIZE

TFSTYLE
TITLE
TOPSHOW
TPOS
TYPE
UNITS
VALUE
VISIBLE

Event Types

CHANGE
DBLCLICK
DESELECT
FOCUS
HELP
SELECT
UNFOCUS

Choice Attributes

ACTIVE
AID

Notes

1. TYPE attribute value equals LIST.

2. Attribute syntax:

```
^$W(window name,"G",gadget name,gadget attribute)=value
```

3. Choice syntax:

```
^$W(window name,"G",gadget name,"CHOICE",
item)=value
^$W(window name,"G",gadget name,"CHOICE",
item,choice attribute)=value
```

4. Event syntax:

```
^$W(window name,"G",gadget name,"EVENT",
event type)=processing routine(s)
^$W(window name,"G",gadget name,"EVENT",event type,event
specification attribute)=value
```

5. The value of the SIZE attribute does not include the gadget's title.

6. A maximum of 1,023 choices can be assigned to this gadget at any one time.

LIST BUTTON

Attributes

BCOLOR
FCOLOR
FRAMED
ID
NEXTG
POS
PTYPE
SIZE
TBCOLOR
TFCOLOR
TFFACE
TFSIZE
TFSTYLE
TITLE
TPOS
TYPE
UNITS
VISIBLE

Event Types

CHANGE
DESELECT
FOCUS
HELP
SELECT
UNFOCUS

Choice Attributes

ACTIVE
AID

Notes

1. TYPE attribute value equals LISTBUTTON.

2. Attribute syntax:

```
^$W(window name,"G",gadget name,gadget attribute)=value
```

3. Choice syntax:

```
^$W(window name,"G",gadget name,"CHOICE",
item)=value
^$W(window name,"G",gadget name,"CHOICE",
item,choice attribute)=value
```

4. Event syntax:

```
^$W(window name,"G",gadget name,"EVENT",
event type)=processing routine(s)
^$W(window name,"G",gadget name,"EVENT",event type,event
specification attribute)=value
```

5. The value of the SIZE attribute does not include the gadget's title.

6. A maximum of 31 choices can be assigned to this gadget at any one time.

LIST ENTRY BOX

Attributes

ACTIVE
BCOLOR
CANCEL
CANCHANGE
CHANGED
CHARMAX
CHOICE
EVENT
FCOLOR
FFACE
FSIZE
FSTYLE
ID
INSELECT
NEXTG
POS
PTYPE
SELECTVAL
SIZE
TBCOLOR
TFCOLOR
TFFACE
TFSIZE
TFSTYLE
TITLE
TOPSHOW

TPOS
TYPE
UNITS
VALUE
VISIBLE

Event Types

CHANGE
CHAR
DBLCLICK
DESELECT
FOCUS
HELP
KEYDOWN
KEYUP
SELECT
UNFOCUS

Choice Attributes

ACTIVE
AID

Notes

1. TYPE attribute value equals LISTENTRY.

2. Attribute syntax:

```
^$W(window name,"G",gadget name,gadget attribute)=value
```

3. Choice syntax:

```
^$W(window name,"G",gadget name,"CHOICE",
item)=value
^$W(window name,"G",gadget name,"CHOICE",
item,choice attribute)=value
```

4. Event syntax:

```
^$W(window name,"G",gadget name,"EVENT",
event type)=processing routine(s)
^$W(window name,"G",gadget name,"EVENT",event type,event
specification attribute)=value
```

5. The value of the SIZE attribute does not include the gadget's title.

6. A maximum of 1,023 choices can be assigned to this gadget at any one time.

7. The VALUE attribute is limited to the M string length.

LONG LIST BOX

Attributes

ACTIVE
BCOLOR
CANCEL
CANCHANGE
CHANGED
CHOICE
EVENT
FCOLOR
FFACE
FSIZE
FSTYLE
ID
NEXTG
POS
PTYPE
SCROLLPOS
SCROLLRANGE
SELECTMAX
SELECTVAL
SIZE
TBCOLOR
TFCOLOR
TFFACE
TFSIZE
TFSTYLE
TITLE
TOPSHOW
TPOS
TYPE
UNITS
VALUE
VISIBLE

Event Types

CHANGE
DBLCLICK
DESELECT
FOCUS
GOBOTTOM
GODOWN

GODOWNBIG
GOTOP
GOUP
GOUPBIG
HELP
SELECT
UNFOCUS

Notes

1. TYPE attribute value equals LONGLIST.

2. Attribute syntax:

```
^$W(window name,"G",gadget name,gadget attribute)=value
```

3. Choice syntax:

```
^$W(window name,"G",gadget name,"CHOICE",
item)=value
^$W(window name,"G",gadget name,"CHOICE",
item,choice attribute)=value
```

4. Event syntax:

```
^$W(window name,"G",gadget name,"EVENT",
event type)=processing routine(s)
^$W(window name,"G",gadget name,"EVENT",event type,event
specification attribute)=value
```

5. The value of the SIZE attribute does not include the gadget's title.

6. A maximum of 1,023 choices can be assigned to this gadget at any one time.

PUSH BUTTON

Attributes

ACTIVE
CANCEL
EVENT
ID
NEXTG
POS
PTYPE
RESOURCE
SIZE
TFFACE
TFSIZE
TFSTYLE
TITLE

TYPE
UNITS
VISIBLE

Event Types

FOCUS
HELP
SELECT
UNFOCUS

Notes

1. TYPE attribute value equals BUTTON.

2. Attribute syntax:

```
^$W(window name,"G",gadget name,gadget attribute)=value
```

3. Event syntax:

```
^$W(window name,"G",gadget name,"EVENT",
event type)=processing routine(s)
^$W(window name,"G",gadget name,"EVENT",event type,event
specification attribute)=value
```

4. The value of the SIZE attribute includes the gadget's title.

RADIO BUTTON SET

Attributes

ACTIVE
BCOLOR
CANCEL
CANCHANGE
CHANGED
CHOICE
EVENT
FCOLOR
FFACE
FRAMED
FSIZE
FSTYLE
ID
NEXTG
POS
PTYPE

ROWCOL
SIZE
TBCOLOR
TFCOLOR
TFFACE
TFSIZE
TFSTYLE
TITLE
TPOS
TYPE
UNITS
VALUE
VISIBLE

Event Types

CHANGE
DESELECT
FOCUS
HELP
SELECT
UNFOCUS

Choice Attributes

ACTIVE
AID

Notes

1. TYPE attribute value equals RADIO.

2. Attribute syntax:

   ```
   ^$W(window name,"G",gadget name,gadget attribute)=value
   ```

3. Choice syntax:

   ```
   ^$W(window name,"G",gadget name,"CHOICE",
   item)=value
   ^$W(window name,"G",gadget name,"CHOICE",
   item,choice attribute)=value
   ```

4. Event syntax:

   ```
   ^$W(window name,"G",gadget name,"EVENT",
   event type)=processing routine(s)
   ^$W(window name,"G",gadget name,"EVENT",event type,event
   specification attribute)=value
   ```

5. The value of the SIZE attribute does not include the gadget's title.

SCROLL

Attributes

BCOLOR
CANCEL
CANCHANGE
CHANGED
EVENT
FCOLOR
ID
NEXTG
POS
PTYPE
SCROLLBY
SCROLLDIR
SCROLLRANGE
SIZE
TBCOLOR
TFCOLOR
TFFACE
TFSIZE
TFSTYLE
TITLE
TPOS
TYPE
UNITS
VALUE
VISIBLE

Event Types

HELP
PDRAG
SELECT

Notes

1. TYPE attribute value equals SCROLL.
2. Attribute syntax:

```
^$W(window name,"G",gadget name,gadget attribute)=value
```

3. Event syntax:

```
^$W(window name,"G",gadget name,"EVENT",
event type)=processing routine(s)
^$W(window name,"G",gadget name,"EVENT",event type,event
specification attribute)=value
```

4. The value of the SIZE attribute does not include the gadget's title.

SYMBOL

Attributes

ID
NEXTG
POS
PTYPE
SIZE
TYPE
UNITS
VISIBLE

Event Types

NONE

Notes

1. TYPE attribute value equals SYMBOL.

2. Attribute syntax:

```
^$W(window name,"G",gadget name,gadget attribute)=value
```

TABLE

Attributes

ACTIVE
BCOLOR
CANCEL
CANCHANGE
CHANGED
CHOICE
COL
COLWIDTH
EVENT

FCOLOR
FFACE
FSIZE
FSTYLE
GRID
HCOLID
HROWID
ID
LEFTSHOW
NEXTG
POS
ROW
ROWHEIGHT
SIZE
TBCOLOR
TFCOLOR
TFFACE
TFSIZE
TFSTYLE
TITLE
TOPSHOW
TPOS
TYPE
UNITS
VALUE
VISIBLE

Event Types

CHANGE
CLICK
DBLCLICK
DESELECT
FOCUS
PDOWN
PDRAG
PMOVE
PUP
SELECT
UNFOCUS

ROW/COLUMN ATTRIBUTES		CHOICE ATTRIBUTES	
ROWHEIGHT	COLWIDTH	AID	RESOURCE

Notes

1. TYPE attribute value equals TABLE.

2. Attribute syntax:

```
^$W(window name,"G",gadget name,gadget attribute)=value
^$W(window name,"G",gadget name,gadget attribute,
rowcol attribute)=value
```

3. Choice syntax:

```
^$W(window name,"G",gadget name,"CHOICE",
ritem,citem)=value
^$W(window name,"G",gadget name,"CHOICE",
ritem,citem,choice attribute)=value
```

4. Event syntax:

```
^$W(window name,"G",gadget name,"EVENT",
event type)=processing routine(s)
^$W(window name,"G",gadget name,"EVENT",event type,event
specification attribute)=value
```

5. The value of the SIZE attribute does not include the gadget's title.

TEXT

Attributes

ACTIVE
BCOLOR
CANCEL
CANCHANGE
CHANGED
CHARMAX
EVENT
FCOLOR
FFACE
FRAMED
FSIZE
FSTYLE
ID
INSELECT
NEXTG
POS
PTYPE
SELECTVAL
SIZE
TBCOLOR

TFCOLOR
TFFACE
TFSIZE
TFSTYLE
TITLE
TPOS
TYPE
UNITS
VALUE
VISIBLE

Event Types

CHANGE
CHAR
FOCUS
HELP
KEYDOWN
KEYUP
UNFOCUS

Notes

1. TYPE attribute value equals TEXT.

2. Attribute syntax:

```
^$W(window name,"G",gadget name,gadget attribute)=value
```

3. Event syntax:

```
^$W(window name,"G",gadget name,"EVENT",
event type)=processing routine(s)
^$W(window name,"G",gadget name,"EVENT",event type,event
specification attribute)=value
```

4. The value of the SIZE attribute does not include the gadget's title.

5. The number of characters that can be assigned to the VALUE attribute is limited by the M defined maximum string length.

MENU

Attributes

ACTIVE
CHOICE
ID
POS
PTYPE

UNITS
VISIBLE

Choice Attributes

ACCELERATOR
ACTIVE
AID
EVENT
MARKER
SEPARATOR
SUBMENU

Event Types

SELECT

Notes

1. Attribute syntax:

```
^$W(window name,"M",menu name,gadget attribute)=value
```

2. Choice syntax:

```
^$W(window name,"M",menu name,"CHOICE",
item)=value
^$W(window name,"M",menu name,"CHOICE",
item,choice attribute)=value
```

3. Event syntax:

```
^$W(window name,"M",menu name,"CHOICE",item,"EVENT",
event type)=processing routine(s)
^$W(window name,"M",menu name,"CHOICE",item,"EVENT",
event type,event specification attribute)=value
```

4. The maximum depth of submenus is seven levels.

5. A window can not have more than 255 menu choices.

6. A choice may not exceed 255 characters in length.

TIMER

Attributes

ACTIVE
EVENT
ID
INTERVAL
PTYPE

Event Types

TIMER

Notes

1. Attribute syntax:

```
^$W(window name,"T",timer name,timer attribute)=value
```

2. Event syntax:

```
^$W(window name,"T",timer name,"EVENT",
event type)=processing routine(s)
^$W(window name,"T",timer name,"EVENT",event type,event
specification attribute)=value
```

3. A window can have a maximum of seven timers.

EVENT

An event object is created and available to each call back routine to reference its characteristics. Before and after each event, this object is undefined. Listed below are the MWAPI defined Event Information Attributes. Implementor's are permitted to define their own beginning with the letter "Z."

CHOICE
CLASS
COL
ELEMENT
KEY
NEXTFOCUS
OK
PBUTTON
PPPOS
PRIORFOCUS
PSTATE
ROW
SEQUENCE
TYPE
WINDOW

Notes

1. Attribute syntax

```
^$E(event information attribute)
```

Index

Other Books from Digital Press

The Art of Technical Documentation, Second Edition by Katherine Haramundanis
1997   300pp   pb   1-55558-182-X

M Programming: A Comprehensive Guide by Richard Walters
1997   384pp   pb   1-55558-167-6

Oracle8 in Windows NT by Lilian Hobbs
1998   350pp   pb   1-55558-190-0

Reengineering Legacy Software Systems by Howard Miller
1997   250pp   pb   1-55558-195-1

SQL Server 6.5: Performance Optimization and Tuning by Ken England
1997   250pp   pb   1-55558-180-3

TCP/IP Explained by Philip Miller
1996   450pp   pb   1-55558-166-8

Visual Basic for Network Applications by Simon Collin
1997   250pp   pb   1-55558-173-0

Windows NT Infrastructure Design by Mike Collins
1998   450pp   pb   1-55558-170-6

Feel free to visit our web site at: http://www.bh.com/digitalpress

These books are available from all good bookstores or in case of difficulty call:
1-800-366-2665 in the U.S. or +44-1865-310366 in Europe.

E-MAIL MAILING LIST

An e-mail mailing list giving information on latest releases, special promotions, offers and other news relating to Digital Press titles is available. To subscribe, send an e-mail message to majordomo@world.std.com.

Include in message body (not in subject line): subscribe digital-press

Printed and bound by CPI Group (UK) Ltd, Croydon, CR0 4YY

03/10/2024

01040345-0006